JEWISH
PEOPLEHOOD

Key Words in Jewish Studies

Series Editors
Deborah Dash Moore, University of Michigan
MacDonald Moore, Vassar College
Andrew Bush, Vassar College

I. Andrew Bush, *Jewish Studies*
II. Barbara E. Mann, *Space and Place in Jewish Studies*
III. Olga Litvak, *Haskalah: The Romantic Movement in Judaism*
IV. Jonathan Boyarin, *Jewish Families*
V. Jeffrey Shandler, *Shtetl*
VI. Noam Pianko, *Jewish Peoplehood: An American Innovation*

JEWISH PEOPLEHOOD

An American Innovation

NOAM PIANKO

RUTGERS UNIVERSITY PRESS
New Brunswick, New Jersey, and London

Library of Congress Cataloging-in-Publication Data

Pianko, Noam, author.
　Jewish peoplehood : an American innovation / Noam Pianko.
　　pages cm — (Key words in Jewish studies)
　Includes bibliographical references and index.
　ISBN 978–0–8135–6365–7 (hardcover : alk. paper) — ISBN 978–0–8135–6364–0 (pbk. : alk. paper) — ISBN 978–0–8135–6366–4 (e-book (web pdf)) — ISBN 978–0–8135–7388–5 (e-book (epub))
　　1. Jews—Identity.　2. Jews—United States—Identity.　3. Jews—United States—Politics and government—21st century.　4. Jews—United States—Social conditions—21st century.　5. Israel and the diaspora.　I. Title.
　DS143.P565　2015
　305.892′4073—dc23

2014040075

A British Cataloging-in-Publication record for this book is available from the British Library.

Copyright © 2015 by Noam Pianko

All rights reserved

No part of this book may be reproduced or utilized in any form or by any means, electronic or mechanical, or by any information storage and retrieval system, without written permission from the publisher. Please contact Rutgers University Press, 106 Somerset Street, New Brunswick, NJ 08901. The only exception to this prohibition is "fair use" as defined by U.S. copyright law.

Visit our website: http://rutgerspress.rutgers.edu

Manufactured in the United States of America

Contents

Foreword by Deborah Dash Moore,
MacDonald Moore, and Andrew Bush   vii
Acknowledgments   ix

Introduction: A Deceptively
Simple Key Word   1

1 Terms of Debate: Jewish Nationhood
   and American Peoplehood   14
   What Is a Nation? Peoplehood's
   European Precursors   17
   The Emergence of Peoplehood   27
   1948, Israel, and a Crisis of Terminology   48
   From Critique to Code Word   51
   Into the American Mainstream   56

2 State of the Question: Enduring
   Entity or Constructed Community   67
   Unity, Solidarity, Statehood   71
   Nationalism, Globalization, and the
   Limits of Peoplehood   82
   Race, Ethnicity, and Peoplehood Studies   92
   Jewish Studies and Jewish Peoplehood   106

3 In a New Key: Can Peoplehood
   Speak to a Global Era?   115
   Jewish: From Periphery to Center,
   from Describing to Defining   119
   Neighborhood: From National to Local,
   from Core to Cohort   125
   Project: From Being to Doing,
   from Essence to Action   129
   Jewishhood Project(s)   133

Notes   141
Index   163

Foreword

The Rutgers book series Key Words in Jewish Studies seeks to introduce students and scholars alike to vigorous developments in the field by exploring its terms. These words and phrases reference important concepts, issues, practices, events, and circumstances. But terms also refer to standards, even to preconditions; they patrol the boundaries of the field of Jewish studies. This series aims to transform outsiders into insiders and let insiders gain new perspectives on usages, some of which shift even as we apply them.

Key words mutate through repetition, suppression, amplification, and competitive sharing. Jewish studies finds itself attending to such processes in the context of an academic milieu where terms are frequently repurposed. Diaspora offers an example of an ancient word, one with a specific Jewish resonance, which has traveled into new regions and usage. Such terms migrate from the religious milieu of Jewish learning to the secular environment of universities, from Jewish community discussion to arenas of academic discourse, from political debates to intellectual arguments and back again. As these key words travel, they acquire additional meanings even as they occasionally shed long-established connotations. On occasion, key words can become so politicized that they serve as accusations. The sociopolitical concept of assimilation, for example, when turned into a term—assimilationist—describing an advocate of the process among Jews, became an epithet hurled by political opponents struggling for the mantle of authority in Jewish communities.

When approached dispassionately, key words provide analytical leverage to expand debate in Jewish studies. Some key words will be familiar from long use, and yet they may have gained new valences, attracting or repelling other terms in contemporary discussion. But there are prominent terms in Jewish culture whose key lies in a particular understanding of prior usage. Terms of the past may bolster claims to continuity in the present while newly minted language sometimes disguises deep connections reaching back into history. Attention must be paid as well to the transmigration of key words among Jewish languages—especially Hebrew, Yiddish, and Ladino—and among languages used by Jews, knitting connections even while highlighting distinctions.

An exploration of the current state of Jewish studies through its key words highlights some interconnections often only glimpsed and holds out the prospect of a reorganization of Jewish knowledge. Key words act as magnets and attract a nexus of ideas and arguments as well as related terms into their orbits. This series plunges into several of these intersecting constellations, providing a path from past to present.

The volumes in the series share a common organization. They open with a first section, Terms of Debate, which defines the key word as it developed over the course of Jewish history. Allied concepts and traditional terms appear here as well. The second section, State of the Question, analyzes contemporary debates in scholarship and popular venues, especially for those key words that have crossed over into popular culture. The final section, In a New Key, explicitly addresses contemporary culture and future possibilities for understanding the key word.

To decipher key words is to learn the varied languages of Jewish studies at points of intersection between academic disciplines and wider spheres of culture. The series, then, does not seek to consolidate and narrow a particular critical lexicon. Its purpose is to question, not to canonize, and to invite readers to sample the debate and ferment of an exciting field of study.

Andrew Bush
Deborah Dash Moore
MacDonald Moore
Series Co-Editors

Acknowledgments

In the middle of working on this study of Jewish peoplehood, I was reminded that my connection to this topic has deep personal and family roots. A few months before finishing this manuscript, my wife, Rachel, and I celebrated ten years of marriage and watched our wedding video. The concluding words of my father's toast, which I didn't remember from the wedding day, struck me. "What they have done is made the words true: the People of Israel lives. To Noam and Rachel, that is really the most important thing that I can pass on as you come to grips in your lives together with questions and you wonder, why am I responsible?"

As the grandchild of Holocaust survivors, I grew up with clear messages of Jewish distinctiveness and the importance of preserving the Jewish people. Whether on a conscious or unconscious level, this project no doubt reflects my own attempts to grapple with the legacy passed on from my parents. I imagine they may have some different perspectives on Jewish peoplehood than the ones I outline in this book. But I hope they realize how much their stories and commitments have shaped my personal and intellectual journey to make sense of Jewish peoplehood today.

My interest and approach to this topic owes a debt to my doctoral advisor, Prof. Paula Hyman (z"l), who passed away as I began working on this book project. Her legacy as a world-class scholar and public Jewish intellectual has inspired me to think more deeply about the relationship between Jewish studies and Jewish communal activism.

At various points in writing this manuscript, I received very helpful feedback from a number of Jewish studies colleagues, including Lila Corwin Berman, Steven M. Cohen, Arnold Eisen, Daniel Heller, Shaul Kellner, James Loeffler, David Myers, Devin Naar, and Shlomi Ravid. I am also grateful to Sue Fendrick for her probing questions and editorial guidance.

Key resources that supported the research and writing of this book came from the Stroum Center for Jewish Studies at the University of Washington, the Samuel N. Stroum Chair of Jewish Studies, and the Lucy S. and Herbert L. Pruzan Professorship of Jewish Studies. I also wish to thank the faculty and staff of the Stroum Center for Jewish Studies and the Jackson School of International Studies for their friendship, encouragement, and partnership.

My career in Jewish studies was made possible by a Wexner Graduate Fellowship, and I remain indebted to the Wexner Foundation for its support and leadership.

The Key Words in Jewish Studies series editors served as critical conversation partners and helped make this a very fulfilling project. Deborah Dash Moore encouraged me to write this book after a discussion several years ago. Since then, she has graciously shared her knowledge of American Jewish history, keen editorial eye, and professional guidance. Andrew Bush contributed his perspective on the manuscript throughout the process. I particularly appreciate his close reading of the text and willingness to push me to strengthen certain arguments. It has been a true pleasure to work with Marlie Wasserman and her team at Rutgers University Press.

My own thoughts about Jewish peoplehood, present and future, have been shaped by watching the inspiring work of my wife, Rabbi Rachel Nussbaum, in building Jewish community. I am very lucky to have a partner with Rachel's wisdom, unwavering support, and generous spirit. We are blessed with three wonderful children, Yona, Mia, and Elisha. Watching them develop distinct personalities and interests has been one of the most rewarding and meaningful experiences in my life. This book is dedicated to Yona, Mia, and Elisha. As you grow up, I hope you will continue to demonstrate in your own unique and novel ways that "the People of Israel Lives."

JEWISH
PEOPLEHOOD

Introduction

A DECEPTIVELY SIMPLE KEY WORD

What does it mean that most American Jews now identify more with the Jewish people than with the Jewish religion? Does this represent a decline in levels of Jewish identity, or present an opportunity to reimagine what connects Jews to one another and to Jewishness? What do the terms that Jews use to refer to their identification with Jewish collectivity reveal not only about the nature of that collectivity, but also about communal attempts to shape and strengthen it in the twenty-first century?

The findings of the 2014 Pew Research Center Survey, "A Portrait of Jewish Americans," provide a window onto the shifting nature of and language for American Jewish group identity. While fewer American Jews describe themselves as religious, they overwhelmingly report a "strong sense of belonging to the Jewish people."[1] At the start of the twenty-first century, Jewish peoplehood (the abstract-noun variant of the Jewish people) has eclipsed religion (as well as ethnicity and nationality) as the conceptual vocabulary for defining what it means to be a Jew, and the group category that captures the ties that bind Jews from around the globe to one another.[2]

The rising significance of peoplehood in the language of American Jewish self-identification is not surprising given the recent communal emphasis on promulgating the idea that affirming membership in the Jewish people—regardless of religious observance, Jewish knowledge, or cultural practices—fulfills the most important expectation of what it means to identify as a Jew. An uptick in the use of peoplehood—especially related to concerns about its dissolution—in the first years of the twenty-first century has generated peoplehood commissions, an organization funded by the Jewish Agency and the Jewish Federations of North America called "The Jewish Peoplehood HUB," an international "School for Jewish Peoplehood Research" based in Tel Aviv, and investment by major Jewish philanthropists in building a sense of peoplehood. It serves as a high priority for American Jewish education, a barometer for evaluating the state of Jewish life today, and a frequent topic for underscoring a crisis in Jewish involvement.[3] After a decade of grave concern about the decreasing relevance of peoplehood, the survey findings raise the possibility that American Jews have responded to a very conscious effort to bolster levels of peoplehood among global Jewry.

The State of Israel, too, has made a significant investment in promoting the concept of peoplehood within Israeli politics and society.[4] For example, the government voted to change the name (at least in English) of The Museum of the Jewish Diaspora to The Museum of the Jewish People in 2005. Since 2011, legislators have been trying to pass a Basic Law (which functions as a constitution in Israeli courts) to define Israel as "the nation-state of the Jewish people"—and more recently, peace negotiations initiated by Secretary of State John Kerry stalled in part over the refusal of Palestinian negotiators to recognize Israel precisely in those terms. Peoplehood serves as the battleground and as a strategy itself for debating the relative strength of American Jewish identity, articulating a conception of the significance of the State of Israel for global Jewry, asserting the nature of Jewish collectivity in the international arena, and conceptualizing boundaries in an age of unprecedented intergroup contact and connection.

The symbolic importance of peoplehood has also been indirectly driven home in American Jewish life through the rhetoric of Jewish communal institutions. Slogans and key phrases such as "We are one," "Never again," "Jewish continuity," "Jewish identity," and "Jewish survival" have all been part of the shift toward thinking about the nature of Jewish collectivity primarily as a people rather than as a religion per se.[5] Together, they put forth a vision of Jews fundamentally sharing a commitment to fighting antisemitism, a dedication to supporting persecuted Jews around the world, a historical experience and mission, and an affirmation of the State of Israel as the primary home of the dispersed collective. Such rallying slogans engender a sense of unity and homogeneity that transcends religious differences, cultural practices, geographic diversity, economic disparity, and political differences—and Jewish people and peoplehood provide a sufficiently flexible (and even ambiguous) terminology of collectivity that affirms this unity across particularity and distinction.

The Pew survey suggests that the increased communal emphasis on peoplehood and external shifts in identity construction has transformed the taxonomy defining Judaism and Jewish identity from categories of religion to peoplehood. Despite the significance of this terminological shift in self-understanding, communal response to the Pew Report has focused on concerns raised by the decline in religious affiliation, rather than noting or celebrating the emergence of new ways of identifying with and defining Jewish collectivity.[6] Headlines about the report might just as easily have hailed the triumph of a relatively new concept in Jewish life.

Two factors limit the perceived optimism about the apparent rise in expressing Jewish identity as belonging to the Jewish people. First, other studies continue to indicate declining levels of Jewish peoplehood in definitions of Jewish identity.[7] It is quite possible that the identification with belonging to the Jewish people reflects as much a none-of-the-above answer as an active and conscious affirmation of peoplehood as a core value. Second, the connotations of peoplehood expressed by the American Jewish communal leadership and the State of Israel over the last several years are not necessarily reflected in a rather amorphous box checked on the Pew survey. In other words, there may very well be a disconnect between the vision of peoplehood espoused by communal advocates and the decision by survey respondents to indicate their sense of belonging to the Jewish people rather than to other, less relevant, categories.

For institutional supporters of peoplehood in the United States and Israel, the concept affirms that Jews are one unified group, connected by a set of secular (not necessarily religious) values, commitments to political solidarity, and historical experiences. These are not necessarily its connotations for Jews, especially younger generations, who were shaped by wider changes in the language of group membership and in American attitudes toward religion, ethnicity, and cultural pluralism. Group affiliations have become more fluid as barriers historically erected by race and ethnicities dissolve, and individuals feel empowered to associate across multiple identity categories. The possibilities for mixing group allegiances and for changing identities fashion an environment well suited for a conception of Jewish peoplehood in which the specific contours are largely undefined. For many Jews who indicated belonging to the Jewish people as their primary mode of identifying, peoplehood may have just provided a useful catch-all category for rapidly shifting conceptions of group attachments in the American context, and thus represents not so much good news as bland news.

With peoplehood taking an increasingly important position in shaping articulations of American Jewish and Israeli life, we are thus at a particularly useful moment to investigate this concept, which has only recently become a subject of scholarly inquiry.[8] Is peoplehood being solidified as a conceptual vocabulary that has the potential to fundamentally reshape meaning of American Jewish identity in a global era? Or is Jewish peoplehood—which emerged in the early decades of the twentieth century, when it did represent innovation—now stuck in an outdated paradigm of collectivity that lacks the flexibility to adapt to demographic shifts, post-ethnic identity patterns, and changing attitudes among American Jews to Israel?

This book attempts to consider the current significance and future relevance of peoplehood by tracing the rise, transformation, and return of this novel term. It tells the surprising and innovative success story of peoplehood beginning in the twentieth century, rather than a depressing narrative of the recent decline of a much older, timeless concept (as many peoplehood advocates would have it). But it also examines where peoplehood falls short as well, along with what it has to offer, as an articulation of Judaism for the twenty-first century. The following three chapters explore these questions: (1) When and why did Jewish peoplehood emerge as a key word in Jewish life? (2) What is at stake for defining modern Jewish identity in today's debates about the meaning of peoplehood? and (3) Can peoplehood serve as the conceptual foundation for a relevant and sustainable definition of Judaism in a global era?

What we might call the logic of Jewish peoplehood, a term that presents itself as encapsulating the unchanging essence of Jewish membership, does not immediately lend itself to a historical analysis of its origins. A recent publication claims that "Jewish peoplehood is not a new concept. It has been central to the Jewish experience and essential to our existence for much of history."[9] This statement, by one of the leading philanthropic supporters of the emergence and prominence of Jewish peoplehood in the American Jewish and Israeli contexts, captures the core claim that is implicit in the very use of Jewish peoplehood. It typifies the escalation of interest in and articulation of Jewish peoplehood over the past decade, including its somewhat defensive posture against those who would argue (as I do here) that peoplehood is a modern innovation rather than a fixed attribute of Jewish collectivity.

This is not to say, of course, that scholars and proponents of Jewish peoplehood deny the emergence of a new English word per se. But peoplehood remains framed primarily as the continuity of a premodern pillar of Jewish belief and practice, rather than as a modern break from historical articulations of Jewish collectivity. An uncritical understanding of the Jewish people as simply the equivalent of (or an overarching category for) the variety of terms that preceded it erases a complex historical effort on behalf of peoplehood's modern pioneers to grapple with and integrate into a variety of possible group constructions. The wide variety of terms linked to concepts of Jewish collectivity reflects internal conflicts, diversity, and fissures in Jewish self-definition and boundary construction across time and space. The relatively recent articulation of and emphasis on the Jewish people, and peoplehood in particular, illustrates the fundamental difficulty of transposing a group self-understanding with a long and diverse history into categories of collective identity developed in the relatively recent history of Western political and social thought. Any attempt to reduce this historical diversity of terms and concepts of Jewish collectivity into a singular, all-encompassing definition of Jewish peoplehood represents a rupture from the very terms peoplehood itself purports to draw on and perpetuate.

As a key word study, this volume takes on the task of understanding the development of the notion of Jewish peoplehood, and how this terminology reflects significant conceptual innovations.[10] It reflects a starting assumption that the development of new key words and phrases for collectivity, such as Jewish peoplehood, is not merely a surface level translation or transition in vocabulary, but articulates significant shifts in how groups perceive and present themselves. In addition, the rise of such new words often—as it does in this case—registers the impact of dramatic transformations in how host societies think about, relate to, and describe individual and group rights. Peoplehood not only reflects but also, by its nature, puts forth disputed claims about Jewish essence and Jewish history.

To avoid the pitfalls of privileging one conception of Jewish peoplehood over another, this investigation views the historical ambiguity and semantic fluidity of the term Jewish peoplehood not as a disadvantage that needs to be corrected (by translating it into a single widely accepted paradigm of collectivity), but as an object of study itself. My goal is to raise questions about the authenticity of any understanding of Jewish peoplehood that presents itself as an essential (core and unchanging) transhistorical concept. Instead, peoplehood's current primacy in North American Jewish discourse belies a complexity and multiplicity of Jewish group definitions and membership boundaries over time. This volume unpacks the claims that peoplehood is a persistent, unchanging part of the Jewish psyche whose recent diminishment reflects a tear in the continuity of Jewish collective consciousness.

An examination of the evolution of peoplehood as a key word allows us to see a process of Jewish identity formation grappling with a set of new conditions—especially the rise of Zionism and the founding of the State of Israel. Jewish peoplehood represents an American Jewish theological, social, and cultural innovation, a largely deliberate intervention into twentieth-century discussions of nationalism, Zionism, and American Jewish identity. The twentieth century fostered and created conceptions of Jewish collectivity (as well as institutions to support them) in response to overwhelming existential threats that Jews faced, the need to ensure the political security of Jews in a world dominated by nation-states, and the unprecedented ability for Jews in certain circumstances to use their resources to rally to protect Jews in danger. These early twentieth-century historical forces fostered a new concept of peoplehood that represented a rupture in Jewish thought—a concept of Jewish collectivity that privileges a largely secular, timeless, yet ambiguous Jewish nature; a solidarity with other Jews facing a common existential threat; and a close connection to the Jewish homeland/state. Using the language of an enduring reality to which Jews must recommit, Jews constructed Jewish peoplehood to convey a new constellation of collective meaning that highlights particular historical aspects of Jewish self-understanding and invents new ones.

The changing and contested meanings of peoplehood stands in for and is an emblematic part of the broader struggle of what it means to negotiate between the sometimes conflicting claims of Americanism, Judaism, and Zionism—for example, the tensions between Jewish nationalism and American pluralism, universal values and particular concerns, religious and ethnic categories of attachment, and positions of power and powerlessness on the international political scene. Few key words provide richer terrain for understanding the strategies that American Jews, from communal leaders to loosely affiliated participants, have utilized to figure out their places in a rapidly changing landscape of identity from the post–World War II nation-state era to today's global possibilities.

Tracing the shifts in the meaning of Jewish peoplehood raises a number of interesting and puzzling questions. Why did peoplehood emerge in the 1930s to denote the meaning of Jewish collectivity just as Zionism succeeded in affirming the status of Jews as a nation through the creation of a state? With a rich vocabulary of group categories in the United States, why does peoplehood endure and even increase in importance as Jews Americanize? Why has the State of Israel recently adopted peoplehood, an English-language term historically absent from Zionist discourse, as an integral part of the state's ideology and self-definition? In answering these questions, we can gain a deeper understanding of the anxieties, debates, and unresolved issues concealed by the term's purported ancient origins in Jewish history and texts.

While a full review of historical continuities and discontinuities that mark millennia of Jewish grappling with questions of difference, boundaries, and solidarity extends beyond the scope of this book, readers will find in these pages new perspectives on the Jewish past that demonstrate the difficulty in directly tracing contemporary ideals of peoplehood backward in time. Looking at Jewish peoplehood as a window onto evolving, fluid, and sometimes contradictory assumptions about membership and inclusion in a group also reveals ways that it relates to and overlaps with other groups' own evolving assessments of the meaning of collectivity.

Instead of looking back to classical Jewish sources or Jewish historical experience, then, to locate the terms of debate for the modern meaning of

Jewish peoplehood, the emergence of Jewish peoplehood can be traced to the United States in the 1930s. Its pioneers were American Jewish leaders, most importantly Rabbi Stephen Wise and Rabbi Mordecai Kaplan, with close ties to the Zionist movement. Exploring their introduction of the term into the English language illuminates the intimate relationship between Jewish peoplehood and the nationalist paradigm of group identity that shaped European Jewish political thought and early expressions of Zionism.

Nationalist paradigms shaped key attributes of peoplehood and dominated the playing field of Jewish group definition in the late nineteenth and twentieth centuries. I employ here the term *nationalist paradigm* to distinguish a wider set of parameters that bind members of a given historical collective group to one another from the singular association of nationalism with political sovereignty and statehood. Modern nationalist paradigms introduced a secular definition of Jewish collectivity that went far beyond (and sometimes did not especially emphasize or even include) statehood, stressing national unity, shared essential characteristics, a common past and future mission, solidarity in the face of external persecution, and the need for Jewish political engagement on the world stage to protect Jewish interests. The nationalist paradigm in general, and Zionism in particular, crossed the Atlantic and contributed in crucial ways to how American Jews thought about collectivity. Tracing the introduction and proliferation of peoplehood captures the ascendency of the nationalist paradigm in the United States through a term too rarely understood as linked to its theoretical roots in streams of political and cultural Zionism.

The link between Zionism and peoplehood reveals the untold success story of Zionism and Jewish nationalism in American Jewish life. Historians have generally claimed that nationalism exerted little impact on Jews in the United States, conceiving of American Zionism as something other than an expression of nationalism.[11] This book demonstrates the ways that Zionist thinking about collectivity, as expressed in the language of peoplehood, is in fact deeply shaped by nationalism. The language of peoplehood translates some of Zionism's fundamental assumptions into a vocabulary that serves as a kind of code word for nationhood, internalizing those assumptions while erasing the term *nation* from the conceptual vocabulary of American Jewish collectivity. Peoplehood, then, is an American innovation not because it rejects Jewish nationalism as the defining framework for defining Jewish collectivity, but precisely the opposite. It enabled Zionism's conception of Jewish groupness to move from the margins to the mainstream of American Jewish life and thought.[12]

At the same time, the introduction of peoplehood as an English-language neologism (largely as a departure from terms like nationhood) in the 1930s and 1940s—as well as its eventual ascendance in the second half of the twentieth century as the dominant terminology for Jewish group identity—reflects the specific historical context of American Jews and Judaism. In translating European ideas about Jewish nationalism into American vocabularies, peoplehood succeeded in affirming an American-Jewish synthesis.

Peoplehood as a term for Jewish collectivity, then, develops in response to the competing claims of Zionism and Americanism, made much sharper by a series of external developments including European antisemitism, World War II, and the rise of statist political Zionism and the Jewish state itself. For some thinkers, peoplehood chiefly functioned as a way to clarify the status of American Jews as a group vis-à-vis both the United States and other Jews around the world; for others, it served to emphasize the content, history, and mission that binds together Jews as a nation. Peoplehood could appeal to American Jews committed to affirming a collective Jewish consciousness without hindering Jewish acculturation and integration within the United States. By paralleling the structure of nationhood without explicitly connecting itself to nation, the addition of the suffix -*hood* provided a bridge between the denationalized connotations of people in the American context and trends in European nationalism and Zionism that influenced American Jewish perspectives on collectivity. Jewish peoplehood emerged and evolved both under the influence of and, at times, in opposition to European nationalism and pluralism in an American context.

The supporting abstract noun peoplehood, then, constructs and gives credibility to a radically new vision of collectivity, by underscoring the historical roots, timeless existence, and essential nature of what is ultimately an innovation. This book focuses on Jewish peoplehood, rather than the Jewish people, precisely because peoplehood—that is, the process of explaining the condition of being the Jewish people, and the consciousness of being a people—constructs the very definition of what constitutes that people. Peoplehood's proponents present it as if it is simply recognizing that there is a condition of being a people that has always been there, while in reality the need to say that a people exists comes first and stimulates the very definition of that people. There is thus no way to divorce particular developments of the peoplehood vocabulary from subsequent uses of the term Jewish people, because the language of peoplehood shapes the meaning of people as much as the reverse. This is a rather counterintuitive claim precisely because it goes directly against the grain of peoplehood's assertion that it reflects an existing reality, rather than shaping or creating that reality.

Yet it is also a claim shared with many other modern groups. One of the strategies of this book is to place the emergence of Jewish peoplehood as the key concept for defining Jewish collectivity and nationhood in conversation with broader trends in scholarship on group identity in the modern period. The past decade has seen significant scholarly work on the concept of peoplehood in general. Berkeley sociologist John Lie and Yale political theorist Rogers Smith both argue that peoplehood—the conscious effort to distinguish particular groups as a people—is a modern phenomenon intimately linked to the emergence of nationalism in the late nineteenth and early twentieth centuries.[13] The modern nation-state, a political unit that claimed to represent a homogenous community among individuals coming from diverse linguistic, religious, and ethnic groups, sparked a process of constructing the idea of specific peoples. "Pre-modern polities were at once incapable of and indifferent to achieving cultural and status integration," Lie agues. "That is, they failed to forge a common national culture or to establish the unity of the rulers and ruled. Hence, attributions of pre-modern peoplehood are proleptic, projecting present understanding onto the past."[14]

Contextualizing Jewish peoplehood in this broader scholarship contrasts with a tendency toward exceptionalism in recent writings on Jewish peoplehood. One of the common claims about Jewish peoplehood is that it reflects the unique case of a historical model of Jewish collectivity that does not fit into the broader categories of groupness in the modern world. According to this narrative, the Jewish case failed to match dominant categories of modern groupness in Western political thought such as race, ethnicity, and nationality.[15] Jewish peoplehood developed to fill a vacuum in modern political thought. Only a new conceptual term could capture perennial characterization of Jewish group identity that recognizes Jews as a religion and a nation, integrates homeland and diaspora populations, and captures the sui generis historical experience of Jewish continuity across time and space.

Peoplehood certainly has allowed Jews to navigate the limits of existing group identity categories. Its semantic flexibility and fluidity enables it simultaneously to encompass and remain distinct from other group concepts such as nation, religion, ethnicity, and race. However, the positioning of peoplehood as a none-of-the-above category belies its primary association with nationhood. Although its beginnings were connected to a critique of state-oriented Zionism, modern Jewish peoplehood has significantly internalized key assumptions about collectivity—such as shared essence, political unity, and connection to a homeland—from the logic of nationalism. In the context of the study of modern peoplehood in contemporary scholarship, the emergence of Jewish peoplehood in close conversation with nationhood makes the Jewish case one example of a broader phenomenon. Articulations of Jewish peoplehood (and its evolution) do resemble the self-articulations and expressions of other modern groups.

The origins of Jewish studies in nineteenth-century Germany helped set the theoretical foundation for defining Jewish peoplehood within the national framework. Today, the close ties between Jewish studies and broader academic interpretation of social, political, and cultural trends provides an opportunity to situate the understanding of Jewish collectivity in a very different context. Indeed, the field of Jewish studies has a potentially transformational role to play in the process of reconstituting the meaning, value, and assumptions of Jewish collectivity. However, there has been a limited level of interest in peoplehood as a research topic or area of specialization.

When the editors of an influential compendium of terms in Jewish religious thought published their volume in 1987, neither Jewish peoplehood nor the Jewish people appeared as entries.[16] (The only related term that was included was *chosen people*.) However, twenty-five years later, the editors of the series on key words, of which this book is a part, did view Jewish peoplehood as a concept worth including and examining critically, as it has remained largely outside the lens of Jewish studies. A generation of modern Jewish historians has transformed how we view the history of Jewish collective self-understanding, but their scholarship has had little direct bearing on communal claims of peoplehood. Though there are certainly scholars of Jewish studies who have contributed to thinking about Jewish peoplehood, no critical, historical analysis of the term has yet been done.[17] Scholarly and popular discussions of Jewish peoplehood have failed to acknowledge the extent to which this key term represents a changing social construction that has evolved over time in response to historical circumstances and to the needs and agendas of Jewish situations. Some scholars accept the idea that peoplehood exemplifies an enduring essential concept that links the various elements of the Jewish experience;[18] others contend that the influence of European Jewish politics, especially nationalism, failed to cross the Atlantic in any substantial fashion.[19] And on the level of both communal discussion and popular conversations, Jews have often used the term *Jewish people* with the apparent intention of distinguishing it from the Jewish nation per se.

One obstacle to critical analysis lies in the term's deceptive simplicity and its now-established position in Jewish discourse. There is little perceived need for (and, I would argue, active if unconscious resistance to) critically analyzing or historically contextualizing a term now so deeply ingrained in communal conversations and individual psyches. The apparent simplicity and familiarity of this key concept enables it to be harnessed in the service of particular ideological or communal agendas, which are revealed, for example, when public intellectuals either lament the demise of Jewish peoplehood or even celebrate a growing shift toward Jewish identity as a personal choice rather than a collective commitment.

A second reason for the hesitation to assess peoplehood involves the high stakes associated with this key word. Peoplehood necessarily evokes the relationship between the Jewish people and the State of Israel. This issue has many implications for often-polarizing discussions and debates among—and about—passionate supporters, caring critics, and committed detractors of the State of Israel. The ideologies of Zionism as a nationalist movement are built on the foundation of certain assumptions about the Jewish people: the people of Israel (*am yisrael*) are linked to the Land of Israel (*eretz yisrael*) and to the State of Israel (*medinat yisrael*). The desire to defend, modify, or delegitimize Zionist claims to all or part of a Jewish national homeland energizes increasingly divergent readings of peoplehood terminology. Delving into the sources and functions of peoplehood in American Jewish life reveals unsettled tensions and contradictions between competing homeland and diaspora claims about modern Jewish life.

Another factor hindering critical study of the Jewish people is that the dominant Jewish communal discourse around collectivity is in tension with scholarly conversations about groupness. The most vocal advocates for Jewish peoplehood in the contemporary Jewish community have adopted a largely essentialist (a set of unchanging shared attributes) vision of Jewish identity and collectivity; are heavily oriented toward the State of Israel; and focus on continuity, in-marriage (descent), and the inexorable reality of persecution. In this view, Jewish boundaries reflect a shared commitment to the State of Israel and an ethnic understanding of Judaism as an identity passed on by descent, situated in a world divided between groups with essential differences and conflicting values. Proponents of these conceptions of Jewish collectivity rarely consider dramatic recent changes in Jewish self-definition, which reflect fluid and even hybrid identities, and a complex relationship to ethnicity and group identity. They merely lament these changes rather than locating them as yet another historical development, and continue to refer to the importance of a transhistorical and constant set of boundaries that define Jewish collectivity. Such lamentation over the loss of Jewish peoplehood today is ironic, given (as we shall see in this volume) the relatively recent (and innovative) emergence of the vocabulary of peoplehood as a constituent element of Jewish identity.

By contrast, historical scholarship on nationalism, ethnicity, race, and other notions of groupness has dramatically altered both descriptive and prescriptive boundaries of groups. Over the last three decades, historians of groups have moved from using their research to support and validate claims of particular groups toward tracing the historical dimensions that shaped constructions of collective identity. The shift from understanding groups as transhistorical entities with essential traits to seeing them as social constructs whose boundaries are largely invented or imagined challenges the sense of historical continuity of particular groups. It raises many questions about the normative value of collective solidarity based on uncritical internalization of inherited historical myths and exclusivist criteria for membership. This scholarly turn has promoted an intellectual environment highly critical of historical or contemporary assertions of the existence or value of group claims.

Also, scholarly shifts toward analyzing, and often affirming, hybrid identities that emphasize cultural dialogue and boundary crossing, membership based on voluntary (as opposed to inherited) identification, and the separation of ethnic identity from political statehood and geography raise further potential tensions. These trends clash with the essentialist and particularist Jewish emphasis on the centrality of the State of Israel, the importance of in-marriage, and the rededication to peoplehood. For example, Israeli historian Shlomo Sand's book *The Invention of the Jewish People* makes an argument about collectivity that uses an analysis of historical construction to articulate a critique of the legitimacy of the modern state of Israel and Jewish nationalism. It should be noted here that revealing the ways that modern nationalism has played a significant role in the construction and reimagination of Jewish collectivity does present some challenges to the narrative of Jewish peoplehood. However, asserting the constructiveness of historical claims does not necessarily lead to the erasure of the contemporary significance of collective claims. Nevertheless, Jewish communal leaders and public intellectuals (including a number of academics among them) often respond defensively to notions of constructedness, experiencing contemporary scholarly approaches to collective identity, nationalism, and ethnicity as only in conflict with their desire to affirm and promote Jewish solidarity.

A critical key word approach to Jewish peoplehood is not meant to do away with concepts of Jewish collectivity, which have played multiple and significant roles in defining Jews and Judaism for thousands of years. Instead, after demonstrating the rupture of today's terminology with historical precedents, this book concludes with an attempt to revitalize and transform conversations about Jewish collectivity in a new key. Our exploration of recent political, cultural, and social trends allows us to consider which conceptions of Jewish groupness might best serve that collectivity in the contemporary context, and capture the imagination of a growing number of Jews alienated by the existing discourse of collective solidarity and peoplehood. The final chapter presents a roadmap for articulating an understanding of Jewish peoplehood that avoids the problematic alternatives for viewing Jewish collective self-understanding—alarmist and essentialist (and/or ethnocentric) on one hand, or merely invented and thus irrelevant on the other.

This volume seeks to create a conversation that bridges the disconnect between Jewish communal essentialism and academic constructivism about the meaning and role of groups. These two positions create a false choice between affirming peoplehood as an unchanging idea and rejecting collectivity as an invented concept used to support ethnocentric claims; the path forward requires navigating between these positions on the legitimacy and value of Jewish peoplehood claims. An essentialist definition of the Jewish people as a stable historical community with a particular unifying essence falls short in a global age in a number of ways, and fails to resonate with audiences sensitive to the historically questionable claims of particular notions of solidarity. From a moral perspective, the dominant rhetoric of the Jewish people can serve to obscure and marginalize ethical concerns about Israel's treatment of its minority populations and the ongoing dilemmas of statehood, especially political debates over the future of the occupied territories.

A sustainable concept of Jewish solidarity needs to acknowledge the ways in which understandings of Jewish collectivity, like almost all other models of collective affinity, evolve and reflect historical development. Taboos surrounding any sustained, complex conversation that might unpack, contextualize, and (re)consider the changing meanings of the Jewish people itself probably (and ironically) contributes to peoplehood's marginalization and delegitimizes efforts to propose alternate models better suited for today's changing patterns of identification and group membership. The continuation of an uncritical use of the term peoplehood in Jewish collectivity would have a negative long-term impact on American Jewish life if champions of the term continue to advocate outdated paradigms of Jewishness that erode, rather than strengthen, the relevance of Jewish membership in a global era. An analysis that historicizes the changing meaning of Jewish collectivity (including recognizing a conceptual dynamism that has in fact characterized Jewish collectivity through history) could actually contribute to its revitalization in contemporary American Jewish life. In order to preserve the possibilities inherent in Jewish peoplehood, the word itself may need to be seriously reconfigured and even transformed, so as to articulate Jewish collectivity in terms unburdened by the assumptions now embedded in the rhetoric of peoplehood.

1 Terms of Debate

JEWISH NATIONHOOD AND
AMERICAN PEOPLEHOOD

I remember standing as a boy on the sidewalks of midtown Manhattan, on a Solidarity Sunday in the mid-1980s, along with thousands of New Yorkers rallying for Soviet Jews. These large gatherings of American Jews working together to free our fellow Jews emphasized and embodied a powerful message that certain bonds connected Jewish people around the world to one another. We chanted and sang the rallying cry "Am yisrael chai" (The Jewish people lives!) for hours. This iconic song, written by Rabbi Shlomo Carlebach specifically for the Soviet Jewry movement, encapsulated a sense of membership in a group with a long past, a deeply felt collective present, and a shared future.

The solidarity that American Jews expressed and experienced with Soviet Jewish dissidents and their cause transcended different languages, cultures, religious practices, and even the Cold War that pitted our countries of citizenship against each other, uniting American Jews in common cause against the Soviet regime. The basis for that solidarity felt so obvious that it hardly had to be articulated: a shared collective history with its experiences of both persecution and endurance, bonds of blood and descent, and an attachment to the State of Israel whose establishment in 1948 created a focal point for Jews around the globe. "Am yisrael chai" was such a powerful concept, capable of inspiring activism and political action for a shared cause—the enduring existence of a distinct transhistorical people.

Looking back over the twentieth century, the Soviet Jewry movement marked a high point in the affirmation of a particular vision of Jewish collectivity and group cohesion.[1] The sense of obligation to protect Jews around the globe was undoubtedly shaped in part by the trauma of the Holocaust and the growing realization and absorption of what American Jewry had been unable to do by way of rescuing their European sisters and brothers from their fate. What defined the Jewish people in this post-Holocaust context of the late twentieth century was the belief that across the diversity of Jewish life, Jews shared an unmistakable set of characteristics and collective goals. The principle of Jewish unity undergirded the need to stand up for one another in the face of unceasing persecution and to work together to fulfill a common mission. Jewish peoplehood came to function as the key term in American Jewish life for articulating these assumptions—and for presenting them as axiomatic.

Two decades after the collapse of the Soviet Union, this sense of unity that links so many members of the world Jewish community appears quiescent. The basic sense of a common denominator of Jewish cohesion so powerfully on display during the Soviet Jewry rallies and felt so deeply during other twentieth-century events, such as the creation of the State of Israel and especially the Six Day and Yom Kippur Wars, has largely dissipated. Contemporary Jews appear far less committed to peoplehood than previous generations, and the dominant communal discourse on Jewish peoplehood is characterized by the conviction that this shift is an alarming sign of a dramatic decline in contemporary Jewish collective identity, with negative implications for Jewish continuity.

Several years ago, two American Jewish scholars, the sociologist Steven M. Cohen and the historian Jack Wertheimer, lamented the dissolution of Jewish peoplehood in an article in the journal *Commentary*, "Whatever Happened to the Jewish People?"[2] After opening the article with a description of the Soviet Jewry solidarity movement in the early 1980s, they compare the then-present situation circa 2006 to what they consider the heyday of Jewish peoplehood:

> Today, less than twenty years later, it is almost inconceivable that the American Jewish community could muster the will to mount so massive a show of unity. It is not just that, at the moment, no large-scale crisis seems to engage the American Jewish *psyche*. Rather, something vital in the *psyche* has changed. Mounting evidence now attests to a weakened identification among American Jews with their fellow Jews abroad, as well as a waning sense of communal responsibility at home.[3]

Cohen, Wertheimer, and many other Jewish communal thought leaders posit this decline based on an implicit set of assumptions about the nature of Jewish collectivity. They underscore a corrosive change to the "vital psyche" of the Jewish people. The affirmation of that collective psyche implies that the shift stems not from an inevitable change in the external historical situation (e.g., the freeing of Soviet Jews in the 1990s), but instead results from a problematic diminution in the substance of Jewish connectivity itself. Their claim thus implicitly rejects viewing events of the 1970s and 1980s as one particular historical manifestation of Jewish peoplehood, and peoplehood itself as inevitably subject to change over time.[4]

It would be difficult to challenge Cohen and Wertheimer's claim that a show of unity like a Soviet Jewry rally would not take place today. What it means to be a member of the Jewish people and what the ties are that bind this collective group together have become far more complicated to conceptualize and enact. In the years since those rallies, the overriding sense of unity represented by centralized Jewish institutions, the State of Israel as focus for diaspora communities, and the plight of persecuted Jews has been eroded by several factors, including high rates of intermarriage, a shift toward individualized Jewish identity, the mass emigration of Soviet Jews, changing attitudes toward the State of Israel, and the decentralization of Jewish communal life in the United States. Wider trends like increasingly permeable identity boundaries and globalization have accompanied these intra-Jewish developments.

But the question "Whatever happened to the Jewish people?" beyond its factual observations implicitly contends that twentieth-century criteria for defining and measuring peoplehood legitimately represent a standard applicable across time and space, a normative set of unchanging beliefs and practices that typify the "Jewish psyche" and transcends changing historical circumstances. One particular set of behaviors—specifically, "weakened identification among American Jews with their fellow Jews abroad, as well as a waning sense of communal responsibility at home"—serves as an indicator of the declining relative strength of the essential quality of Jewish peoplehood.[5] This specific definition of what it means to be part of the Jewish people may also suggest one reason why the recent Pew report's findings of a rise in identification with the Jewish people did not garner more optimistic celebration among concerned Jewish communal leaders.[6] The survey respondents' conception of peoplehood lacked the level of political conviction and call to activism on behalf of world Jewry that would match a particular criterion for peoplehood—that is, a high level of identification with Jews abroad and responsibilities to the local Jewish community.

But is there an unambiguous, unchanging, and timeless basis for defining the essence of Jewish peoplehood, as Cohen and Wertheimer imply? Do changing models of Jewish individual and collective expression represent a decline in a transhistorical criterion for peoplehood? Or is there another way to interpret changing attitudes as a reflection of the ongoing evolution of the meanings and practices of Jewish collectivity, and of Jewish peoplehood—one of many expressions of that collectivity, and one that is itself relatively new and innovative rather than timeless and immutable?

This chapter charts the evolution of Jewish peoplehood as shaped by both Zionist conceptions of Jewish nationhood and English-language notions of people as a group category aligned with the democratic values at the core of what it means to be American. I focus primarily here on these modern terms of debate, rather than precedents from Jewish texts or history, as the most important sources of modern Jewish peoplehood to demonstrate the recent genesis of the term. The first section of this chapter argues that Jewish peoplehood's defining features have clear etymological and theoretical precedents in terminology linked to European and European Jewish nationalism developed in the nineteenth and early twentieth centuries. In particular, Jewish peoplehood brings forward three aspects of the nationalist paradigm of collective identity: rigid boundaries between national groups, the assertion of a shared essential national quality, and the shift to grounding collective narratives in secular history rather than religious narratives. The second section traces the transition from nationhood to peoplehood in the American context. It focuses on why a new terminology was needed, what made peoplehood particularly useful, and how it came to represent a critique of and corrective to certain articulations of Jewish nationalism even as it drew heavily on aspects of nationalist logic. The third section traces the rise of Jewish peoplehood post-1948, shaped not only by the emergence of the State of Israel but also by a deepening attention to peoplehood in American public debates about identity politics, such that Jewish peoplehood came to be presented as transhistorical and essential—in a sense asserting, through this relatively new term, its own timeless authenticity.

This approach challenges the implicit claim that one can meaningfully ask the question "Whatever happened to the Jewish people?" without first probing the historical origins of the specific constellation of meanings associated with peoplehood—an analysis that goes against the very grain of peoplehood's representation. Reconceptualizing the role of this word—from an enduring concept to a recent innovation—and tracing its evolution from an American alternative to the limited terms for collective identity in diaspora culture, to one that supports key Zionist concepts, raises a fundamental question about Jewish peoplehood that contrasts with the view that this veteran concept is now in decline: How did peoplehood, a neologism from the 1930s, shift in a few decades from being a marginal idea developed unsystematically to respond to a new set of early twentieth-century opportunities and challenges, into a (and perhaps even *the*) core defining component of Jewish identity and the dominant taxonomic category for Jewish collectivity in the second half of the twentieth century and beyond?

What Is a Nation? Peoplehood's European Precursors

The seemingly close linguistic link between *am yisrael* (the people/nation of Israel) and Jewish peoplehood might lead the reader to ask legitimately here: Isn't Jewish peoplehood basically just an English translation of the Hebrew phrase *am yisrael*? Though the lineage of Jewish peoplehood as a central concept throughout Jewish history is in fact often traced precisely through this connection, that association is tenuous. Certainly the conception of Jews as a collective group has this and many other precursors in Jewish sources, practices, and institutions. Historical antecedents for referring to Jews as the Jewish people include a rich Hebrew conceptual vocabulary, with terms that emphasize a shared divine election (*am segula* [a treasured nation], *knesset yisrael* [congregation of Israel]), territorial sovereignty (*am yisrael, beit yisrael* [house of Israel]), and tribal bonds (*b'nei yisrael* [children of Israel], *shivtei yisrael* [tribes of Israel]). Biblical sources as early as the Book of Esther called the collective *Yehudim* (Jews). Words in other Jewish languages include the Yiddish *der yidn* (the Jews) or the Ladino *la uma* (the [Jewish] nation/ethnoreligious group).

However, the dominant contemporary English translation of these terms, Jewish people, has no direct antecedent in Hebrew or any other Jewish language. Furthermore, the addition of *-hood*—a suffix connoting the condition of groupness itself—is itself an innovation, with no historical precedents at all (nor does there seem to have been any other abstract noun describing that condition of the Jewish collective). The fact that the English key word Jewish people lacks a clear antecedent (as does its abstract noun form, Jewish peoplehood) signifies that its use does not chiefly reflect translation.

Based on the list of possible terms to select as the source for English-speaking Jews to refer to their own group identity, neither the most historically common term for referring to Jews individually and collectively (*yisrael*, or Israel) nor any other single historical key term has taken center stage in Jewish communal discourse. The Jewish people might better reflect a combination of the translation of *am* (as in *am yisrael*) with that of *yehudi* (Jew/ish), but the term *am yehudi* appears nowhere in traditional Hebrew sources. And a Hebrew analogue for peoplehood, *amiyut*, has only entered the Hebrew language recently, as a new word translated from and created to serve as a parallel to peoplehood, attempting to represent in Hebrew the hood-ness that is asserted in the English (and largely American) term.[7]

Moreover, translations of the Hebrew terms *am* and *yisrael* into "people" and "Jews/Jewish," respectively, represent subjective interpretations. The modern *Even-Shoshan Hebrew-Hebrew Dictionary* renders *am* as "a large collection of people with a shared ancestry, history and generally a spoken language and most of whose members are concentrated in a specific state [*medina*, as in *medinat yisrael*, or the State of Israel]."[8] Based on linguistic comparison of the use of *am* in the biblical context, the Brown-Driver

Briggs lexicon of the Hebrew Bible suggests "kinsman" as the most appropriate translation of the ancient term.[9] These two sources—one written by an Israeli Hebraist shortly after the founding of the state and the other created by nineteenth-century Christian biblical critics—illustrate two divergent historical meanings of the Hebrew word *am,* the former largely territorial and cultural, the other ethnic and perhaps even biological. The multiple possible connotations of *am* in these dictionaries make references to the term as an antecedent for modern Jewish peoplehood an argument based more on reading contemporary interpretations of collectivity back into Jewish sources rather than on translating a singular and constant historical concept into an English word.

A far more obvious choice for an English term to refer to the Jewish collective would have been Israel (the English rendering of *yisrael*). Israel—the new name, meaning "godwrestler," given to the patriarch Jacob in the biblical book of Genesis—stands out in biblical and rabbinic literature as the most common single term (or the most prevalent second noun in construct noun phrases) used to refer to the collective, as well as to one of its members. Indeed, before 1948, Israel referred to Jews regardless of geography and political status; for example, nineteenth-century American Jews most often used Israelite (as well as Hebrew) to refer to themselves.[10] But today Israel refers almost exclusively to the Jewish state, whose early leaders made a conscious decision to name itself the State of Israel rather than several other proposed options.[11] From a Zionist perspective, the phrase *am yisrael* seems implicitly to make a historical case for the modern nation of Israel as the heir to the legacy of the Bible—but that association of Israel with citizenship in a modern state would have made little sense before the state's establishment, when Israel applied equally to Jews in the homeland and the diaspora.[12]

Reflecting a juxtaposition of *Jewish* and *people* (the latter grounded in a selective translation of *am*) with the addition of *-hood,* Jewish peoplehood is as much a new creation as a translation of longstanding terminology. Furthermore, the grammatical construction of the term peoplehood, as opposed to people alone, implies a focus on the fact of collectivity, rather than the basis of cohesion or practices of membership. Indeed, the suffix *-hood,* according to the Merriam-Webster dictionary, means "individuals share a specific state or character (as in brotherhood)."[13] Peoplehood, referring to the Jewish people with an abstract noun, renders the existence of some particular condition or quality as a given, and focuses on the very idea of sharing an abstract commitment of being part of a people, rather than on that condition or quality per se. The recent language of peoplehood, then, has fostered a circular definition of the term, with the condition of being a people—and articulating that condition—as its defining mode, and an end in and of itself. In that sense, peoplehood begs the question of what the nature of Jewish collectivity is, and moves directly to argumentation about and meta-analysis of how and what the people are and should be doing as a reflection of that collectivity.

Beyond this strictly terminological rupture within Jewish self-articulation, recent Jewish studies scholarship reveals a diversity of expressions over time of Jewish groupness that conflict with contemporary uses of peoplehood and its claims of timeless and singular endurance characterized by clear boundaries, secular political unity, and attachment to the modern state of Israel. Significant historical counterexamples illustrate permeable boundaries between Jews and others,[14] focus on religious principles and law,[15] and downplay territory as the central aspect of Jewish collectivity.[16] The disconnect between these and other diverse premodern conceptions of Jewish collectivity and the recent language of peoplehood reflects, in large measure, the impact of nationalism on post-emancipation Jewish life and thought, as well as the historical context of the late nineteenth and twentieth centuries in the United States. In this chapter, we examine each in turn.

The functional and linguistic antecedents of the English word peoplehood emerged in Europe during the nineteenth century; somewhat paradoxically, post-emancipation opportunities for Jewish integration and acculturation prompted new vocabulary for defining Jewish distinctiveness.[17] The process of Jewish emancipation, which began in France at the end of the eighteenth century and spread in fits and starts across Europe during the nineteenth century, promised Jews citizenship and full membership in the national community.[18] At the same time, emancipation demanded high levels of conformity to a set of cultural, linguistic, social, and behavioral norms. Conflicting pulls toward integration and separation had divergent outcomes: unprecedented acculturation for Jews accompanied by a novel focus on boundary preservation and notions of an essential difference between Jews and non-Jews (even while these differences were rapidly disintegrating).

The logic of modern nationalism played a central role in navigating the tension between acculturation and differentiation. Jews from across the political and religious spectrums incorporated key aspects of the modern nationalist paradigm of identity and collectivity into their thinking and language, even while many of them struggled to distance themselves from nationalism's assumptions and explicitly embracing the category of nation for their own definitions of Jews as a distinct group.[19] As an expression of Jewish collectivity linked to premodern sources and associated with diasporic expressions as well as statist ones, peoplehood can easily be disconnected with the study of Jewish nationalism. This creates the illusion that modern nationalism is disconnected from historical definitions of Jewish peoplehood.[20]

Nationalism's defining role in shaping nineteenth-century conceptions of Jewish group identity surfaces more clearly against the backdrop of the contested and capacious meanings of nationalism in this period.[21] Today, nationalism is intimately associated with the principle, established following the First World War, that each nation has the right to its own territory and political sovereignty, giving each particular ethno-national group control of its own political destiny.[22] In contrast, the historical nationalist paradigm of identity, as opposed to this intimate connection with statehood, understood national boundaries and the meaning of membership beyond political sovereignty and statehood, and offered novel frameworks for thinking about collective groups and boundaries.

The conceptual precursors to peoplehood, then, emerged at this earlier moment when the relationship between nation and state remained inchoate, and many conflicting visions of national identity battled for broad acceptance. Our term nationalist paradigm is useful here for distinguishing between nation-state nationalism and the broader set of assumptions about collectivity identity associated with nationalism as it evolved during the nineteenth and early twentieth centuries, which contributed to the evolution of key terms related to Jewish collectivity. That wider paradigm dominated the political discourse across Europe. As a new concept, the meaning of national identity remained open for debate.

Budding nation-states, long-lasting multinational empires, and minority communities all negotiated the relationship between collective groups, territory, and political authority through engagement with the nationalist paradigm. That negotiation hinged on the question famously posed by French philologist Ernest Renan, "What is a nation?"[23] The question required answering several fundamental issues about the meaning of national membership. Is membership in a national group an innate quality passed down through blood or a voluntary association? Are territorial and/or political borders necessary for national consciousness? What role does language and/or culture play in identifying the ties that bind group members to one another? How much diversity can national groups tolerate before dissolving as a discrete group?

The modern constructions of Jewish collective identity that paved the way for the introduction of peoplehood in the 1930s originated in the broader milieu of European thinkers and politicians debating these questions. Jewish thinkers and leaders recognized the stakes of the debate about the definition of a nation, and participated by developing Jewish analogues to various categories of national membership. Among the most important of the categories which functioned as precursors to peoplehood are the Yiddish *folk* (connected closely to the German *Volk*), German *Stamm,* and Russian *narod*.²⁴ These terms translate somewhat interchangeably as "people," "ethnic group," or "tribe"—affirming a timeless sense to these concepts.²⁵ But these key words all developed while intellectuals and political leaders debated the idea of nationalism and its implications for different groups in the nineteenth and early twentieth centuries.

My goals in identifying the emergence of these precursors to peoplehood are twofold. First, that identification will illustrate the pre-origins of peoplehood in a rich discourse of European Jewish politics that was well known to the émigré intellectuals who brought peoplehood to the fore of American Jewish life. Second, it will highlight a set of shared assumptions based in the nationalist paradigm that remain highly influential on assumptions about peoplehood to this day. Peoplehood's precursors helped shape an eventual essentialist definition of Jewish collectivity rooted in secular history, protected by rigid boundaries based on descent, language, or culture, and unified by a shared mission for humanity.

The meanings of *folk, Stamm,* and *narod* were somewhat overlapping and contested, both within their Jewish and non-Jewish contexts. For example, the German *Stamm* affirmed a collective consciousness based on a shared history. In Germany, Jews spoke of themselves as Germans of the Jewish *Stamm* (tribe).²⁶ Historian Till van Rahden argues that the concept "provided the lowest common denominator between those Jews who considered themselves a religious community and those who thought of themselves as an ethnic group, a nation, or even a 'race.'"²⁷ In addition to providing a palatably vague reference to the Jewish tribe's common descent and history, *Stamm* suggested a harmonious balance between particular and universal objectives. As the Viennese rabbi Adolf Jellinek described it, "[The Jew] is particularistic enough, stable enough, subjective enough not to be absorbed by other people; he is however also sufficiently universalistic, enthusiastic, progressive, and objective not to persist in insolent and rigid isolation. . . . The Jewish Stamm is therefore truly chosen for its mission."²⁸ Jews could be one of many Stämme (tribes) in the Hapsburg Empire fully dedicated to a set of shared universal principles and yet remain distinct.²⁹ This articulation demonstrates a common trope in modern Jewish thought—the claim that Jews are distinct precisely because they embody the group most committed to integration and universal principles. The logic attempted to mitigate the tension between integration and separation by affirming particular ties as the basis for contributing to the broader polity.

In the Eastern European context, the Yiddish word *folk* (closely linked to the German *Volk*) shaped Jewish visions of collectivity with more concrete delineations of what constitutes difference. *Folk* offered a more robust set of national characteristics, including a culture, language, spirit, and even homeland. The preference for *folk* in the Eastern European context reflects the ability to mold the term to the context of living in multinational empires where social, cultural, and linguistic differences remained far clearer. For example, the historian and theorist of Jewish nationalism Simon Dubnow created the Folkspartei ([Jewish] People's Party) in 1906, to advocate for territorial autonomy within the Russian Empire.[30] The concept of folk in Yiddish emphasized the spiritual, cultural, and territorial bonds among Jews that justified autonomy within the broader empire.

Dubnow's choice of the Yiddish *folk* probably also reflects the influence of the Russian word *narod*. Like the German, *narod* is based on an understanding of a particular set of cultural practices and folklore that distinguished each group within the Russian Empire. Influenced by the Russian search for the pure folk culture of the *narod*, Jewish intellectuals attempted to capture the unique practices, rituals, and folkways of the Jewish *narod*.[31] During the nineteenth century, *narod* could either mean the residents of a state or "an ethnic group without political autonomy or even a tradition of statehood."[32] The fact that *narod*, like *folk* and *Stamm*, did not necessarily have political claims made all these terms well suited for negotiating between defining the collective through a shared political allegiance to a state and other ethnic, cultural, or religious claims about the nature of Jewish particularism.

As with people and peoplehood, all three of these terms had popular abstract-noun variants—*Volkstum* (character of the ethnic community), *Stammbewußtein* (tribal consciousness), and *narodnost* (national principle)—which affirmed the very existence of collective groups in the use of terms to discuss the nature, essence, or consciousness of these communities.[33] All these terms answered the question of what the unique qualities and essential traits are of a given national group. But, by building on the prominence of these terms and their associated abstract nouns, Jewish national claims could affirm distinct boundaries while demonstrating the fundamental parallels between Jews and other collective groups (both the majority population and other minority communities).

Situating terminology associated with Jewish national identity in the nineteenth century within the marketplace of European nationalism opens up the study of peoplehood to insights from the field of nationalism studies. Until the 1970s, the study of nationalism mainly considered national groups as fixed (albeit evolving) communities. Scholarship focused on tracing the path of these seemingly timeless entities. More recently, scholars studying nationalism have traced the ways in which national movements (re-)imagined their collective identity, exploring how these shifts actually represented a rupture with premodern categories. Rather than nations creating states, historians of nationalism argue that states actually created national groups.[34] Interpreting the evolution of peoplehood as a variety of modern nationalism sheds light on the key word's innovation in conceptualizing the Jewish collective. The nationalist paradigm introduced a self-conscious vocabulary of Jewish difference that emphasized a particular nature, rigid boundaries, and a connection to a homeland.

One of the primary changes to group identity introduced by nationalism was a shift toward a more self-conscious and intentional affirmation of collectivity than premodern articulations of membership. According to the historian of nationalism Benedict Anderson, group identity existed in premodern religious communities (not just Jewish ones) as "unselfconscious coherence."[35] There was little need to define the collective because identity was so deeply rooted and self-evident in practice, myth, social interactions, culture, and external political boundaries. One would be hard-pressed to find a premodern thinker focusing explicitly on the terminology and definition of collectivity.

Nationalism's emphasis on collective bonds across historical periods and geographic territories stimulated efforts to define and affirm group boundaries explicitly that had previously been both implicitly assumed and organically nurtured through local webs of relationships. Indeed, one of the foundational assumptions of the nationalist paradigm is the possibility of constructing clear distinctions between insiders and outsiders around quantifiable and measurable criteria. As nationalists endeavored to construct useable pasts to justify collective cohesion, their narratives argued for a high degree of separation and delineation between collective entities over time. This perspective introduced strict categorization of national groups and the mutually exclusive logic of membership.[36] Clear rubrics of national identity were superimposed over the blurry and messy category and community boundaries that existed in practice.[37] The nationalist paradigm shaped what historian Rogers Brubaker describes as "the tendency to take discrete sharply differentiated internally homogenous, and eternally bounded groups as basic constituents of social lives."[38] The emergence of nationalism in fact erected a new model for group identity, including an emphasis on Jewish blood and race, that was far more exclusive, rigid, and monolithic than premodern notions of collective difference.[39]

Each national group's distinctiveness was linked to a particular set of characteristics. The importance of an essentialist definition in articulating the nature of differences between national groups can be seen in a classical formulation of the nationalist paradigm. In his famous 1882 lecture, Ernest Renan defined the nation as a "soul, a spiritual principle" that links members to one another and across time.[40] A parallel development occurred in the identification of the particular set of cultural or ethical ideas that the group has to share with the world. One of the goals of tracing the evolution of nations throughout time was to discover their unique spirit.[41] National groups, it was assumed, shared a core essence that could be identified as unique to each throughout history. Intellectuals referred to the particular spirit or culture of a collectivity over time; nationalist leaders and historians dedicated efforts to identifying the set of cultural attributes that differentiated each nation in order to provide a record of past contributions and future mission. The quintessence of Judaism was portrayed as a cultural connection to texts that defined ethical principles, which had differentiated Jews from their neighbors since the biblical period. Jewish culture embodied a set of ethical principles, which emerge in each historical epoch and contribute to moral progress toward ever more harmonious interactions between different groups. The Jewish people, then, existed to spread a particular mission based on their commitment to universal moral standards.

A final element of theories of collectivity that, influenced by nationalism, emerged in nineteenth-century vocabulary of groups is a shared secular history and mission. According to Anderson, a key intellectual transformation undergirds the shift from premodern religious communities to modern national identities, namely, a parallel shift in the apprehension of time.[42] Anderson argues that classic religious communities "linked by sacred languages had a character distinct from the imagined communities of modern nations."[43] In order to think about a particular group as a nation, there had to be a shift in that group's own conceptions of time and history.

Premodern religious communities like Judaism viewed the world through a mythic lens that conflated the past and present. The present was understood through a cosmic narrative that connected particular events to broader themes.[44] Nationalism introduced a shift away from each individual viewing him/herself as part of a cosmic theological narrative of the relationship between God and the Jewish people. Instead, the nation is conceived as a collective secular group that marches forward together over time, developing its particular characteristics and shaping its historical milieu.

A very different interpretation of the past and its relevance for the present and future emerges with the rise of secular history in the modern period. This turn to a secular history reflects the impact of the nationalist paradigm on collective identify formation. This does not mean that expressions of national collectivity cannot be religious or have religious elements integrated into their narrative. But the perceived need to explain the Jewish past through the language of scientific history introduces an innovation in Jewish views of the past and, with it, the nature of group solidarity.[45] The significance of the Jewish people's past as the primary basis of solidarity leaves the realm of cosmic storytelling and enters the secularized flow of time from one event to another that can be understood in a sequential fashion. For instance, Jewish intellectuals presented the Bible as an example of the role that the Jewish nation played in evolving moral and political concepts in the ancient world.

As theological significance lost currency in the modern world, the historical development of a particular group became a key criterion for legitimating and defining that group's identity. Historians of the Jewish people wrested authority away from rabbinical interpreters to identify national characteristics and patterns. For secular Jewish historians, the purpose of Jewish history was to understand how the collective moved together through time and what those temporal experiences demonstrate about national character. The need to compare and contrast Judaism with other collectivities made the role of the historian increasingly important. The arbiter of collective importance and value moved from theological considerations to an ability to demonstrate scientifically through historical evidence the merits of a particular group, and its unique contributions that could be highlighted when viewing the collective past from the perspective of the present. It is not a coincidence that the first historical studies of Jewish national history emerged in the middle of the nineteenth century. Influenced by the age of nationalism, great modern Jewish historians, such as Heinrich Graetz and Simon Dubnow, narrated the history of the Jewish people through the lens of modern nationalist historiography. Their turn to secular history was linked to a new way of understanding groups and their distinct roles in the world.

The construction of a secular national time with a clear historical narrative fostered the articulation of the origins of a national group, generally in a specific territorial homeland. Zionism emerged as the Jewish ideological movement that developed under the influence of the nationalist paradigm to underscore territory. The spectrum of Zionist thought ranged across a variety of different visions for defining and actualizing these concepts that defined Jews along a spectrum between national group with political sovereignty and confessional religious community.[46]

Major camps included political Zionism, which pushed for the creation of a Jewish homeland in Palestine and the simultaneous rejection of diaspora Jewish life; cultural Zionism, which viewed the Land of Israel as an intellectual center that would invigorate the enduring life of Jews in the diaspora; religious Zionism, which understood the return to Palestine as the beginning of the messianic era; and revisionist Zionism, which sought military strength and maximal territorial control.[47] All these Zionist paradigms of Jewish collectivity shared the assumption that the Jewish people required a national center in a homeland and the corollary belief that Jews living outside the homeland would not have the same opportunities to actualize full membership in the collective.

Until the 1930s, mainstream Zionism remained agnostic on whether establishing a nation-state was the primary goal of the movement.[48] It was not until relatively late in the development of the vocabulary of Jewish collectivity that an autonomous and sovereign state emerged as an integral part of defining the Jewish nation. One of the elements that now stands as arguably the key constituent component of Jewish peoplehood—the State of Israel—was not a central concern for most expressions of Jewish collectivity in the late nineteenth and early twentieth century.

The emergence of a new vocabulary for defining Jews within the nationalist paradigm—at the very moment in which various responses to integration and enlightenment thought fragmented Jews' beliefs and practices—introduced a set of tools for articulating the parameters of Jewish collectivity. This meant new emphasis on the homogeneity of Jews, rigid boundaries distinguishing Jews from non-Jews, an essential, often ethical, core to Jewish membership, and a secular historical narrative that surpassed earlier theological claims as the basis for collective ties. These attributes, as well as the tremendous ambiguity about their details, are brought forward in the emergence of peoplehood in the United States.

But peoplehood reflects two distinctions from its European antecedents. First, peoplehood develops against the backdrop of American nationalism and the unique politics of pluralism that emerged in the United States. Second, peoplehood materializes as a key word just as political Zionism and its statist aspirations gain widespread support. One of the factors differentiating Jewish peoplehood from its functional and linguistic antecedents is that peoplehood must contend with a far more established definition of nationhood that more closely aligns nation and state.

The Emergence of Peoplehood

In the summer of 1942, Rabbi Mordecai Kaplan, the American Jewish thinker most closely associated with peoplehood, delivered the opening address to participants in the Reconstructionist Summer Conference. A report from the proceedings of the conference outlines Kaplan's remarks at the opening session. In framing the theoretical basis of his vision for

American Judaism, he insisted on the importance of preserving the distinction "between nation, nationality, and nationhood." He continued, "The first, nation, should be regarded as the name applied to any group that has all or almost all of the characteristics commonly implied in the term; nationality should refer to any group which is striving to become a nation; nationhood should refer to those bonds of unity which make a group either nationality or a nation."[49] Kaplan's audience appeared skeptical about his attempt to parse nation and its related nouns into distinct typologies. Given the terminological hairsplitting, several conference participants offered suggestions of "alternative phrases for the term 'nationhood.'" These included "peoplehood," "nationality-hood," and "religious nationalism." (In 1942, peoplehood likely sounded as strange and non-obvious as "nationality-hood" sounds today.)[50]

While we don't know what if anything Kaplan said in reaction to these suggestions on that day, 1942 marks a turning point in his vocabulary. Until this point, there were no references to peoplehood in Kaplan's writings; a few months later, Kaplan presented this word (suggested to him, according to the above report, by someone else as one of several choices better than his own terminology of nationhood) as "basic to the whole Reconstructionist position"![51] By 1948, Kaplan had integrated peoplehood into his central platform with the publication of *The Future of the American Jew*, the text that would introduce peoplehood to a wide readership in the United States.[52]

It is rare to have such explicit records of why and when influential introducers and popularizers of key words decide to first use them at all. Here, in the case of Jewish peoplehood, we have a historical window into the emergence of the term, in the form of a story about the thinker who helped transform it from a marginal English label for the Jewish collective into what would become by the beginning of the twenty-first century its primary vocabulary. Far from reflecting a deliberate process of selecting terminology, the adoption of peoplehood by one of its most important popularizers seems unsystematic and even accidental.

The specific word chosen is in some ways far less important than its direct link to nationhood and Kaplan's decades-long commitment to Zionist thought. This account of Kaplan's unplanned shift from his early reliance on nationhood to his adoption of peoplehood illustrates one of this book's central claims: the nationalist paradigm of group identity entered American Jewish thought and shaped the construction of collectivity in American Jewish life precisely—and ironically—through the terminological shift away from nationhood to peoplehood.

Often viewed as an exceptional Jewish community untouched by European politics, Jews in the United States were also affected by principles of identity articulated in European nationalism as they wrestled with notions of collectivity on American soil. In the decades preceding the emergence of Jewish peoplehood in the United States, the nationalist paradigm transformed the meaning of Jewish collectivity. The cornerstones of that paradigm—clear boundary markers that underscored each group's unique shared history and future mission, distinct from others—permeated conceptions of Jewish collectivity across established divides between homeland and diaspora, religious and secular expressions of Judaism, and even national and anti-national articulations of Jewish politics. These constituent elements, as well as a strong connection to a homeland advocated by Zionism, would serve as the theoretical foundation of the new term Jewish peoplehood.

The transition from nationhood to peoplehood in the American context beginning in the 1920s and 1930s invites this question: Why did a set of nationalist-inspired assumptions demand a new terminology at all? The answer, as we shall see, involved several interrelated developments, including the increasingly strong association of nationhood with statehood, the pressure to define Jewish collectivity as fully compatible with American democracy, and the need for American Jews to create a unified voice to advocate for the rights of European Jews with the rise of Hitler. Peoplehood would become the bridge between European internationalization of the nationalist paradigm and the Jewish American experience.

Peoplehood's early Jewish adopters were, like Kaplan, committed Zionists interested in translating Jewish nationalism into terms acceptable in the U.S. context and weaving them into the fabric of American Jewish identity. As American religious leaders sensitive to the challenges facing American Jews at a time of increased nativism, they recognized the limitations of explicitly adopting the terminology of nationalism. In Kaplan's own work, peoplehood came somewhat haphazardly to represent his innovations in Jewish thought, which in part internalized, and yet at times critiqued, conceptions of collectivity derived from the nationalist paradigm.

The success of the term peoplehood can be attributed in part to the resonance of the people with American democratic ideals, and to the ambiguity of the term itself, which does not appear in English dictionaries until the late 1960s.[53] Peoplehood came to offer a largely blank slate that alluded to many elements associated with nationhood, while avoiding the highly charged language of nation, increasingly inflected with statist connotations, that divided American Jewish leaders in the 1930s and 1940s. The emergence and success of Jewish peoplehood as a key word thus reflects far more about the particular political and social challenges of American Jews in the twentieth century than the historical Jewish language of collectivity.

American Zionism: Imagining a Nation of Nationalities

The impact of European nationalism and Zionism on American Jewish thought can be appreciated by understanding the shift that peoplehood represented in English language terminology for Jews and their collective status in the early twentieth century. Terminology for Jewish groupness in the United States from the seventeenth-century arrival of Sephardic Jews from Curaçao until the early twentieth century was quite diverse, but the terms that would come to dominate diaspora Jewish self-understanding by the last half of the twentieth century—Jews as a religion, people, or ethnicity—had not yet played a meaningful role in Jewish vocabulary. On the contrary, some words that are quite foreign to our contemporary parameters of vocabulary for Jewish collectivity in the United States—such as *race* or *nation*—served as earlier American terms for articulating Jewish groupness.

Proper nouns like *Israelites, Hebrews,* and the *chosen people* were widely used until the early twentieth century.[54] From the eighteenth century until the middle of the nineteenth, the first two terms had both national and racial connotations in American discourse about the Jewish collective entity. Early documents such as the famous letter from the Newport community to George Washington refer to Jews as a group of shared descent.[55] Although vocabulary later associated with race described Jews until the early twentieth century, these terms possessed softer connotations, closer to what we now refer to as an ethnic group or people.[56] Indeed, the language of Jews as a race (one generally considered within the parameters of whiteness) was considered largely unproblematic in American and Jewish vocabulary until the rise of American nativism and European antisemitism in the 1920s and 1930s.[57]

The rise of nationalism and Zionism in Europe and the United States after the First World War introduced new intellectual and political forces into discussions about the meaning of Jewish collectivity, and so the nationalist paradigm entered into American Jewish life as an increasingly visible and influential framework of Jewish collective identity. Indeed, definitions of Jews as a nation began to replace previous vague and overlapping concepts of groupness such as Israelites and Hebrews. Several important American Jewish intellectuals who would later be central to the emergence of peoplehood turned to the category of nation. Still several decades before the establishment of a Jewish state, nation offered a concept potentially compatible with Americanism. Zionism's redefinition of Jews as a nationality thus served as a basis for redefining American Jewish life and American pluralism more broadly.

Leading Zionist intellectuals such as Kaplan and scholar and American public intellectual Horace Kallen joined others in the pages of important

Jewish publications such as the *Menorah Journal* in referring to Jews as a nation. The cultural Zionism of Ahad Ha-am (the pen name of Asher Ginzberg) inspired them, and they borrowed from European Zionism the idea that Jewish national status was a function of shared culture (Kallen's focus) and religious folkways (which was Kaplan's) rather than a primarily political or territorial attachment.

Two of the most important statements of American Jewish collectivity for Jewish and non-Jewish audiences in the first third of the twentieth century both embraced the terminology of Jews as a nation. Kallen's famous essay "Democracy vs. the Melting Pot" developed the concept of America as a nation of nationalities.[58] Rejecting the melting pot vision of America, Kallen wrote one of the most enduring articles about the politics of group difference in the United States. Considered the chief inspiration for American cultural pluralism, the essay argued that what made America unique was its recognition of its various immigrant communities' cultural differences. Kallen highlighted the ability of immigrant Jews to preserve their own collective national identity as the epitome of how national minority groups could hold onto their cultures, languages, and social structures and yet remain fully part of American society. Judah Magnes, a leading Reform rabbi, voiced a similar vision of America as a "republic of nationalities" in articulating his vision of an America that rejected the melting pot model, writing that "[a] national soul is as precious and as God-given as is the individual soul."[59]

Kallen's influential writing on the Jewish nation and its relationship with other national groups in the United States also demonstrates the permeation of descent and racial logic into a range of collective definitions of the Jewish people. For Kallen, national life was a secular cultural group identity, passed down through parents and grandparents; his famous statement encapsulated this understanding: "Whatever else [a Jew] changes, he cannot change his grandfather."[60] Scholars have viewed this claim about the nature of identity as evidence that Kallen's concept of nation was grounded in descent as constitutive of group identity.[61]

As for Kaplan, due to his conscious decision in the 1940s to shift his key term for Jewish collectivity from nationhood to peoplehood, few remember his original commitment to Jewish nationality. But the concept of Jews as a nation characterized much of Kaplan's work. In his first five decades writing about Jews and Judaism, he shared Kallen's use of the language of nation and nationality, and the theme saturates the most sustained and influential theoretical discussion of the Jewish people in twentieth-century American Jewish thought, Kaplan's 1934 *Judaism as a Civilization*.[62] However, the received legacy of this text has obscured the author's commitment to the terminology of nationhood in this path-breaking book.

From his first published essay, "Judaism and Nationality" (1909), to his final book, *The Religion of Ethical Nationhood* (1970), Kaplan made it his mission to define Jews as exemplars of a more progressive type of nationalism that separated the historical bonds of national groups from the political ties of citizenship.[63] His writings prior to Israel's establishment contrasted Jewish nationalism and his particular, non-statist understanding of Zionism with paradigms of nationalism that emphasized territory and sovereignty as primary markers of group membership. Kaplan viewed "absolute national sovereignty" as "liable to . . . destroy the very foundations of human civilization."[64] Jewish nationalism modeled the antidote to these trends: cultural diversity, solidarity across geopolitical boundaries, and non-coercive criteria of inclusion.

When Kaplan published his magnum opus in 1934, he had decided that the best conceptual vocabulary to describe the Jewish collectivity was nationalism—but with a caveat. The notion of nation would need to avoid association with a state and territory in order to reflect the Jewish political tradition. For Kaplan, Jewish nationhood offered a model of collectivity that he called "ethical nationhood" or "international nationhood," relying on a shared mission of heterogeneous interaction rather than a model that promoted the division of the globe into homogenous units—both an ethical model for other national groups and the best path to Jewish survival.[65]

Kaplan witnessed the rise of fascism in Europe and recognized the repercussions of unfettered nationalism for European Jews. In a telling incident, on a trip to Jerusalem in the late 1930s, he was sparked by events in Europe to write in his diary about the dangers of statist nationalism and its potential to strip minority citizens of their rights. His entries show his reflections on Jewish nationalism as he sat in Jerusalem, thinking about Zionism, the future Jewish state, and the problematic nature of nation-states.[66] Interestingly, his private words written as Nazism was unfolding emphasize not a commitment to a state as an instrument to protect its Jewish constituents, but his concern that a Jewish state never be an instrument of discrimination against minorities within it.

Kallen and Kaplan represent two examples of the presence of the nationalist paradigm of boundary formation at the heart of American Jewish notions of difference and collectivity. They demonstrate how the categories of nation and nationality emerged as highly plausible language for defining Jewish collectivity in the United States in the early twentieth century. The turn to nation reflects not only the influence of the logic of the nationalist paradigm in American Jewish thought, but also the largely forgotten possibility of a Zionism that advocated a type of collective status that challenged the conflation of national group and political state.

Zionism appealed to Kaplan as a movement capable of shepherding a new worldwide era of depoliticized nationalism. Instead of contributing to the division of the world into discrete territorial units with homogeneous national populations, Zionism would underscore the practical and moral limitations of national sovereignty. Modern democracies, including the United States, Kaplan insisted, should follow the teachings of Jewish nationalism, which he hoped the Zionist movement would embody, and refrain from demanding any degree of ethnic, religious, or cultural conformity of its citizens.

Jewish nationality in Kallen's and Kaplan's hands exemplified early twentieth-century attempts to make sense of what it meant to be an American in light of the growing U.S. immigrant population, and presented a collective vision that reflected the broader context of identity and nationalism in early twentieth-century politics, even as it served as a corrective to emerging trends in European and American nationalism. After World War I, the association of nation and state dominated nationalisms. As President Woodrow Wilson articulated in the Fourteen Points at the Versailles Peace Conference, each national group on principle would have its own homeland and political sovereignty.[67] The Jewish nation, as Kallen and Kaplan saw it, offered a counterexample—a national group whose solidarity transcended a political unit or specific territory, instead of one whose primary goal was the establishment of an ethnonational state with a homogeneous population. Jewish nationhood offered a different model, available to all nations—one that viewed the endurance of multiple national groups in the same political state and the endurance of a given national group in multiple locations as the most effective guarantee of international harmony.

Efforts to define Jews as a national group were not merely scholarly or theoretical. Jewish organizations attempted to translate the idea of minority national identity into institutional reality. In 1909, a group of New York City Jewish leaders, including Kaplan, established the Kehillah (the Jewish community) to unify communal life for New York City's Jews. Founders of the organization aimed to create a representative body to attend to Jewish education, social welfare issues, and communal policy as well as defend the rights of Jews. The experiment lasted from 1908 until 1922, and illustrated the perceived viability of organizing American Jews along the lines of a distinct corporate community within the United States.

Kallen and Kaplan employed the term *Jewish nation* in their writings because Zionism made Jewish national terms familiar to American Jews. But the language of Jewish nationhood per se in the American context lasted perhaps two decades, when nationhood was still inchoate enough to suggest rich diasporic possibilities. As statist Zionism emerged as Zionism's dominant form around World War II, the language of Jewish nationality declined. Neither Kaplan nor Kallen managed to establish the vocabulary of their brand of nationalism as the key term for the Jewish people in the American context.

By the time he published *The Future of the American Jew* in 1948, Kaplan recognized that his own attempt to mold the language of nationalism to fit his vision of the Jewish case had failed to make an impact on either Zionism or American nationalism. As a result, he eventually adopted an alternative term that he could define outside of the influence of nationalism as it came to be understood in the second half of the twentieth century: peoplehood. The DNA of Jewish nationalism remained in this new terminology, but the dramatic changes of the 1930s and 1940s that were transforming the language of nationalism, bringing unprecedented antisemitism and building toward a Jewish state in Palestine, meant that new language was needed. New terminology could promote the nationalist paradigm through the back door without disrupting the evolving demands of an American Jewish synthesis at a particularly threatening historical moment of both European and American antisemitism.

Peoplehood's Progenitors

The rise of Nazism in Europe and increasing support among American Jews for Zionism in the United States reopened existential questions about how American Jews should define themselves as a group. Articulations of Jewish collectivity during this period largely focused on external questions of how American Jews should respond to issues involving the global Jewish community, rather than on internal questions of culture and historical group self-definition, as American Jews felt an increased sense of marginalization as Americans. Their need to unite to advocate for Jews in Europe and Palestine provoked tension between collective pressure to help global Jewry and concerns that such assertions of solidarity might threaten their own precarious situation at home.

This tension surfaced in increasingly heated debates about whether Jews should define themselves as a religion (as advocated by the Reform movement) or as a nation (the Zionist position). This historical situation stimulated the need for a new vocabulary, as American Jews searched for a term that could negotiate between those competing pulls and articulate a consensus across ideological splits within the broader Jewish community. These circumstances promoted a logic that led several different thinkers in different institutional contexts toward the same term.

Reform rabbi and passionate Zionist Stephen Wise, head of the American Jewish Congress, enthusiastically championed peoplehood.

Under his leadership as honorary president, the American Jewish Congress in 1932 developed a plan to galvanize support for the creation of a world Jewish congress to increase pressure on the U.S. government to protect European Jews from increased antisemitism. The new organization would be dedicated to fighting the spread of Nazism.

In a speech delivered in Zurich and reported by the *New York Times,* Wise "urged the convocation of a congress both as a means of asserting the 'peoplehood of Israel' and protesting against anti-semitism." Wise introduced peoplehood as part of his attempt to mobilize a collective Jewish response to European antisemitism, and his belief that it would take American Jewry, "those not yet smitten by anti-Semitism," to take the lead in organizing a global response.[68] The association of the peoplehood of Israel with protests against antisemitism reflected the origins of peoplehood as a new term related to opposing external persecution and an existential threat. Wise also linked peoplehood to the idea of brotherhood, understood as a shared sense of obligation and connection that would warrant the creation of a political entity—a congress. Indeed, Wise declared, "The only Jews who will be shut out of the congress," he said, "are those Jews who shut themselves out by denying the brotherhood and peoplehood of their people."[69]

Wise's use of peoplehood to justify a world Jewish congress that would be united in the face of external threat echoes in logic and terminology a famous passage in Theodor Herzl's *The Jewish State* (1896). After explaining the economic, political, and social roots of modern antisemitism, as well as why Jewish persecution will continue until there is a state of the Jews, Herzl wrote: "We are one people (Volk) —our enemies have made us one without our consent, as repeatedly happens in history. Distress binds us together, and, thus united, we suddenly discover our strength. Yes, we are strong enough to form a State, and indeed, a model State."[70] As a founder of the Federation of American Zionists (the forerunner of the Zionist Organization of America) and a delegate at the Second Zionist Congress in Basel (1898), Wise no doubt was familiar with Herzl's argument and its logic. Born in Budapest during the process of German reunification and raised in a German-speaking milieu in the United States, Wise probably understood the nationalist connotations of the German term *Volk* and its connotations in Herzl's writing.[71] The concept of *Volk* evolved in German political discourse in the early nineteenth century both to refer to subject nationalities of the Dual Monarchy and to define the unified group of subjects that would constitute the sovereign polity. Indeed, Wise commented that the 1932 organizational meeting in Geneva, held not far from the site of the First Zionist Congress in 1897, was "worthy of any Parliament in the world."[72] While the explicit terminology of nationalism or Zionism was absent from Wise's speech, political Zionism's view of an external threat as the catalyst for Jewish unity and the need for an organized political response to antisemitism permeates Wise's explanation for Jewish peoplehood.

In English, however, the connotations of people (and thus peoplehood) had fewer nationalistic and exclusivist overtones than its German equivalent. The different meanings of this identical concept in two languages enabled Wise to translate Herzl's nationalist logic into a code word calibrated for an American milieu. A vocal Zionist, Wise understood the limitations of using terms associated with nationalism for building a broad consensus among Jews in Europe and the United States, especially given the dramatic rise of antisemitism that increased anxiety among Jews about defining themselves as a distinct national group. Justifying the call for a world Jewish congress on the grounds of peoplehood rather than nationhood could largely neutralize the potentially divisive politics of Zionism.

Notably absent from Rabbi Wise's various statements is any reference to the cultural, spiritual, or historical content that unites the Jewish people. If indeed Wise's push for peoplehood developed from his engagement with Herzl's political Zionism, that is not surprising. Political Zionism focused on protecting Jews rather than revitalizing Judaism. A definition of unity focused on solidarity avoided potential fragmentation among different visions that might undermine Wise's primary goal of building consensus to support collective political goals. However, this vision for a world Jewish congress illustrates only one of the early Zionist-inspired definitions of peoplehood.

Another version of Jewish peoplehood articulated on American soil, also influenced by Zionism and the nationalist paradigm, emerged in the 1930s and 1940s—but this version primarily addressed internal questions about Jewish identity vis-à-vis Zionism and Americanism. American Jewish intellectuals inspired by Ahad Ha-am's vision of cultural Zionism viewed the nationalist paradigm as a crucial avenue for galvanizing Judaism in both homeland and diaspora, highlighting the role of Jewish nationality in reviving American Jewish life and culture. Both these uses—one chiefly reflecting political Zionism's call for unity and solidarity in the face of external threats, the other having more in common with cultural Zionism's focuses on the revival of Judaism as an internal project—adopted the language of peoplehood to navigate the status of American Jews, negotiate a new set of parameters for the American-Jewish synthesis, and translate Jewish nationalism into an American context. While the two approaches were not mutually exclusive, they represented two distinct uses of peoplehood as a way of articulating the most important goals of strengthening the Jewish collective. One prioritized galvanizing American Jews to build a Jewish nation for Jews at risk; the other sought to mold American Jews into the nationalist paradigm so that they might in turn serve as an ideal model.

In the latter camp, the largely forgotten identities of the earliest innovators of the new peoplehood terminology will likely surprise those primarily familiar with Kaplan as the eventual promulgator of peoplehood. Although Kaplan became the most significant—and enduring—representative of the cultural Zionist-inflected peoplehood camp, he was a reluctant and even half-hearted latecomer to use of that language. A number of leading, Zionist-leaning Reform rabbis in addition to Wise had in fact turned to peoplehood in the two decades before Kaplan integrated the key word into his own writings, and marshaled it toward similar ends at a time when Zionism represented a minority position in the Reform movement. Their adoption of the term demonstrated the attraction of peoplehood terminology for the purpose of integrating Reform's emphasis on Judaism as a religion with Zionism's advocacy of Judaism as more than a faith.

Reform rabbi and, initially, Zionist supporter Morris S. Lazaron discussed peoplehood in his 1921 *Journal of Religion* article "The American Jew: His Problems and His Psychology."[73] The article, intended for the non-Jewish readers of the scholarly journal, defended American Jews as a group misunderstood as unpatriotic, clannish, and even a social/criminal menace. Instead, Lazaron argues that the psychology of Jews makes this group particularly inclined toward patriotic attachment and commitment to the United States. Lazaron grounds his defense of Jews as full participants in the American polity by repeating twice within a few pages the explicit declaration that "Jews are not a nation." To further assuage potential doubts about American Jews' allegiance to their host country, Lazaron adds the claim "many Jews of the world are opposed to the creation of a Jewish nation."[74]

But Lazaron's distancing from political claims that might suggest dual loyalties did not change his commitment to the idea that "the Jews are a nationality." It is precisely in defending his distinction between Jews' status as a nation (which he denies) and defining their status as a nationality that Jewish peoplehood appears in possibly its earliest published form. "In addition to the bond of union as believers in the same religion, Judaism, there is the consciousness of peoplehood—the realization that we belong to a people, the Jewish people."[75]

The status of nationality, unlike a nation, Lazaron suggests, is a category of cultural and historical significance that has no political bearing on Jews' loyalty and commitment to the United States. Indeed, he says, the status of nationality normalizes American Jews, because in America there are as many nationalities as there are people who have come here from other lands.⁷⁶ "Jews are a nationality," he writes, "because they have a consciousness of peoplehood and the spiritual background of a people—a common past, a common history, common sacrifice and suffering the same language and literature, a common hope and ideal, and a common faith"—a nationality, but not a nation, without any territorial or political implications.⁷⁷ The emphasis on what we might call a spiritual allegiance not just to Judaism but also to the Jewish people demonstrates the influence of cultural Zionism that emphasized revitalizing modern Jewish culture rather than the development of a state apparatus per se.

Explaining this distinction, rooted in the logic of cultural Zionism, Lazaron echoes the terminology and logic of Jewish integration into a multinationality state that had been developed by Kallen in his 1915 essay "Democracy vs. the Melting Pot."⁷⁸ Lazaron writes, "America declares: You serve me best when you serve me as a Jew!"⁷⁹ Lazaron's perceived need to remind his readership that there is an alternate concept of nationality that makes no political claims demonstrates the challenges for an American Jewish thinker who is attracted to ideas of Jewish national identity but who is also sensitive to perceptions that defining Jews as a nation in the American context might raise questions about their loyalty. As a corollary, a proactive retort to attacks on Jews for favoring Jews from other countries over non-Jewish Americans, Lazaron stressed that "[the] Jewish people is not obliged to defend the opinion of individual Jews."⁸⁰

By the 1940s, Lazaron would go on to a visible position as one of the founders of the American Council for Judaism, a group of Reform rabbis who publicly distanced themselves from Zionism's definition of Jews as a national group.⁸¹ But in the 1920s, Lazaron, like Kallen and Kaplan, was still a Zionist-inspired American intellectual, struggling to integrate his attraction to reframing Judaism in the Zionist paradigm and his concern about increased levels of nativism in the United States. The language of peoplehood helped him articulate a national status compatible with American citizenship and the already accepted status of Jews as a religious denomination in the United States.

For this to work, Lazaron had to critique two key aspects of Zionism. First, living in the ancient homeland did not represent the only possibility for full membership in the Jewish nation. Second, nationality, or peoplehood, did not promote a secular vision of Judaism, but one that integrated its religious component into the broader historical, cultural, and social practices of Jewish life. Moreover, Lazaron explicitly distanced peoplehood from the idea of automatic solidarity with Jews around the world! Defining peoplehood from the perspective of American Jewish identity—portraying Judaism as a religion and a nation compatible with American concepts of identity, and decoupling peoplehood from unity and solidarity—distinguished this articulation from the one Wise would develop a decade later.

Lazaron was not alone among leading Reform rabbis in his articulation of peoplehood as a compromise position between Judaism as a religion and political Zionism. At the 1934 Central Conference of American Rabbis (CCAR) meeting, Zionist rabbi Abraham J. Feldman critiqued the "exponents of 'secular nationalism' who refuse to recognize religion as the basic element of the Jewish tradition and the 'religious sectarians' who refuse to recognize the element of peoplehood that has persisted in the Jewish tradition."[82] Peoplehood occupied the middle ground between the antireligious position of much of Zionism and the fundamentally creedal definition of classical Reform Judaism. Among leading Reform thinkers in the 1930s, peoplehood worked effectively to both reject secular Zionism and expand the view of Judaism beyond faith, to include such key aspects of the nationalist paradigm such as history and culture as well as religious practice. Finally, for these Reform rabbis, peoplehood also served to integrate these aspects of that paradigm into their definition of American Reform Judaism.

Their influence registered in the adoption of the term *people* in the 1937 Columbus platform adopted by the CCAR, Reform Judaism's rabbinical organization. Interestingly, however, the Columbus platform does not include peoplehood, despite its previous uses. Perhaps the word *people* produced greater consensus within the Reform rabbinate. We might think of a terminological spectrum that spans nation, nationality, peoplehood, people, and religion, with people standing as a compromise between peoplehood and religion—lacking associations that had already developed between peoplehood advocates and Zionist conceptions of the Jewish nation.

Mordecai Kaplan: The Late and Half-Hearted Prophet of Peoplehood

Though Kaplan would ultimately be remembered as the figure who introduced peoplehood to American Jews, his centrality in its popularization makes it all the more important to understand his reluctance to use the term as a new key word for the Jewish collective. While he remains an integral part of the story of peoplehood in the American context, especially through his influence on a cadre of followers who would spread his vision through American Judaism in the second half of the twentieth century, for the first sixty years of his life Kaplan largely focused his thinking and writing on defining Jews as a nation and Judaism as a religious civilization. He had placed the meaning of Jewish nationalism at the forefront of his thinking since his first publication in

1909, but he does not seem to have used the term peoplehood before 1942.[83]

Kaplan long emphasized an internal focus on the needs of the Jewish people in the American setting, largely depoliticizing claims of statist nationalism and emphasizing the worldview of cultural Zionism. He dedicated his thought to a definition of Judaism that included cultural, social, and even political elements as fully compatible with American democracy, but its primary focus was not on external issues. His vision of Zionism highlighted Palestine as a cultural center for nourishing the Jewish nation around the globe and Judaism as a civilization that extended across national boundaries.

Like Stephen Wise, Kaplan knew Herzl's use of *"Wir Sind ein Volk"* as a basic assumption of Zionism.[84] His familiarity with this important political Zionist belief demonstrates the close connection between Herzl's vision of a unified Jewish collective in the face of the external challenges confronting Jews in the modern period and Kaplan's understanding of peoplehood. For Kaplan, the Jewish question—the question of Jewish status as a minority group within nation-states—consisted of a single set of challenges that demanded a shared response. As a result, Kaplan's articulation of peoplehood assumes, like Wise, that Jewish solidarity and unity remain crucial components of peoplehood.

However, Kaplan's understanding of the practical implications and desired implementation of this unity resembled the cultural Zionist direction espoused by Lazaron rather than the political focus articulated by Wise. Establishing a shared political voice to address threats facing Jews was less important to him than the revival of Jewish culture in both the diaspora and homeland. Moreover, Jewish culture for Kaplan included a far deeper appreciation of the role of religious practice and sources than the more secular approach championed by Ahad Ha-am. But how did Kaplan's reading of Zionism evolve into his contribution of peoplehood as a key word in American Jewish life?

The transition from nationhood to peoplehood represented both a significant terminological rupture from Kaplan's earlier vocabulary of nationhood and an insignificant ideological shift from his prior vision of Jewish nationalism. Rather suddenly, between 1942 and 1948, Kaplan elevated peoplehood to the center of his program for American Judaism, and eventually gained a reputation as its intellectual progenitor. The shift from nationhood to peoplehood does not seem to signify an intentional change in his own thinking. Instead, the peoplehood turn developed because of the increasing limitation of nationalist terminology in the context of state-oriented Zionism and the threat of annihilation raised by Nazism in the 1940s. He thus turned to peoplehood out of the same logic and dearth of adequate alternate vocabulary that inspired Lazaron, Wise, and others.

The word itself was not important to Kaplan. But peoplehood (because it was disconnected from nation) provided an accessible and politically neutral concept that would allow him to continue putting forth his existing theory of Jews as a national group whose political significance actually provided an alternative model of nationality—one that did not equate nationhood solely or even primarily with statehood. He had held on to the language of nationhood until the early 1940s, yet he ultimately felt it had simply become too inflected with statist connotations to be useful or desirable.[85]

The parallel with Lazaron's parsing of the same terms twenty years earlier shows Kaplan's own thinking still operating largely in the context of the discussion of nationalism from the 1920s, when the definition of the term and its various correlated concepts was hotly debated after World War I. At the same time, the record of Kaplan's 1942 Reconstructionist Summer Conference talk mentioned above indicates a new degree of sensitivity to the limitations of the conceptual vocabulary that had defined his project since the early twentieth century. Splitting semantic hairs between nation, nationality, and nationhood demonstrates Kaplan's perception that it was increasingly important to clarify seemingly slight terminological distinctions between these three concepts because they actually had significance. Nation was not unproblematic; it needed to be explained, delimited, and distinguished from other related, softer terms.

For decades, Kaplan had advocated a vision of Jewish nationalism that opposed exclusionary, *Volk*-ish, political and territorial models, and nourished particular historical and cultural communities in their progress toward greater levels of integration with others and greater ethical behavior. But the meanings and connotations of nation were rapidly changing and highly contested. The member of the audience at the talk challenged Kaplan's use of nation with this argument: "The Supreme Court of the United States, when using the term nation, always refers to a group which occupies a definite geographical area."[86] The source of this reference cannot be determined from the publication, but it indicates that national terminology had specific resonances with territory in American public discourse. The changing landscape of nationalism clearly left Kaplan word-smithing, spending time explaining his ideas through rather esoteric terminological distinctions. His sensitivity to the difficulties of terminology was on target, but, it seemed, he had not gone far enough.

With the increasing association of nation and state, Kaplan suggested two relatively new terms. First, he needed *nationality* to expand the definition of nation to include Jews outside the homeland. Second, Kaplan tasked *nationhood* with bridging the two different terms of Jews as a nation in Palestine and a nationality in the United States. The meaning of nationalism in general, and Jewish nationalism in particular, constricted his argument. But Kaplan's speech indicates his enduring commitment to understanding Jewish collectivity through the paradigm of nationalism, even if he had to work increasingly hard in the midst of World War II to distinguish Jewish nationalism from the ethnocentric, militaristic, and territorial expressions visible in the global conflict. The exchange recorded after his talk strongly suggests that Kaplan's peoplehood ultimately did not arise from his own thinking, but from brainstorming by his disciples who found wanting his own stubborn attempts to retain the inadequate language of nationalism while questioning some of its emphases.

The pressure from his closest students and followers at this gathering seems to have convinced Kaplan. Peoplehood quickly moved to the center of his platform for the reconstruction of American Judaism. At the 1944 Reconstructionist conference, he started his remarks with this claim: "Our religion and culture derive from our peoplehood."[87] In 1948, peoplehood anchors *The Future of the American Jew,* which becomes the book that provides the association of the term with Kaplan's legacy.

As a critique of statist definitions of Jewish nationhood, the language of peoplehood was compatible with Kaplan's much broader argument about the role that Zionism would have in transforming American Jews, and American pluralism as well. Similarly, Lazaron, whose writings in the 1920s about nationality and peoplehood were clearly influenced by cultural Zionism, went on to view peoplehood as distinct from what emerged as political Zionism in the 1940s—although for Lazaron, this ultimately meant rejecting Zionism altogether.[88] Kaplan envisioned the establishment of a unified cultural and ethical voice across various Jewish populations. Nationalism, he felt, in the pre-state years, still had the opportunity to shape American Jewish life in a different fashion, before the link between nation and state left little room for other models of national existence and self-understanding.

In addition to Kaplan's increasing struggle to differentiate nation and state in his own thinking, a broader Jewish communal debate about the vocabulary of Jewish groupness arose in the American Jewish community. Concerns with the serious challenge to the compatibility of Zionism's definition of Judaism as a nation with American Judaism likely fueled a search for a new vocabulary. Before 1948, mainstream American Jewish organizations, such as the American Jewish Committee, rejected the language of nationalism to refer to Jews and defined themselves as non-Zionists.[89]

More radical organizations also arose in this period to add additional momentum to the move away from the definition of Jews as a nation. In 1942, leading Reform rabbis established the American Council for Judaism to distinguish Reform Judaism from Zionism. They advocated strongly for the preservation of the ideals of classical Reform Judaism, which emphasized Judaism as a religious creed and thus challenged the influence of Zionism on American Jewish group definitions. For this group, which included Lazaron, Zionism reduced Judaism to a secular, political force that removed the religious essence and created dual allegiance problems for American Jews.[90] Use of the terms *nation, nationhood,* and *nationality* (and certainly *nationalism*) became a litmus test in public debates between Zionists and non-Zionist American Jewish leaders.

Peoplehood's importance as a compromise term in negotiations about the role that national definitions of Jewishness might play in the United States is captured vividly in a 1942 article by Kaplan's close disciple, Rabbi Milton Steinberg. Steinberg, a key participant in Kaplan's early Reconstructionist circle, had been present a few months earlier when the audience member suggested peoplehood as an alternative to nationhood and its attendant terms. Clearly upset about the rising criticism of Zionism, Steinberg wrote a polemical piece in strong opposition to the American Council for Judaism. Responding to the critique of Zionism as secular and not religious, he argued: "Accustomed to defining Judaism in terms of religion, they naturally resent any attempt to characterize it in terms of nationhood. But on this score ... they are quarrelling over a word not substance. For they themselves concede that Judaism is more than a religion."[91]

Steinberg instead argues that the issue is merely one of vocabulary. "There is a large plus beyond religion," he explains. "To characterize religion [together with this 'plus'], Zionists use the words 'nation' and 'nationhood.' Non Zionists seem to dislike the words. They prefer to speak of 'people' or 'religious-cultural heritage.' ... since they find certain words distasteful, they are entitled [to] not employ them. But they should recognize that it is names over which they are stickling."[92] Steinberg goes on to say that Zionism is not political (!)—viewing it as the engine of Jewish cultural renaissance, rather than of physical or political commitment to a Jewish state to the exclusion of living in the United States and loyal American citizenship. Neither, he contends, is Zionism secular, so it is fully compatible with being an American patriot and part of Jewish religious culture.

Steinberg's assessment of how to avoid a highly visible public break between leading Reform rabbis and Zionism emphasized the significance that peoplehood played for a thinker at the center of Kaplan's circle. Steinberg's analysis of the tension as a debate about terms rather than content had a rather simple solution—introduce terminology acceptable to proponents of both positions, Jews as a nation and Jews as a people, to agree on a word that represents what they both think anyway. Indeed, with a range of positions already embedded in the term peoplehood—from Lazaron's turn to peoplehood to clarify his rejection of political claims to Wise's embrace of peoplehood to promote a strong Zionist-oriented political agenda—precedent existed for both sides of the debate about the relationship of American Jews to Zionism to see their own position reflected. However, even Steinberg's own statement a few months earlier that "Zionism is a complete philosophy of life, asserting the peoplehood of Israel, and the presence in the heart of Judaism of cultural as well as religious elements" undermined his attempt to pit the debate as merely a question of vocabulary.[93] For Steinberg, the equation between Zionism and peoplehood was integral, and thus for that reason alone his attempt to position peoplehood as a neutral solution was somewhat misleading.

In the same Reconstructionist publication that featured Steinberg's argument that the debates were really over words, Kaplan made his first public call for peoplehood as a defining term for his Reconstructionist program: "We insist that the concept of Jewish peoplehood, which is basic to the whole Reconstructionist position, involves the translation of ethical principles into concrete laws and institutions."[94] Kaplan focuses here on the universal ethical component of Judaism, a type of national cultural offering that makes Jewish identity seem more rather than less compatible with American ideals of democracy. But the content for which peoplehood serves as a container keeps it a cultural Zionist, and therefore nationalist, expression.

A 1944 article by Samuel Dinin written in collaboration with Kaplan (and two other figures who would soon help popularize peoplehood in a variety of publications, Rabbi Ira Eisenstein—Kaplan's son-in-law—and Eugene Kohn) captured the use of peoplehood as a vessel for basic assumptions of nationalism: "It [peoplehood] connotes a common language, a common literature, historic memories, common hopes and aspirations, a link with a land, as well as a common religion."[95] The constituent elements of peoplehood remain inextricably indebted to the nationalist paradigm with the addition of the element of religion—while stripping the theological power of election from the meaning of religion—though Kaplan explicitly used religion chiefly to affirm the moral status of Jewish collectivity and the role of Judaism's ethical component in shaping the cultural practices of the nation.[96]

We the People: American Political and Religious Context

The direct link between the pioneers of peoplehood as a new English-language term and Zionism's articulations of Jewish collectivity demonstrates a primary ideological basis for this key word, and reveals its roots, among other things, in a translation into English of Herzl's vision of the Jewish *Volk*. At the same time, the term's appeal lies in its ability to serve a series of very important functions in an American milieu. Peoplehood moderates the particularistic and exclusivist connotations of the German term. Moreover, people and peoplehood in the American context implicitly emphasize democratic ideals of inclusion, tolerance, and individual freedom. The gap between the German *Volk* and English *people* created an opportunity to fuse Zionism's view of Jewish collectivity with American ideals of democracy and individual freedoms beginning with "We the people," and made the use of peoplehood in the American context an excellent choice for those seeking to balance particular Jewish and universal American commitments and bridge the definitions of Judaism as a nation and a religion.

While peoplehood had not previously been used as a term referring to Jews, related English phrases, such as the chosen people and American peoplehood, paved the way for Jewish peoplehood's introduction in the first half of the twentieth century—and its rapid internalization in the second half of the twentieth century. First, it benefitted from the rich association with the term *people* in the American context as a group united by a shared commitment to democratic government and freedom from tyranny. Second, it resonated with not only Jewish but also Christian writings about Jews as the chosen people, affirming Jews' historical place as a community with a special relationship to the country's dominant religious tradition.

Parsing the roots of Jewish peoplehood in American soil highlights its resonance with American values and with familiar language for the Jewish collectivity in this largely Christian country. As the language of the Constitution and other defining American documents such as the Gettysburg Address ("We the people," "government of the people, by the people, and for the people") indicates, people as an idea was a familiar, fundamental, and beloved concept in American political thought and national identity. Indeed, it stands in contrast to the term *nation* in defining the basis of citizenship in the state. While *nation* (from the Latin *natio*, birth) underscores the cultural or familial connection of members of a polity, the term *people* focused on a collectivity built on shared principles of freedom from oppression, self-government, and democratic values. American nationalism had adapted the word people to define the collective group of citizens, stressing America's self-definition of patriotic bonds based on civic national identity, as opposed to the ethnic models more prominent in Europe.[97] The implication was that national ties and patriotic allegiance developed from a shared commitment to democracy and freedom.

Peoplehood enjoyed rather limited use in the American context. Where it was used, it emphasized the right of a group to decide to live as members of a free and sovereign country. For example, American diplomat and social activist Elihu Burritt writes in 1871 in one of the earliest examples: "We have just learned, and other nations are learning, to number all the inhabitants of the national domain into the grand totality of its peoplehood, and to give the rule to its majority."[98] Peoplehood here justifies democratic self-government and sovereignty of a collective group, from the level of individual states in the Union to the entire country.

The connotations of people-framed group solidarity within the core narrative of American democracy and its own historical justifications for self-government. Moreover, it balanced particular collective recognition with universal principles—providing a potential logic and vocabulary for any group to equate American political ideals with navigating between particular and universal concerns. People had the diverse rhetorical functions of affirming the national status of Jews as a free people in Palestine, articulating a national identity in the diaspora, and linking Jews as individuals (however implicitly) with a historical commitment to core principles of the United States in the American context. All of these offered modifications to Zionism—downplaying the term *nation* and its increasing association with statehood, including diaspora communities as equal members in the world Jewish community, and connecting Jewishness and Americanness—while remaining anchored in the broader nationalist paradigm.

These early examples are important because they suggest that the eventual selection and broad adoption of peoplehood built on an existing vocabulary that was familiar and appealing in the American context. However, at the same time that the prevalence of these terms created a fertile basis for and influence on the use of peoplehood, they contained elements that later users of peoplehood rejected. It is particularly ironic that the earliest English terminology for Jews as a chosen people—referring to their divine election—is antithetical to the thinking of advocates of peoplehood in the first half of the twentieth century, and especially to Kaplan, whose rejection of chosenness was and remains a cornerstone of Reconstructionist Judaism.[99]

Considering the relationship between peoplehood and the chosen people underscores the subtle negotiation between internalizing well-known American categories and introducing new constructions of Jewishness. Peoplehood both echoed and challenged the language of Jews as the chosen people, a common rhetoric referring to the Jewish collective in the United States. There were two fundamental problems with the associations of chosenness with the Jewish people. First, the term underscored a theological vision of election that painted Jews in a negative light, emphasizing their insularity. Second, the association of Jews with the chosen people also conflicted with modern claims about collectivity. When Christians referred to the Jewish people, it was primarily to harken back to a historical collectivity in the biblical period. The chosen people was largely neutralized of its problematic connotations when referring chiefly to ancient Israel, avoiding a tension with the definition of Judaism as one of several religious creeds in the United States. For these reasons, Zionist activists in the United States interested in making contemporary claims about the collective status of Jews were unlikely initially to turn to the language of people. Instead, terms associated with nationalism such as *nation, nationality,* and *Hebrews* dominated the discourse of the figures interested in defining Judaism in collective terminology.

In addition to the Jewish people being an unappealing term for Zionist-oriented Jewish thinkers, it was also potentially problematic for non-Zionist Reform Jewish leaders. The association of chosenness with Jewish particularism and separatism limited the potential utility of calling Jews a people even among Reform integrationists. Conceptualizing Jews as a religion created parity between Jews and Christians, while depicting Jews as a people underscored perceptions that Jews remained arrogant in their self-understanding as superior and unique. The chosen people was too universal for Jewish nationalists (because Christians could marshal it to apply to Christians, the new elect) and too particular for Reform Jews. But peoplehood—a softer term than the Jewish people—would eventually provide the advantage of resonating with American ideals of democratic inclusion without any baggage of Jewish chosenness.[100]

Attaching -hood to people offered an implied terminological synthesis of, or meeting point between, American democratic ideals of individual freedoms, Christian vocabulary for relating to Jews, and Zionism's claims about nationhood. This resonance worked to legitimate Jews' rights to national status in Palestine as well as their response to the oppression of European Jews. In the American context, the affirmation of Jews as a people situated a Jewish parochial story within universal claims of American citizenship. Peoplehood offered safe conceptual vocabulary with which to integrate Zionism into American-ness without directly confronting the question of whether Jews constituted a religion or a nation; it also avoided existing politicized terminology of race and chosenness. Peoplehood blurred increasingly strong categorical differences between secular and religious expressions of Judaism, national particularism and American patriotism, and pro- and anti-Zionist factions of American Jewish life.

Peoplehood also allowed Jewish thinkers to hedge the competing pulls of Zionism and Americanism. Its power lay in its ability to embrace two different sides of the modern Jewish experience in one word without surfacing too many contradictions. Peoplehood stood in opposition to classical Reform's narrow and often anti-Zionist definition of Judaism as a religion, but also eschewed the strict secularism of most political Zionism. It facilitated American Jews' advocacy of the separation of citizenship and patriotism from specific religious, ethnic, or national criteria. In Kaplan's work in particular, peoplehood forged a middle path between American Judaism and statist Zionism by demanding that both poles reconsider their foundational assumptions.

Peoplehood's most significant asset as a key word may have been its lack of firm content, along with the advantage of a new term that provided a big tent just as existential issues about Jews' present and future were leading to fragmentation and internal discord. It contained the seeds of two trajectories of its use: as a kind of code word of support for political Zionism, and as a critique of the entire idea of homeland and the Jewish state. Both of these political positions exploited the relatively blank slate of peoplehood, whose resonance with, but lack of firm theoretical grounding in, both American ideals of democracy and Zionism's commitment to nationhood made it an effective rhetorical instrument for addressing perceived needs of American Jews in the interwar period. While the question of whether or not Zionism would in fact lead to the creation of a Jewish state in Palestine was still open, the two different visions of Jewish nationalism in peoplehood generated little controversy. But the establishment of Israel in 1948 and the triumph of David Ben-Gurion's vision for the relationship between the Jewish people, the new state, and the Land of Israel further facilitated the victory of political, state-oriented version of Zionism. As we see below, peoplehood then emerged as a key word in the polemical debate between statist and non-statist supporters of Jewish nationalism, and also crossed over into academic scholarly work on group identity and into American identity politics.

1948, Israel, and a Crisis of Terminology

Once the Jewish state was established, Kaplan became more convinced that the ship had sailed on *nation, nationality,* and *nationhood,* and that a new word was both necessary and acceptable. "Not nationhood, but peoplehood," Kaplan wrote in *The New Zionism,* "would be the objective . . . since it would have to embrace the entire House, or Community, of Israel."[101] Kaplan required a replacement for the "concept of 'nationhood' as applied to the Jews" because the term "had come to be closely identified with statehood and was therefore in need of being replaced by the concept of 'peoplehood.'"[102]

The language of nationalism and Zionism had become too closely associated with national sovereignty for Kaplan to use it effectively. This increasingly statist orientation, he believed, would create a rift between Jewish populations by reinforcing two disparate and even incompatible categories of Jewish identity—as a majority national culture in the homeland and a minority religious community in the diaspora. A robust sense of solidarity would endure only if an alternate concept established a shared understanding of the meaning of Jewish collectivity as distinct from both political citizenship and religious creed. By affirming peoplehood as an alternative to nationhood, Kaplan could continue his lifelong vision of promoting Jewish nationalism as a theoretical and practical alternative to the nation-state paradigm.

Kaplan's deliberate introduction of the term as a replacement for nationhood illustrates how the use of peoplehood in the lexicon of Jewish identity originated in the perceived failure and inadequacy of existing vocabulary, rather than in either a longstanding, transhistorical pattern of usage, or some systematic, collective process of developing a key term. Without Kaplan's need to identify a viable language of collectivity and his somewhat arbitrary choice of peoplehood, this volume on a key term in Jewish studies would likely have focused on other language in its exploration of changing notions of Jewish collectivity.

Ironically, however, Kaplan did not intend for peoplehood itself to develop into *the* key word for categorizing Jews as a group split between homeland and diaspora populations. Indeed, he would likely be shocked to know that peoplehood has become perhaps the most common contemporary English term for referring to Jews as a collectivity. "The term 'people,'" he wrote, was to be used "merely in anticipation of the particular category that a conference is likely to agree on as the appropriate one for the Jewish corporate entity to assume."[103] Of course, no such conference ever took place. But Kaplan's desire to reconsider this terminology reflected his understanding that peoplehood was a provisional term. While others adopted it, Kaplan in the end returned to nationhood in his final book, *The Religion of Ethical Nationhood,* published in 1970.

Kaplan may not have been particularly invested in the specific term he put forth as a placeholder, but he did have his finger on the key tension facing the terminology of Jewish collectivity after 1948. The decision to name the Jewish state Israel (with the many assumptions about Jewish collectivity it represented) was probably the most dramatic, proactive intervention into the naming of collectivity in Jewish history. Yet one man, soon-to-be prime minister David Ben-Gurion, chose the name, shortly before the declaration of the new state in May. This decision would confound the relationship among the historical term for the Jewish people, Israel; Israeli citizens (both Jewish and non-Jewish) of the State of Israel; and the territory of the Land of Israel.

Ben-Gurion wanted citizens of the new state to inherit the most common term for Jews from the biblical period forward, symbolizing the new state's role as the authentic telos of Jewish history. As American Hebraist Simon Rawidowicz subsequently complained to Ben-Gurion in a series of letters in 1954 about the choice of Israel, that name introduced ambiguity into the vocabulary of Jewish collectivity.[104] For centuries, Israel (that is, *am yisrael*) had served as the primary name in Hebrew for members of the Jewish people, most of whom lived outside the Land of Israel. With Israeli citizens (both Jewish and Arab) now called Israelis, what would Jews who were not Israeli citizens call themselves, especially in Hebrew and especially as a collectivity?

Rawidowicz challenged the bold terminological claim made in the identification of the Jewish people wholly with the State of Israel, despite the small minority of the global Jewish population living there. Both he and Kaplan, among others, were frustrated with the direction of Zionism and felt that their efforts had been completely overshadowed. Ben-Gurion had succeeded in supplanting the diversity of interwar Zionisms with a doctrinaire claim—one that left American Jewish theorists without a usable vocabulary for affirming collectivity as distinct from political citizenship and sovereignty. This rupture in the vocabulary of collectivity between homeland and diaspora communities endures today as an underlying and unresolved tension in defining the Jewish people. But there is little awareness of the semantic implications and legacy of the decision to call the state Israel, wresting the term away from its diverse and mostly diasporic meanings and placing it squarely into the statist nationalist paradigm.

The name of the state, with its instantiation of Jewish nationhood, created a crisis of vocabulary for the American Jewish community, a dearth of language that could link English terms either to Hebrew antecedents, now associated with citizens of Israel, or to the most familiar modern concept of collectivity, nationhood. The crisis of terminology and ideology, explicit and conscious for Kaplan and Rawidowicz, generated a wider terminological shift away from nation to people after 1948, reverberating beyond the few intellectuals who consciously challenged statist Zionism's articulation of national membership and boundaries. The ambiguity and fluidity of various terms that had been used in English now receded in the face of a much more concrete and narrower definition of the Jewish nation as associated with the Jewish state. Nationhood became even less compatible with minority identity in the United States. As a result, before the term *ethnicity* would achieve popularity, new terminology had to emerge to navigate between the claims of what today might be called a transnational Jewish collectivity and Jews' status as a minority in the United States.

Moving outside the work of a few thinkers that we have seen in the previous section, peoplehood gained wider currency among American Jews in the 1950s.[105] Thus Kaplan's struggle to replace nationhood with peoplehood anticipated the need for a far more flexible articulation of Jewish collectivity that would appear urgent after 1948. Despite his initially lukewarm commitment to it, peoplehood's dramatic rise indicated its resonance as a suitable post-1948 English alternative to nationhood, though the term's enlarged profile deviated from Kaplan's vision of peoplehood as a critique of statist Zionism.

For the increasingly marginalized community of intellectuals still consciously trying to differentiate statist and non-statist models of Jewish collectivity, the language of peoplehood continued to represent the possibility of an alternative to and a critique of Zionism's definition of Jews as a national group associated with a state. But increasingly supporters of the new state's centrality in American Jewish discourse employed the term because they were apprehensive about affirming nationality directly at a time of Jewish insecurity in America. Both the Jewish people and peoplehood became comfortable code words pointing to the centrality of the Jewish state for Jews around the globe.

Peoplehood then proliferated even further in the 1960s, when it crossed over from internal Jewish conversations to enter American identity politics. Its usage shifted as did its meaning. The Jewish innovators of peoplehood had used the term as an ambiguous hybrid of national and religious components; neither political nor cultural dimensions of Jewish peoplehood emphasized descent or race. But the language of peoplehood entered American political discourse with a far greater openness to race, which played a central role in the term's adoption by civil rights and eventually Black Power leaders in the 1960s. This increasing association of peoplehood with race represented a potential challenge to understandings of Jewish peoplehood as a collective bond rooted in religious traditions and national culture, but the racial undertones of the American concept of peoplehood would subsequently in turn shape rather than threaten the Jewish model, as it would come to incline toward a focus on descent and tribal allegiances at least as much as religious or cultural similarities.

From Critique to Code Word

Between 1940 and 1959, the number of references to Jewish peoplehood in the corpus of English-language books scanned by Google expands dramatically from a starting point very close to zero (an increase of about

9,800 percent).[106] The explosion of peoplehood during this period can be traced directly to the writings of Kaplan and his large group of followers. Several prominent scholars and public intellectuals, such as Horace Kallen, Jacob Agus, and Salo Baron, reviewed Kaplan's book in prominent Christian and Jewish publications and underscored his contribution of peoplehood.[107] Many of Kaplan's students, such as Jack Cohen, Ira Eisenstein, Eugene Cohen, Jacob Agus, and Arthur Hertzberg, published articles that brought peoplehood to academic journals, popular books about Judaism, and other Jewish publications.[108]

Peoplehood could both support Zionism and underscore difference with the increasingly statist focus of Jewish thinking about collectivity after 1948. Kaplan himself worked within Zionist organizations to try to effect change, always perceiving that Zionism still represented the Jewish movement best suited to revitalize Jewish life around the world. Through the movement of Conservative Judaism, Kaplan sought to bring national religious organizations under the umbrella of Zionism. He led the charge for building closer institutional bridges between the largest denomination of American Jews and the international umbrella for the Zionist movement. As the Zionist Organization was reconstituting itself as the World Zionist Organization to provide a representative body of international Zionist groups, Kaplan pushed United Synagogue (the Conservative movement's congregational arm) to join. While the close link between American Jewish religious organizations and the Zionist movement is today obvious, in 1959 this was still an issue to be debated.

This potential institutional affiliation represented a chance for Kaplan to actualize his vision of Zionism—the definition of Judaism as a national group linked by a commitment to a "non-creedal religious civilization."[109] This description of the nature of Jewish collectivity, from Kaplan's 1957 *New Zionism*, captures the terminological tension in Kaplan's effort to find a position that included a deep appreciation for Jewish religious practices and sources along with a fundamental theological position far closer to secular nationalism. For Kaplan, the nationalist paradigm at the heart of Zionism remained central to his thinking, and the assumption of the Jewish people as one collectivity—along with a corollary concern with fragmentation—characterized his writing. Kaplan thus championed affiliation with the Zionist movement in peoplehood terms. "The time has come when the very existence of the Jewish people demands that all Jewish religious forces identity themselves with the Zionist movement." The idea of a unified Jewish people committed to Zionism remained fundamental. Indeed, he wrote, "Only thus can the common concern of all Jews for the State of Israel as the homeland of Judaism demonstrate the spiritual unity of the Jewish people."[110]

However, Kaplan's Zionism, expressed for a time in the language of Jewish peoplehood, included a significant critique of post-1948 Zionism as support for the political positions of the state. Ben-Gurion promoted an ideology of statism that prioritized a specific definition of Zionism within the state itself. He considered Israeli citizenship as the central expression of membership in the Jewish people. Residing in the homeland was the only way to live a fully Jewish life. By contrast, Kaplan viewed cultural Zionism precisely as a catalyst for revitalizing American Jewry and creating a new context for religious and cultural practices.

For Kaplan, the Jewish nation's most significant attribute existed in its religious tradition that included a distinct philosophy of nationalism, integrating its religious sources and practices as a constant reminder of the need to foster a greater level of harmony in the world by steering nationalism away from its exclusivist, territorialist, statist variety. Building a homeland like any other national homeland was not the end goal, but a crucial step to implement new models of national ethical nationhood with members across the globe. Kaplan's desire to have United Synagogue affiliate with the World Zionist Organization reflected his attempt to adjust the direction of post-1948 Zionism to integrate religio-ethical principles and to recognize the new country's role as a catalyst for Jewish life all around the world. Less than a decade into Israel's existence, Kaplan continued to understand Zionism's role as the engine of Jewish peoplehood, which he contrasted with statehood as the basis for a new Zionism.

Other critiques of Zionism using the language of peoplehood did not aim to change the movement, but instead to differentiate Jewish collectivity from Zionism altogether. The most vocal Jewish champion of peoplehood as an alternative to Zionism was the political philosopher Hannah Arendt. Arendt contrasted two distinct definitions of Jewish collectivity. In 1948 she explained the distinction as follows: "In Palestine we have a Hebrew nation, in the Diaspora a Jewish people."[111]

Arendt viewed these two identities as complementary in the early years of the state. However, as she grew increasingly frustrated with the Arab-Israeli conflict, Arendt contrasted the Jewish people with developments of Jewish nationalism. Jewish nationalism prevented coexistence and moral engagement with the Arab population in Palestine that would befit the Jewish people. In the face of reaction to her coverage of the Eichmann trial in 1961, Arendt made a clear break from Zionist assumptions about the Jewish people. In response to her book *Eichmann in Jerusalem: A Report on the Banality of Evil,* which suggested that Jewish leaders had helped the Nazi regime, the Zionist historian Gershom Scholem accused Arendt of lacking "'love of the Jewish people' or *Ahabat Israel.*"[112]

Arendt's response cuts to the core of assumptions about peoplehood—chiefly, solidarity and the importance of placing the protection of fellow Jews above other considerations—that had developed since the 1930s. She responded, "I have never in my life 'loved' any people or collective—neither the German people, nor the French, nor the American . . . indeed the only kind of love I know of and believe in is the love of persons."[113] She questioned the premise that one can have a natural commitment to a broad group.

Her second response challenged secular notions of nationalism. Despite Arendt's own secularism, she considered the replacement of love of God with love of people as problematic, leaving the people to "only believe in itself."[114] The inner focus and elevation of a collectivity above all other values relegates Zionism to a vision of peoplehood unchecked by self-aggrandizement. Arendt's peoplehood clearly breaks from Zionism in questioning the assumption that love of one's people comes before other considerations. In this she resembles Kaplan, who intentionally included in his platform God and Jewish religious tradition as a moral ballast to the particularistic emphasis of the nationalist paradigm's elevation of the collective.

The language of peoplehood ultimately failed to unseat statist Zionism. Its role as a critique of state-focused Zionism, and an alternative to it, was eclipsed in the 1950s by the emergence of peoplehood as a kind of code word to help generate support for the State of Israel largely as articulated through political Zionism. In this capacity, peoplehood continued the role it had served from its entry into Jewish conversation beginning with Rabbi Stephen Wise's 1932 speech. American Zionist leaders in the 1950s utilized peoplehood to navigate between affirming a commitment among American Jews to the State of Israel and patriotic attachment to the United States.

The desire for a characterization of the Jewish collectivity that could undergird support for the emerging state (without threatening a sense of Jews as loyal U.S. citizens and good Americans) reflected both internal tensions in the Jewish community about the relationship with the new state, and enduring postwar anxiety about acceptance of Jews as full Americans. Debates about defining Judaism as a nation or people instead of a religious community continued after the founding of the state, and it was peoplehood that grounded these arguments: American Zionists distinguished between nationhood and peoplehood, while their non-Zionist opponents highlighted the extent to which peoplehood language was ultimately rooted in national claims. In a 1952 report covered by the *New York Times*, the American Council for Judaism (ACJ) critiqued Zionism's contention that Jews constituted "some kind of separate entity which they identify as a 'nationalism,' a separate 'peoplehood' or 'culture.'"[115] Leaders of the ACJ saw peoplehood as equivalent to nationhood, imposing an involuntary association of Jews that conflicted with their primary identity as a voluntary religious community. In 1961, following the inclusion of organizations such as United Synagogue in the Twenty-fifth Zionist Congress, the ACJ published a pamphlet that associated Jewish peoplehood with "another phrase for a separate body-politic overseas to serve Zionist Israel purposes."[116]

The argument about whether peoplehood was equivalent to nationhood peaked in 1964 when the Zionist Organization of America (ZOA) sought the blessing of no less than the U.S. State Department to counter the ACJ's claims that Jewish peoplehood imposed any sort of obligation on American Jews that might hinder their full commitment to their American citizenship. The assistant secretary of state, Philip Talbot, wrote a letter to the head of the ZOA, Dr. Max Nussbaum, and Rabbi Philip S. Bernstein, chairman of the American-Israeli Public Affairs Committee (AIPAC), agreeing with the ZOA's position that "the Jewish people concept was not political, but emotional, spiritual, and cultural."[117] Interestingly, the ZOA report that highlighted this event a few pages later also contained an article declaring that "the ZOA organized its national aliya committee in the belief that the ranks of its nation-wide constituency would be attracted by the potential for self-fulfillment and the living of a complete Jewish life inherent in aliya."[118] This latter statement reaffirmed Israel's centrality to Jews and its importance as the only place they could fulfill their Jewish national identity.[119]

Peoplehood, for many of its proponents, did include the fundamental principle of statist Zionism that living in the state was the only way to live as a complete member of the Jewish people, and could be used to advocate for American Jews to move to Israel. Peoplehood gave American Zionists language to endorse enthusiastically the mission of aliyah (immigration to Israel by diaspora Jews) in post-1948 Zionism along with its attendant notions of Jewish peoplehood as best reflected in Jewish statehood, while still remaining ambiguous enough to receive the blessings of a high-ranking U.S. government official.

In debates with the ACJ, which was increasingly critical of Zionism, peoplehood assumed a position as the bedrock of Jewish identity. The decision to pursue an official stamp of approval from the U.S. government demonstrates how peoplehood was a crucial concept for American Zionist organizations interested in continuing to galvanize support for political Zionism and its worldview of Jewish collectivity. That worldview presented the Jewish collective as a secular nation, the people of Israel, whose members may be dispersed but in which full membership demanded citizenship in the State of Israel. In the battle to marginalize the ACJ's challenge to the claim that American Jews automatically had an association with the State of Israel, a counterargument emerged. "Any group that seeks to dissect Judaism and to carve it away from such essential elements of its being as Jewish peoplehood, and the central role of the land of Israel, is belying it."[120] In less than two decades, peoplehood had emerged as a key term, gained legitimacy as the approved American language for supporting Israel and its centrality, and established itself as an essential element of collective Jewish identity.

A deepened political Zionist version of Jewish peoplehood rhetoric emerged with the rise of the Soviet Jewry movement and further solidified peoplehood's evolution. Peoplehood justified linking the plight of American Jews with Soviet Jews, whose Jewishness was quite limited after the prohibition of religious observance in the USSR. Political Zionism's narrative of protecting persecuted Jews around the world and its goal of massive aliyah also facilitated appeals to Jewish peoplehood as an excellent rallying cry for international support for the Soviet Jewish community. This logic is evident, for example, in comments of the president of the ZOA, who argued that the challenges facing the Soviet Jewish community are not religious problems, but nevertheless "the Jewish community there is an integral part of Jewish peoplehood, deeply rooted in historical and cultural traditions."[121] The communal focus on Soviet Jewry infused new energy and strength to the logic of peoplehood that had been introduced in the 1930s. Once again, there was a clear external need to protect Jews; moreover, the context of the Cold War meant that protecting the individual rights of Jews oppressed under communism simultaneously affirmed Jews' patriotic attachment to American ideals. The peoplehood discourse was perfectly positioned to integrate parochial concerns for protecting Jews with American civic responsibility.

Into the American Mainstream

From the late 1940s until the late 1960s, peoplehood brought the nationalist paradigm and support for the State of Israel from the margins of the American Jewish community into the mainstream, from the work of intellectuals into popular American Jewish life. But as a term reintroduced to English by Jewish intellectuals, it had not yet crossed over into non-Jewish conversations about group identity in the United States. In the late 1960s, however, peoplehood rapidly gained currency in American English as a key word for American identity politics.

Use of the term outside the Jewish community can be charted by comparing the number of references to Jewish peoplehood and peoplehood in books published between 1965 and 2000.[122] Until 1965, the use of peoplehood in English-language books mirrored the rise of Jewish peoplehood. Key texts on American pluralism written by such Jewish intellectuals as Julius Drachsler, Oscar Handlin, Nathan Glazer, Will Herberg, and Marcus Lee Hansen did not include peoplehood in their vocabulary for discussing various models of American pluralism.[123] The absence of the term even in the work of intellectuals (many of them Jewish) demonstrates that peoplehood was simply not a key term in discussions about what it means to be an American in the first two-thirds of the twentieth century.

However, in the mid-1960s, references to peoplehood exploded, while the number of books including the term Jewish peoplehood remained consistent. Why did peoplehood cross over into broader conversations about identity politics?

While it is impossible to trace the precise process by which this crossover took place, a key text helped transform peoplehood from internal Jewish vocabulary to an element of the debates about identity politics—and particularly the Black Power movement—that fundamentally shook American perceptions of minority groups and their role in American society: sociologist Milton Gordon's influential 1964 book *Assimilation in American Life: The Role of Race, Religion, and National Origin*.[124]

Gordon's book provided a sociological model to understand the endurance of racial, religious, and national entities in the United States. Gordon proposed an alternative that could navigate between the Anglo-conformity of the melting pot theory and cultural pluralism. His vision of American assimilation explained and validated group difference while also affirming the hypothesis that such groups will likely melt away in a generation or two.

The language of peoplehood formed an integral part of his argument about the nature of group ties. Gordon's definition of peoplehood is "the social-psychological element of a special sense of both ancestral and future-oriented identification with the group. These are the 'people' of my ancestors, therefore they are my children, and they will be the people of my children and their children. . . . But in a very special way which history has decreed, I share a sense of indissoluble and intimate identity with this group and not that one within the larger society and the world."[125] Gordon argued that the category of peoplehood thus encompasses ties that could include one or more of the common categories of nation, race, or religion.[126]

Writing just as the concept of ethnicity was emerging as a key word for articulating difference in the American milieu, Gordon defined ethnicity as a marker rooted in the bonds of peoplehood. We gain an insight into his understanding of the relationship between these two terms, peoplehood and ethnicity, in his explanation that "a convenient term for this sense of peoplehood is 'ethnicity' (from the Greek word 'ethnos,' meaning 'people' or 'nation')."[127] From Gordon's vantage point, the available understandings of peoplehood could and should be translated into the language of ethnicity, a term that would soon, in turn, eclipse peoplehood as the broad concept used to navigate between race, religion, and nationality in the American context. Like the early Jewish peoplehood proponents, Gordon aimed to assure the American people that "structural and cultural pluralism in moderate degrees [is] not incompatible with American democratic ideals"—on the contrary, group identity is in fact the greatest expression of American social values.[128]

In some ways, Gordon's peoplehood functions similarly to how it was used in the Jewish community during the 1950s and 1960s. First, it created an alternate category that merged the sub-categories of religion, race, and nation that Jewish peoplehood advocates saw as misleading single categories for defining Jewish collectivity. Second, it was fundamentally secular in nature, while still including religion as a key potential attribute shared by a group.[129] Third, in Gordon's view, peoplehood bonds are distinct from, and not at all in tension with, political loyalty to the United States. "My point is not that Negroes, Jews, and Catholics in the United States do not think of themselves as Americans. They do. It is that they also have an 'inner layer' sense of peoplehood which is Negro, Jewish, or Catholic."[130] Gordon concludes his book with the hope that there will be sufficient integration to ensure that "prejudice and discrimination will disappear" but also argues that "the sense of ethnic peoplehood will remain as one important layer of group identity."[131] Peoplehood, a hybrid of religious and national connections, establishes the perfect balance between melting away particular identities and insular, clannish allegiance that generates antipathy from other groups.

Gordon aimed to minimize prejudice and validate enduring ties of immigrant and ethnic families and sub-groups. However, he did not believe that these peoplehood bonds would remain past the first or second generation. In addition, his thinking has a strong basis in issues of class and race as well as religion and national culture, although peoplehood gave this Marxist-oriented sociologist a wider rubric than class alone as the basis of understanding group solidarity.

How did Gordon, not only a Marxist but a Jew, come to encounter conceptions of peoplehood from the 1940s and 1950s in their Jewish communal context and adopt the term in 1964? In a short autobiographical account in a later book, Gordon described himself as a "Yiddishe Yankee" and linked his academic interest in issues of group identity to his own youth as a Jew growing up in rural Maine.[132] He narrates experiences of antisemitism, which may have contributed to his interest in critiquing melting-pot theories with their limited tolerance for immigrant diversity.

His encounter with peoplehood language itself in the context of the Jewish community can likely be traced to his noteworthy focus on the debates about American Jewish life between the ACJ and the American Jewish Committee (AJC). As we have seen, in the 1950s these two Jewish groups debated the relationship between American Jews and the State of Israel. At the heart of their argument was the assertion by the ACJ that Jews were a religion (not a people) and had no collective attachment to the new state. The AJC disagreed and argued that Jews constituted a people whose commitments to Jews around the world did not undermine their loyalty to the United States. Gordon's *Assimilation in American Life* pays a significant amount of attention to the Jewish case, and indicates his awareness and implicit critique of the ACJ and its emphasis on defining Jews solely as a religion, rejecting any connection to the State of Israel.

Gordon credits the AJC and the ACJ (two key players in the debate about the validity of peoplehood) as devoting "the most extensive and most considered thought to problems of social structural adjustment in the American scene."[133] While Gordon does not mention Zionism directly, the debate that he refers to as the most significant conversation about group identity in the United States was primarily over the question of Jewish nationhood and peoplehood. Undoubtedly Gordon would have been heavily exposed to peoplehood in his research, which included not only reviewing written documents and debates but also interviewing representatives of four Jewish agencies—the most of any peoplehood group in his study.[134] While the debt to specific Jewish thinkers remains unclear, Gordon's text translated the conceptual vocabulary of peoplehood from Jewish thought into mainstream American culture. Like the model that Jewish thinkers had been developing for two decades, the term peoplehood in Gordon's hands articulated a category broad enough to include particular religious, national, and tribal bonds, yet permeable enough to allow for the integration of American democratic ideals and for loyal American citizenship.

In the years following the publication of *Assimilation in American Life*, peoplehood played a limited but significant role in the ethnic debates of the late 1960s and early 1970s. The distinguished scholar of American religious history Martin Marty credits Gordon with popularizing "the concept of 'peoplehood,' which is the 'sense' of an ethnic, racial, or religious group. The word turns up frequently in literature on ethnicity and new movements."[135] Gordon's text paved the way for a category of collectivity that supported the revival of tribal allegiances, racial groupings, and national claims of minority communities in the late 1960s.

However, a significant difference occurred in the shift from the internal language of peoplehood developed by Jewish intellectuals to the broader term popularized initially in Gordon's writings. The Jewish peoplehood innovators, such as Wise and Kaplan, were religious thinkers who constructed peoplehood as a language for articulating what they considered a unique merger of religion and nationality in Jewish tradition. Supernatural beliefs or religious law were not meaningful for these liberal rabbis, but the category of Jewish peoplehood fundamentally envisioned religious communities as the basis of enduring and ethical collective groups. And, as Marty's description notes, Gordon's legacy added race into the mix—a part of collectivity absent from Jewish writings on peoplehood.

Gordon's peoplehood reconfigured the way in which religion and race interacted as the primary criteria of minority group identity in the United States. Religion had been a fundamental basis of Jewish peoplehood as well as a fundamental category of American pluralism. Visions such as Kallen's, which did underscore descent, largely shied away from considering the place of race, especially for African Americans, in cultural pluralism. Scholars and public intellectuals advocating for models of pluralism rather than conformity generally remained concerned with groups considered white, ignoring the racial basis of social hierarchies within the United States. Gordon raised the visibility and relevance of racial distinctions in his expanded articulation of peoplehood, including African Americans as a sub-group. (He also insisted on the importance of class in shaping groups' self-concepts and collective identity.) His secular language emphasized descent, shared history, and future mission, which resonated far more with nationality rather than religion as creed. His language of transmitting a collective identity to "my children and their children" reflected racial and cultural, rather than creedal, definitions of that identity.

This shift from religion to race is evident in contrasting Gordon's 1964 work with another classic text on American sociology published about a decade earlier. In his 1955 volume *Protestant, Catholic, Jew*, Will Herberg introduced a slightly different perspective on the primary divisions of American ethnic groups. Herberg was a sociologist who had studied at the Jewish Theological Seminary and was quite aware of Kaplan's vision of Judaism as a religious civilization. Herberg's portrait of American pluralism more closely resonated with Kaplan's insistence that peoplehood encapsulated nationhood plus religion. In identifying the three distinct groups in the United States, he solidified Jews—barely 2 percent of the population!—as one of the three defining American religious groups.

Herberg's book reflected the importance of the category of religion as a primary conceptual box for making sense of the Jewish people in the second half of the twentieth century. American Jewish integration hinged on transforming the group as parallel to other religious traditions, rather than ethnic communities, though Herberg acknowledges that these religious identities, for all three communities, are closely linked to ethnic connections and often have less to do with religious belief. Herberg's tripartite division of American ethnic groups into religious categories raised religion to a status as a primary differentiator between American groups. This important book—which was also the first major work to popularize the concept of identity—reflected an emphasis on religious affiliations as the basis for unmeltable group bonds. It echoed Kaplan's religious orientation and provided Jews with a clear language of where its group fit into the American landscape of pluralism. Herberg, like Kaplan, had constructed a category of group identity based on the model of traditional religious civilizations that added ethnic and cultural practices to religious beliefs. Underscoring religion downplayed the crucial role of race in dividing American society. Moreover, by equating Judaism with a religious civilization, other Jewish intellectuals could implicitly counter nativist claims about Jews' racial otherness. Linking peoplehood with religion, rather than race, located Jews as white.

Gordon's divisions across religious, racial, and national lines were far broader than Herberg's. Jews now paralleled not only Protestants and Catholics, but also "Negros," "Japanese Americans," and "Italian Americans." Writing in the midst of the civil rights movement and sensitive to the importance of social class as a crucial lens for understanding American sociology, Gordon expanded the discussion of peoplehood from its original Jewish national-religious basis to include ethnic groupings and racial categories. Ironically, the translation of peoplehood from the Jewish into the academic and popular American context challenged the primacy of religious culture. Gordon's peoplehood understood religion as one component but put the term into the American context with other equally useful criteria for defining the peoplehood roots of ethnic identity.

Gordon's inclusion of race as a component of peoplehood may partially explain the adoption of the term by leaders of the civil rights movement in the mid-1960s.[136] Black nationalists involved in the Pan-African movement, as well as Black Power leaders, adopted peoplehood as a key term in explaining their struggle for civil rights in the United States. For example, the politician and Black Power leader Adam Clayton Powell endorsed self-defense "to achieve the full dignity of black peoplehood, which is in the great American tradition of self-defense."[137] Black Power leader Stokely Carmichael placed peoplehood at the center of his call for black people to define their own needs and gain a political voice: "We are going to build a concept of peoplehood in this country or there will be no country."[138] Peoplehood promoted pride and solidarity among African Americans in the United States with a separatist demand for recognition.

The concept of peoplehood in early American Jewish articulations had been meant to highlight cultural differences and downplay ascribed hierarchies associated with race, but the new vocabulary of peoplehood in the 1960s and 1970s reinforced racial logic. Within a few years of entering the wider discourse of identity in the United States, peoplehood shifted from its roots as an accommodationist language of synthesis for American Jews as a religious minority to being a key word in a confrontational movement that raised the visibility of racial fragmentation and demanded radical changes in American pluralism.

Peoplehood's place in the Black Power movement provoked mixed reactions among Jewish communal leaders the late 1960s.[139] Dr. Jerry Hochbaum, addressing the Council of Jewish Federations and Welfare Funds in 1969, laid out the opportunities and challenges: "The Black evolution, with its emphasis . . . on Black peoplehood . . . had indirectly produced an unexpected dividend for the Jewish community, a rise in Jewish self-identity." At the same time, however, Hochbaum worried that the Black Power movement had brought "an increased antisemitism and anti-Israel feeling." Similar concerns were expressed at a National American Jewish Congress Women's Division meeting, where participants spoke out "against black racism while supporting the strivings of the black community for identity and peoplehood."[140] The spread of peoplehood put Jews into a quandary, by normalizing the category but changing the conscious permeability in Jewish conceptions of peoplehood. The Black Power movement transformed peoplehood into a category that underscored separatism, to a degree absent in Jewish advocates' conscious attempts to define peoplehood precisely in ways that would erase, not heighten, the tensions between groups and national identities.

Was the spread of peoplehood good for the Jews? It was a mixed blessing for Jewish leaders dedicated to a strong sense of Jewish identity, collectivity, and attachment to Israel. The wider cultural shift away from melting-pot imagery and toward pride in one's identity shifted social pressure away from assimilation and affirmed an assertion of ethnic roots. At the same time, however, Jewish communal leaders such as Hochbaum viewed this inward focus on a group's self-interest as fostering the very intergroup tensions that Jewish peoplehood had been calibrated to harmonize.

Another potential difficulty for Jews lay in the embrace of peoplehood by a community recently marginalized and persecuted on the basis of race. Kaplan's notion of nationhood, and later peoplehood, had consciously attempted to shift Jewish group identity away from the language of race and an emphasis on biological descent precisely at a time when racial science was emerging. Kaplan saw national culture and religious folkways as a means of implicitly critiquing what he felt were the racial undertones of liberal Jewish self-definitions. In *Judaism as a Civilization*, Kaplan criticized the Reform movement for strengthening "[Jewish] unity by means of the theory of Jewish racialism."[141] Kaplan feared that without a clear supernatural mission, which he rejected, or national cultural connections, Jewish group identity would rely on descent to make the case for unity. The implicit hierarchy of racial conceptions clashed with Kaplan's belief that Jewish peoplehood in fact had the mission of overcoming prejudices he associated with racial conceptions.

In the Jewish context, peoplehood had in fact moved Jewish categories of collectivity away from explicit racial associations. Especially after the Holocaust, it was important that peoplehood be employed to support Jewish efforts to distance Jews' own articulations of difference from the category of race. The association of racial difference with inferior status in the United States and with the racially motivated genocide of World War II pushed the term *race* outside the discourse of Jewish identity, and Jews have continued to be seen increasingly simply as white—by others and by themselves.

But the new linguistic and ethnicity-oriented parallel between Jewish and black peoplehood that emerged in the 1960s complicated the relationship between racial and peoplehood notions of Jewishness. The emergence of ethnic pride and identity politics strengthened the hold of ethno-racial categories for collective self-understanding, yet actively rejected political and social hierarchies historically associated with racial distinctions. Identity politics challenged racial oppression by celebrating membership in historically disenfranchised racial groups. Novel possibilities for articulating the political and cultural role of race offered a vocabulary that affirmed the value of descent and biological markers in establishing group identity. Kallen (despite his association of identity with one's grandparentage), Kaplan, and other early Jewish cultural pluralists had wanted to dissociate Jews from racial categories; but paradoxically, Jews could now actually facilitate their integration into a culture increasingly interested in ethnic differences by emphasizing their particular boundaries based in family ties and even a link to a territorial homeland.

Ethnicity both problematized and supported distinctions built on racial conceptions of difference that now assumed a more integral place in the wider peoplehood discourse. The concept of ethnic groups and identities had increasingly replaced the vocabulary of nation and race in the United States following World War II, and provided a convenient solution to the conundrum of how to navigate the advantages and disadvantages of racial categories. The language of ethnicity avoided the negative connotations of race but preserved its underlying logic of group identity as based in descent, moving the emphasis from blood alone and including a set of linguistic, cultural, and social patterns.

However, American historian David Hollinger notes that the transition from race to ethnicity with the help of peoplehood in the 1970s and beyond was, for most groups, ultimately one of semantics. For example, the major ethnic groups included on census forms and in population studies (Caucasian, African American, Hispanic, Asian, and Native American) still mirrored the spectrum of categories that had been used to differentiate racial boundaries.[142] Hollinger underscored this point in his description of the parallels between the ethnic pentagon that developed in the United States and the racial categories that preceded them (white, black, brown, yellow, and red). In other words, the change in vocabulary did not reflect a change in the nature of an ascriptive color as the biological basis for ethnic groups. America remained a nation of nationalities, now often referred to in the vocabulary of ethnic groups, defined primarily based on the color of one's parents—even for Jews, despite the fact that they did not fit strictly into the color scheme.

The acceptance of peoplehood as an American concept moved an originally Jewish concept to the center of American pluralism, but also dramatically shifted and widened the term's meaning, which in turn exerted an impact on Jews and organized Jewish life. The rhetoric of Jewish peoplehood increasingly reflected the broader social turn of the term, as Jews also shifted toward more parochial, inward-facing definitions of Jewish collectivity. As Hochbaum reported to the Jewish Federation audience, a heightened sense of Jewish identity in response to the assertions of peoplehood more broadly led to "greater demand for Jewish institutions to concern themselves only with Jewish interests."[143] The emergence of black peoplehood resonated more with the logic of peoplehood introduced by Stephen Wise: Jews, like African Americans, faced external persecution and needed to create mechanisms to support one another in the face of outside threats. Kaplan's vision of peoplehood as a collective movement that encouraged intergroup pluralism and placed the pursuit of ethical ideals as the goal of particular attachments had limited compatibility with the new peoplehood in the context of racial politics and separatist movements.

The shift in peoplehood rhetoric and practices in the late 1960s and 1970s took place as Baby Boom leaders of Jewish organizations were coming of age. They absorbed ideas in an American milieu that defined peoplehood as part of identity politics, which focused on self-interest and particularist agendas. Those politics infused a generation of Jews with a pride in Jewish collectivity, which paralleled the ascriptive identities of other ethnic groups. Thus racial logic colored Jewish communal and intellectual discourse even while the term *race* was rarely if ever explicitly deployed. This proclivity toward racialized notions of Jewish boundaries reflected the influence of racial logic in shaping diversity in the United States.

American Jews could now be most American by emulating the political movements of African Americans and other minority groups seeking to redress decades of racism in the United States. Jewish discourses of difference once again reverted to early models that blurred the distinction between ethnicity and race, viewing biological continuity as primary markers of collectivity. Indeed, a sociologist of American ethnicity, Mary Waters, suggests that one of the reasons that American ethnicity persists, despite its largely symbolic nature, is "because of this ideological fit with racist beliefs."[144] Thus, the tendency in Jewish conceptions of collectivity to blur symbolic ethnicity with racial bonds of membership reflects a much broader tendency in American ethnic communities.

This backdrop of post-1960s peoplehood categories as more closely linked to racial categories allowed Judaism's own focus on matrilineal descent to function with limited criticism; in fact, the notion of a fixed identity based on descent rather than choice or learned characteristics actually gave a legitimacy to a Jewish identity based on birth. Descent emerged as a reasonable and effective criteria for making claims about the Jewish group that transcended the increasing diversity among modern Jews and the weakening of religious practice and shared cultures as a viable basis for solidarity. The adoption of peoplehood as a key word in identity politics allowed a racial logic, based on connections of biology and descent, emphasizing in-marriage and eventually continuity, to permeate American Jewish thinking about collective identity in the 1970s and beyond.

The changing meaning of peoplehood only further complicated the ambiguous relationship of American Jews with dominant frameworks of racial and ethnic difference that came to define group identity in the United States. Jews' liminal role as both white and a racial or ethnic other over time enabled Jewish language of collectivity to encompass multiple (and even competing) categories in order to take advantage of different possibilities each category offered. Ethnic and racial categories delineate group boundaries based on the very simple equation of membership with kinship; for a community with a diversity that ranges from ardent atheist intellectuals to ultra-Orthodox traditionalists, yet seeks a unifying language, the confusion between race and ethnicity is a distinct advantage. Cultural differences can be overlooked when racial ideals identify difference using the sole criteria of blood. At the same time, since race served as the key division between groups, dominating the vocabulary of group difference, and as the key criteria for distinguishing between enfranchised and disenfranchised groups, separating Jewish identity from racial terminology would become necessary in order to maintain Jews' status as white and thus eligible for political, social, and economic integration.[145] The shift toward viewing peoplehood in the context of identity politics enabled Jews to think about themselves in the language of nationalism and descent, while still articulating less parochial language of Judaism as a religion and culture that avoided any association of Jews with racial or national categories.

This analysis of the key terms of historical debate—nationhood and peoplehood—and the trajectory of Jewish peoplehood over the last several decades provides an important context for understanding the contemporary state of the question regarding the significance and relevance of peoplehood. While peoplehood initially challenged a nationalism that served primarily as a political program to achieve sovereignty and to discredit diaspora expressions of Judaism, it shifted from being part of a conscious critique of political Zionism's definition of Jewish collectivity to serving as a synonym for support for the Israeli state and its objectives.

This perspective offers a different interpretation from that of nostalgia for the halcyon days of the Soviet Jewry rallies. Instead of the modern heyday of Jewish groupness representing the best of the Jewish people's essence as a collective entity, that historical moment was the last hurrah of a very particular historical model of peoplehood defined by Zionism and the existential concerns of Jewish survival. The Soviet Jewry movement expressed the last chance to put the nationalist paradigm of Jewish collectivity into practice. The threat of Israel's destruction in the Six Day and Yom Kippur Wars, and Jewish persecution in the former Soviet Union in the 1970s, catalyzed a high-intensity model of collectivity that focused on protecting, defending, and normalizing Jews as equal American citizens and national players on the international stage. As we see in the next chapter, this evolutionary reading of changes in notions of Jewish peoplehood suggests that the instruments for measuring the state of Jewish peoplehood in communal discourse fail to capture the crucial feature that can truly be said to be the essence of the history of Jewish thinking about Jewish collectivity: its conceptual fluidity and semantic elasticity, its ability to constantly reimagine and transform the meaning, categories, and boundaries of groupness to reflect changing historical circumstances and needs and ideological and cultural trajectories.

State of the Question

ENDURING ENTITY OR CONSTRUCTED COMMUNITY

In 2005, the Museum of the Jewish Diaspora in Tel Aviv embarked on an ambitious plan to reinvent itself as the Museum of the Jewish People—in Hebrew, Muzayon Am Hayehudi.[1] This transformation reflects an attempt to respond to important ideological changes in thinking about Jewish collectivity that have taken place since the museum was first built in the 1970s. It provides us with a helpful bridge for moving from the earlier terms of debate to this chapter's analysis of contemporary meanings of Jewish peoplehood. As we shall see, peoplehood's recent reemergence as a key word in both American Jewish and Israeli contexts reinforces a trajectory in the second half of the twentieth century focusing on ethnic solidarity, the State of Israel, and family-like ties. At the same time, an epistemic shift in the study of nations and identity has challenged these core aspects of peoplehood.

The museum's original and enduring organizing principle reflects a set of assumptions, grounded in classical Zionism, about the inevitable fate of Jews in the diaspora—that is, either assimilation or extinction—and the centrality of the Land of Israel and the State of Israel in bringing new life to the Jewish people after two millennia in exile. The museum concretizes this narrative in a permanent exhibit of diaspora life that starts with an enlarged facsimile of the Arch of Titus with its depiction of Jews leaving the homeland in 70 C.E.; proceeds to display empty, lifeless models of Jewish communities in the subsequent nearly two thousand years of diaspora living; and concludes on the top floor (representing and enacting ascent—*aliyah*—in its architecture) with an exhibit of renewed Jewish life in the Land of Israel. Rising three stories in the center of the museum is a dark room commemorating the six million Jews killed in the Holocaust. The message is not subtle: the State of Israel marks a return to the ancient and ideal paradigm for Jewish collective existence, ensuring group survival over and against the existential threat of the diaspora.

Recognizing the dated nature of this narrative grounded in classical Zionism's rejection of the diaspora, the museum organized scholars, communal leaders, and philanthropists to reshape the very concept of a diaspora museum into a revamped institution that tells its story through a less obviously ideological lens—or, perhaps more accurately, that tells that story through a different ideology, that of multiple vibrant Jewish centers contributing to the survival of the Jewish people as an entity. As one of the curators of the new exhibit told me on a guided visit to the museum, the dominant paradigm of Jewish collectivity has shifted over time from negation of the exile to positive recognition of Jewish life in areas formerly known as the diaspora, and a new paradigm of peoplehood has emerged. While the first paradigm actively privileged Jewish life and Jews living in the State of Israel, the new peoplehood paradigm values both homeland and other lands, and seeks ways to promote a sense of collective ties that transcend location, religious practice, and diverse cultures. The challenge, as this curator sees it, is how to tell the story of the entity called the Jewish people as an expression of Jewish collective identity in the past, present, and future.

Despite the museum's interest in reshaping itself and moving away from early Zionist narratives, its transition still exemplifies a conventional commitment to nationhood (despite its peoplehood terminology) as the key concept shaping American Jewish and Israeli definitions of what it means to be part of the Jewish people. The growing emphasis on peoplehood raises as many issues as it addresses, responding as it does to shifts in internal Jewish understandings of Jewish national identity yet seemingly ignoring recent shifts in wider thinking about nations and groupness. Efforts by the new Museum of the Jewish People to tell *the* story of the Jewish people, highlighting the defining characteristic of the Jewish experience over time, illuminates the challenges of reworking nationalist claims through the language of peoplehood, given its links to the same theoretical set of assumptions.

As explained to me by the curator, one of the texts guiding the museum's understanding—or, I would argue, misunderstanding—of the important role of museums in telling the story of Jewish peoplehood is a work discussed in the previous chapter, Benedict Anderson's influential book *Imagined Communities*. Anderson refers in that volume to the ways that museums—along with censuses and maps—have shaped collective self-understanding in the modern period.[2] Yet Anderson is a curious voice to cite as authorization and imprimatur, given the broader context of his interest in museums.

Like most contemporary scholars of nationalism, Anderson does not define the meaning of national collectivity as something essential that has existed throughout time. Instead, the point of his work has been to demonstrate how various communities began to imagine themselves in novel ways at the beginning of the modern period—specifically, to articulate themselves as peoples and nations. In this context he writes: "The census, the map, and the museum . . . profoundly shaped the way in which the colonial state imagined its dominion—the nature of the human beings it ruled, the geography of its domain, and the legitimacy of its ancestry."[3]

The work of scholars like Anderson, whose understanding of the modern nature of national groups typifies the academic approach to the topic today, undercuts any portrayal of a consistent historical entity called the Jewish people, whether it has singular or multiple geographic focal points. Recent scholarship on nationalism raises a far more fundamental question than simply "homeland versus homeland and diaspora?" regarding how a museum of Jewish peoplehood could best reflect and promote the story of the Jewish people over the last several thousand years. The very assumption that a collective group can be defined as unified across geographic boundaries, historical periods, and cultural markers is questioned by scholars like Anderson, who argue that collective identity does not reflect real bonds, but instead the imagination of individuals shaped by a variety of historical circumstances. A museum's attempt to narrate one coherent story about the Jewish people from its origins in the biblical period to its current manifestations around the world—even with a new narrative—would seem to be at odds with Anderson's analysis of the modern construction of collective boundaries.

In fact, in response to a question from this author raising that very tension, this particular museum professional expressed discomfort with the idea that building an exhibit tracing the origins, key practices, beliefs, and tribal bonds of the Jewish people would reflect as much about the contemporary need to tell that story as about the historical reality of that group. This revamped museum exhibit about the Jewish people, it would seem, is—like the vast majority of Jewish institutional voices both within and outside of Israel—not positioned to respond to deep scholarly claims questioning the concept of a well-defined Jewish collectivity across space and time, linking Jews to a singular shared story.

Interestingly, in making clear her ideological distance from those who would doubt this sort of assumption by examining the idea of the Jewish people critically, the curator gestured with one hand beyond the walls of the museum toward the university academic offices nearby. She wanted to indicate that her museum's view of the Jewish people is distinct from the logic of just such critical scholars, including not only Anderson but also Shlomo Sand, a scholar based—like the museum itself—at Tel Aviv University. Sand's controversial book *The Invention of the Jewish People* also calls into question the very idea that there is such a thing as the Jewish people with a history from the ancient Land of Israel to the present day.[4]

This window onto one of the most visible communal institutions dedicated to preserving and teaching about the history of the Jewish people captures the contested nature of the meaning of Jewish peoplehood today. Previous Zionist articulations of Jewish collectivity, with Israel as the center and Jewish life in the diaspora as a lesser entity, have been displaced by the search for a new definition of how the two centers of global Jewry—North America and Israel—relate to each other, but a more comprehensive rethinking of Jewish collectivity in light of the significant intellectual, political, and social transformations of the last few decades has not yet emerged. As a result, popular conceptions of the Jewish people remain ambiguously and precariously perched between still-outdated (if revamped) models shaped by Zionism and paradigms of postmodern identity and critical scholarship eroding the perceived legitimacy of historical and political claims.

The museum's efforts to rethink itself as a museum of the Jewish people places its curator and consultants in an emblematic position, representing a far broader predicament. Its staff is struggling to articulate a narrative of Jewish peoplehood today that tones down some nationalist claims without undermining the validity of the assertion of a collective group with a historical link to a homeland and shared tradition. Yet any attempt to make the language of the Jewish people and peoplehood relevant and present a new paradigm for Jewish collectivity has to come to terms with the extent to which both scholarship and popular understandings of group identity have shifted away from making essential, transhistorical claims about the features linking individuals with a greater collective. In a sense, the struggle simultaneously to engage with the scholarship of nationalism and keep at a distance the most critical questions raised by that scholarship is the core dilemma faced by contemporary attempts to define the meaning, relevance, and value of the Jewish people. How can this term and the term peoplehood be relevant today without either reifying outdated and overly simplistic modes of self-understanding, or imploding under postmodern pressure to deconstruct essentialist claims and globalization's erosion of particularist boundaries?

Three divergent paths have emerged. One is the Jewish peoplehood promoters supported by American Jewish organizations and the State of Israel. Still deeply influenced by the nationalist paradigm, peoplehood advocates double down on the function of peoplehood as a code word for modified Zionist claims about the meaning of Jewish collectivity. The rhetoric of peoplehood serves as a ballast against post-Zionism and the perception of a distancing between American Jews and Israel.

A second path, represented by scholarship on nationalism, religion, ethnicity, and race, reflects a critical turn over the last three decades. The building blocks of twentieth-century group self-understanding and scholarly rendering of the nationalist paradigm—static boundaries, essential characteristics, and shared histories—have been replaced by understandings and expressions of porous borders, fluid identities, and constructed histories. These trends pose a number of normative and practical challenges to precisely those assumptions about the Jewish people that were solidified by the modern turn to the nationalist paradigm in the twentieth century. The gap between the divergent paths of mainstream Jewish communal dedication to peoplehood in the nationalist paradigm and modern academic studies on peoplehood cannot be bridged by simply selectively integrating bits of scholarship into communal institutions and their existing narratives.

There is a third path—like the first, specifically interested in Jewish peoplehood, but from a scholarly perspective—that might seem like the perfect synthesis of the other two approaches. The work of some scholars of Jewish studies—especially historians and cultural theorists—takes seriously the construction over time and contextual nature of Jewishness and Jewish groupness. However, in significant ways, this scholarship falls victim to the same split. These scholars generally stay out of the communal peoplehood discourse (which is then not strengthened by an investigation into the constructed nature of Jewishness), and with good reason—those who participate in that discourse are generally not interested in critical scholarship on group identity, since it problematizes their peoplehood agenda.

We turn in this chapter to examine these three approaches to peoplehood—Jewish communal, general scholarly, and Jewish studies—and the clash between these different perspectives over key aspects of the nationalist paradigm. This enables us to understand the tensions that arise when trends in Jewish communal institutional life are explicitly put in conversation with a scholarly reevaluation of fundamental nationalist claims about collective identity—and see in more detail how scholarship in Jewish studies does not resolve that tension. Just as the terms of debate had their roots in mid-twentieth-century nationalism and Zionism, the state of the question of the meaning of the Jewish people today is closely linked to the rapidly changing meanings of nationalism and ethnicity in cultural and scholarly conversations.

Unity, Solidarity, Statehood

In 2011, the Commission on the Jewish People, a program of the UJA Federation of New York, sponsored a global task force on peoplehood education. The members of the task force introduced their report as follows:

> Throughout Jewish history, the notion of Jewish Peoplehood, of being part of *klal yisrael*—the Jewish Peoplehood notion—was embedded in

Jewish life and was transmitted organically in a myriad of implicit and explicit ways via the rich fabric of Jewish communal actions and family life. In contemporary times, however, as the composition, culture, and demographics of Jewish life undergo unprecedented transitions, the Peoplehood consciousness that was once organic and integral to Jewish identity cannot be taken for granted. Indeed, the vision of Jewish Peoplehood is at risk of disappearing.[5]

This statement is emblematic of the rhetoric of many peoplehood initiatives that have emerged since 2000 by or with the support of American Jewish and Israeli state-associated organizations. Peoplehood, according to that rhetoric, is an indubitable and perennial aspect of Jewish identity that faces extinction for the first time in Jewish history, unless efforts succeed to counteract the recent changes and challenges of modernity.

This presentation of peoplehood stands in direct contrast to the actual development of the term Jewish peoplehood, which, as we have seen, emerged in the last century as a rupture from premodern conceptions of collectivity, and was inspired by and drew on concepts taken from nationalism. Indeed, the transitions highlighted in the above quotation as undermining peoplehood actually helped to create the concept in the first place, by putting Jewish thought in conversation with ideas of modern nationalism and Americanism.

The new vigor that characterizes Jewish peoplehood conversations in the last decade of the twentieth century, and especially in the first decades of the twenty-first century, merits analysis. Why has peoplehood made such a strong comeback, fueled by the investment of the organized American Jewish institutional framework in tandem with the Israeli government and philanthropic foundations? Does this renaissance of Jewish peoplehood language represent a continuation of the trajectory established in the middle of the twentieth century, or a new framework for promoting peoplehood in theory and practice?

The term peoplehood had limited currency in Jewish communal publications and initiatives in the last decades of the twentieth century. For example, according to a search of the Berman Jewish Policy archive, an online repository of Jewish communal material, between 1980 and 1995 there were fewer than ten articles with peoplehood in the title.[6] However, the same archive contains almost one hundred articles with peoplehood in the title published between 1996 and 2014.[7] The proliferation of literature in communal publications related to the topic reflects a concerted effort to promote the term, as well as investment of significant resources by major Jewish philanthropists around the globe in the study and popularization of the concept. Peoplehood has also served as a major focus of the State of Israel through the work of the state agency, the Jewish Agency for Israel, an organization historically tied to promoting aliyah and settling the Land of Israel.

A few key events between 2000 and 2011 exemplify the sudden emergence of this new attempt to promote a definition of peoplehood through an enormous, unprecedented investment of time, institutional energy, and money.

- In 2000, UJA-Federation established the Commission on the Jewish People.
- In 2002, the Jewish Agency for Israel established the Jewish People Planning Institute.
- In 2003, the Nadav Foundation was created "to support and advance Jewish peoplehood."
- In 2005, the Israeli Knesset voted to approve a bill to rename and reconfigure Beit Hatfutsot (the Museum of the Jewish Diaspora) as the Museum of the Jewish People and the Center for Peoplehood Education (in 2009, Israeli philanthropist Leonid Nevzlin gave $6 million to remake the museum).
- In 2007, participants in the General Assembly of the United Jewish Communities focused on the theme of peoplehood, and each attendee received a free copy of the book *The Case for the Jewish People: Can We Be One?* by Erica Brown and Misha Galperin.
- In 2011, Israeli legislators submitted a Basic Law proposal to define Israel as "the nation-state of the Jewish people."

The state of the conversation today has some internal variety, but overall many shared assumptions characterize the recent peoplehood phenomenon. A few themes repeat across various articulations of Jewish peoplehood, chief among them an instinctive sense that peoplehood exists and unifies world Jewry. We "just feel it," one commentator remarks.[8] The existence of a primary bond between Jews around the world seems unquestionable and axiomatic. The all-important nature of Jewish peoplehood, along with a simultaneous sense that the concept faces unjustified criticism, can be seen in the quasi-legal language employed: one makes a case for peoplehood. They are also reflected in concerns over a crisis of peoplehood. Discussions often take an alarmist tone with references to "the death of the peoplehood" or its "unraveling."[9] Cases and articulations of crises come about in response to perceptions that something essential is under attack.

The focus on unity as the bulwark against the destruction of peoplehood is so important that a number of metrics have been developed to measure its level among various Jewish communities. For instance, a

"Peoplehood Index" and dashboard of Jewish peoplehood bonds measured by criteria of "Hard Power" have emerged to measure and increase levels of Jewish unity.[10] Interestingly, this Peoplehood Index's measure of "degree of shared identity" is primarily assessed through self-reporting of a feeling of connectedness, rather than actual engagement in expressions and enactments of Jewishness. This rhetoric skews discussions of peoplehood into organizing policy positions that promote simplistic divisions between us and them in marking the boundaries of Jewish collectivity.

Recent articulations of Jewish peoplehood also underscore the external perils unifying Jews to one another. The threats of antisemitism and efforts to delegitimize Israel are often emphasized. One example of a combination of the two appeared in the decision by the Nadav Foundation to grant their "Peoplehood Award" in 2010 to the creators of "We Con the World," a satirical video poking fun at the international outcry against Israel following the Israeli Navy's storming of a Turkish flotilla off the coast of Gaza.[11] The video, the award citation asserts, "made many Jews feel proud in a time of conflict and tension for our people." Solidarity, this citation suggests, occurs when Jews come together to refute unfair criticism of Israel.

With an emphasis on external threats, rather than internal unifying characteristics, the actual internal ties that unite Jews to one another remains vague. Peoplehood's rhetoric and literature stress values, heritage, and unifying goals, but they are rarely identified beyond a general language of *tikkun olam* (usually translated in contemporary contexts as "repairing the world"). One of the more prominent published examples of this trend toward identifying a set of Jewish characteristics that are rather vague is the aforementioned volume *The Case for Jewish Peoplehood: Can We Be One?* which provides an important window onto the new discourse of peoplehood. Authors Brown and Galperin focus on finding an essential unity that is necessary to "make a strong case for Jewish continuity."[12] Their articulation of peoplehood underscores the enduring influence of the nationalist paradigm: "We need to be part of an extended family with a vision, a unique mission in the world. Part of that mission involves seeking social justice for all people. More of that mission involves nurturing Jewish literacy, Jewish values, and Jewish solidarity with Israel and Jews the world over."[13]

Similar to the paradigm of Jewish peoplehood developed by the term's pioneers, *The Case for Jewish Peoplehood* builds on the foundations of nationality by emphasizing an essential mission, ancient textual sources read as shared history, and a familial conception of group ties. The work also implicitly highlights a mythic past and the centrality of the homeland: the Jewish nation's particular mission, echoing initial articulations of Jewish nationality in the 1920s and 1930s, should embrace a vision of particularism that best promotes universal harmony and justice.

The contemporary ethical mission concept shares another aspect with earlier connotations of peoplehood and its European antecedents. The rhetoric of ties linking Jews to one another lack a clear articulation of what it is about Jewishness that should be preserved beyond the importance placed on an ambiguous essence. For example, a recent report to the Museum of the Jewish People's board of governors described the "essential question" around the story of the Jewish people as follows: "What is the secret underlying the continuous vital and creative endurance of the Jewish people?"[14] The assertion that such a blueprint exists linking Jews to one another suggests a set of empirical commitments whose articulation and preservation would ensure Jewish continuity. But these values are rarely articulated beyond broad slogans that belie the fragmentation of values within Jewish communities.

This affirmation of a shared set of Jewish values, literacy, and solidarity precisely at a moment of increasing internal fragmentation illustrates Anderson's "imagined community." Indeed, it is particularly interesting to note repeated references to Anderson's imagined communities among proponents of peoplehood—all sharing the misreading I heard in the Museum of the Jewish Diaspora.[15] Imagined communities are indeed resources for Jewish leaders interested in generating a feeling of solidarity—but they are social constructs, and none of the peoplehood proponents who invoke Anderson's work do so with his acknowledgment of this construction or his critical lens that questions the existence of any group as a group prior to the socially constructed category that describes it. These leaders seem to ignore entirely the word *imagined* in his phrase—by which, of course, Anderson does not mean imaginary, but called into being by acts of imagination—and often use or rely on social science to portray as essentially real what is actually constructed.

The imprecise use of scholarship such as Anderson's "imagined community" to buttress the existence of shared collective principles avoids the surfacing of internal contradictions that could fragment the claims of unity. The current embrace of peoplehood, unlike the earlier articulation of Mordecai Kaplan and his followers, sidesteps any potential conflicts between Jews' universal mission and the State of Israel as the engine for enacting it. Whether or not the State of Israel is in fact the center of Jewish activism toward universal justice is never addressed, so this modified commitment to statism is allowed to exist (in the world of this text and others like it) in harmony with rhetoric of ethical nationalism; the authors do not explore the on-the-ground, concrete, and specific social and political issues that would of necessity highlight tensions between the two.

One reason that the tension between a shared commitment to Jewish values and the implementation of these values is difficult to address in the context of peoplehood is that peoplehood increasingly functions as a code word for supporting both the State of Israel and Zionist assumptions about the relationship between Israel and the diaspora.[16] The rise of Jewish peoplehood as key term over the last decade reflects its role in strengthening the centrality of the State of Israel in response to recent historical circumstances. The second Intifada began in late 2000, initiating what would be almost five years of intense conflict between Israelis and Palestinians. Israelis felt incredibly isolated, and feared the diminishment of American Jewish support. At the same time, the fundamental organizing principle of Zionism, the emphasis on aliyah and the corollary negation of the viability of diaspora Jewish life, had outlived its usefulness with the immigration of almost one million Soviet Jews, on one hand, and the richness of the North American Jewish communities on the other.

Peoplehood reemerged on the scene at the time that a new approach to thinking about the relationship between the state and Jews around the world was necessary. One can see the shifting attitude of the state in the reframing of the Jewish Agency for Israel in order to embrace peoplehood. Historically, the Jewish Agency stood for aliyah and state building. It was the face of Zionist negation of the diaspora and a gateway to support Jewish immigration to Israel. Under its new chairman, former Soviet dissident Natan Sharansky, the Jewish Agency has now adopted the American Jewish term peoplehood and is attempting to popularize the relatively obscure Hebrew analog, *amiyut*.[17] The Jewish Agency, in the words of its executives, seeks to be the convener of a conversation about Jewish peoplehood. A sense of the interchangeable nature of support for the state and Jewish solidarity has been nourished by the Agency's embrace of peoplehood as an integral part of its mission.

This marks an interesting shift in the use of peoplehood, from an American context grappling with the impact of Zionism on American Jewish life to one increasingly centered in Israel and its state institutions. Though the language of people and peoplehood emerged in English as a way of translating Zionist principles into terms acceptable in the United States, that language has now come full circle as Zionism itself struggles with changing attitudes toward nationalism and post-Zionist critiques of its own history.

Peoplehood offers Israeli leaders several advantages over more entrenched concepts such as Zionism or Jewish nationalism. Once official Zionist organizations, such as the Jewish Agency, realized the need to temper the statist aspects of their vision of Jewish nationalism, peoplehood provided an alternative, softer, vision of Jewish nationalism—one that had already been accepted and articulated by many established American Jewish organizations. Facing the reality that the State of Israel will not ingather all diaspora Jews, as well as growing concerns about the distancing of American Jews from Israel, the Jewish Agency can use peoplehood as a less demanding and diaspora-friendly version of Zionism. Its embrace of peoplehood marks a shift from being an organization rooted in political Zionism's rejection of diaspora Jewry to one that accepts cultural Zionism's vision of Israel as the organizing principle of diaspora Jewry.

The classical Zionist hierarchical elevation of peoplehood as best expressed through Jewish collective life in the State of Israel—as well as the importance of supporting the State of Israel personally, materially, and politically—largely remains, even if the state per se is not the explicit centerpiece of definitions of peoplehood. As Jewish Agency for Israel (JAFI) executive Alan Hoffman argues, "Israel exemplifies the very idea of peoplehood."[18] Birthright Israel, the free trip for young American Jews to spend ten days in Israel, is hailed as an example of "building peoplehood power."[19] A report by the Reut Institute, an Israeli think-tank, acknowledges that Israelis are no longer all in Israel, but still gives diaspora Israelis a central role as "catalyst for Jewish Peoplehood."[20]

The language of a new openness to diaspora communities notwithstanding, the most recent incarnation of Jewish peoplehood represents return to the nationalist paradigm to preserve Zionist claims, largely by repackaging that vision of Jewish collectivity in terminology calibrated to appeal to Jewish audiences who likely would have hesitations about explicitly nationalist claims. The shift reflects continuity with conceptions of peoplehood that emerged in the second half of the twentieth century on American soil, stressing unity and solidarity as well as statehood as the fundamental pillars of Jewish peoplehood. This model not only underscores the shared internal cohesion of Jews despite different practices and religious beliefs, but also preserves intact the homeland-diaspora dichotomy while still focusing on the need for political power to defend the collective against outside threats.

Major programs like Birthright Israel, the focus on *mifgashim* (encounters) between Jewish Israelis and American Jews, and the Jewish Agency of Israel's adoption of peoplehood as one of its primary pillars all provide highly visible examples of a shift away from the explicit language of Zionism while positing the homeland as the engine of Jewish identity formation in the diaspora and the involuntary nature of Jewish membership based on one's birth. These programs reflect the State of Israel's enduring interest in shaping a narrative of Jewish identity based on Zionist assumptions about the secular, political, and territorial nature of collective identity.

Peoplehood has thus largely replaced the sharp division of the Jewish world into Israel and diaspora, a binary seen by many as outdated.

However, the key word's popularity in English and relative obscurity in Hebrew contribute to and certainly also reflect the perpetuation of Zionism's categorical distinction and hierarchy between homeland and diaspora communities. Peoplehood's advocates focus on Jews outside of Israel connecting with Israel—and far less on how Israeli Jews view their own identity as Jews, linked to a people beyond their own citizenship and their fellow Jewish Israeli citizens.[21] The new name of the Museum of the Jewish People illustrates the difference between English and Hebrew adoption of peoplehood. Significantly, despite the new English name of the museum, its Hebrew name as indicated on the museum's stationery retains both old and new: "Beit Hatfutsot / Muzayon Am Hayehudi"—keeping the Zionist message of diaspora (*tfutsot*) while incorporating the word *am*, which can mean nation as well as people. It would appear from the decision not to change the museum's name in Hebrew that this is a rebranding meant chiefly to appeal to English speakers, and to be used in conversation with them for philanthropic and political ends. English-speaking diaspora Jews are portrayed as needing a sense of peoplehood because they are increasingly distanced from Jewish organizations and the state. However, Hebrew speakers can continue to use their existing conceptual terminology that articulates nationalist claims. Israelis don't need peoplehood because they de facto have a greater sense of it, just by being citizens of the State of Israel. It is not surprising, then, that there has been little traction for the new word *amiyut* in Israel, and even less acceptance from Israelis for the idea that there should be a shared concept of peoplehood associating them with communities outside the state.

As peoplehood has played an increasingly dominant role as a code word for supporting Israel and placing the relationship with the Jewish state at the core of Jewish collectivity, peoplehood advocates' methods of assessing levels of collective solidarity are difficult to distinguish from the ways they would or do assess support for the State of Israel.[22] For instance, a recent study of American Jewish leaders explicitly congratulates establishment leaders who champion particularity- and solidarity-oriented expressions of peoplehood, rather than "a celebration of Diaspora cultures, including an implicit or explicit rejection of Israel's centrality for American Jews."[23] This understanding of peoplehood reflects its strong association with a commitment to the State of Israel, and a corresponding devaluing of diaspora activities and local religious engagement, implicitly considered in opposition to peoplehood attachment.

The extensive use of peoplehood and political support for the State of Israel as overlapping terms suggests that the distinctions Kaplan hoped to emphasize have been largely ignored.[24] Indeed, Jewish peoplehood, ironically, would now undergird the institutions of a state-oriented Zionism that Kaplan had marshaled it to challenge. Mainstream definitions of peoplehood have evolved—just as nationalism has—in the direction of blurred boundaries between national collective identity and state sovereignty. The narrow use of the language of peoplehood in the organized American Jewish communal and Israeli institutional peoplehood discourse highlights a novel (if staid) aspect of its most recent revival. Efforts to explore alternate models of collectivity, distinct from the dominance of Israel, would actually reflect a much closer link to the countercultural reasons for which Kaplan initially selected the term in the mid-twentieth century; instead, established institutions employ it as a way of preserving Israel's primacy and shoring up the status quo.

Making national political claims around ties of Hebrew language and Jewish peoplehood are more complicated at a time when large numbers of new immigrants from the former Soviet Union have settled in Israel. Peoplehood provides a category to integrate a large number of Russian Jews with tenuous Jewish identities into the State of Israel. Between the 1990s and early 2000s, Israel absorbed almost one million formerly Soviet immigrants. After decades under communism's prohibition of religious learning and practice, these immigrants needed to be integrated into Israeli and Jewish identities. However, the Israeli religious establishment contests the Jewishness of many Russian immigrants. Under the Law of Return, the state considered immigrants with one Jewish grandparent and their (not necessarily Jewish) spouses as eligible for automatic Israeli citizenship. A secularized definition of peoplehood more easily enables the inclusion of this part of the population within the Jewish collectivity. A symbolic identity that is secular, ethnic, and ambiguous could integrate even Jews cut off from Jewish life and practice for decades.

The desire to shift the collective basis from religious to national definitions may explain the absence of religion from communal definitions of peoplehood. The revived post-2000 articulation of peoplehood is deeply secular, with almost no explicit associations with religious orientation. Sidestepping religion, peoplehood's emphasis remains on terms (such as values, heritage, and mission) from which a reader or listener might make her own link to religion but need not. This contrasts with earlier articulations of peoplehood, the most famous of which (Kaplan's) described the Jewish people as an "evolving religious civilization" to differentiate a conception of Jewish collectivity rooted in religious texts, traditions, and practices from the territorial and political nation-state paradigm.

The historical bookends of the Soviet Jewry movement as the highpoint of American Jewish solidarity and Russian émigrés now at the center of institutional and financial support for peoplehood thirty years later are worth considering.[25] The journey of dissident icon Anatoly Sharansky, the object of American Jewish solidarity, to Natan Sharansky, Jewish Agency chairperson and proponent of peoplehood, provides an interesting lens through which to think about the changes in the rhetoric of peoplehood. The movement to free Soviet Jews focused on universal ideals of freedom of religion and democracy. The rhetoric of peoplehood articulated by the Jewish Agency now emphasizes preservation of the Jewish people rather than claims of ending religious persecution.

Peoplehood's uptick also indicates efforts by leaders of the American Jewish community to address structural and demographic shifts endangering legacy communal institutions, especially Jewish Federations. The increased use of peoplehood in communal events, publications, and institutional programs emerged just as pillar organizations of the American Jewish community began to recognize a set of existential challenges, as their models of philanthropy failed to attract new generations of supporters. These conditions created fertile ground for growth of a revised peoplehood concept, one that on the surface distanced itself from an older model for defining Jewish collectivity in the Israel-diaspora framework, while still affirming through the back door many of that model's assumptions.

The push for continuity in the 1990s had failed to reinvigorate local Federations and their allied institutions. Moreover, the call to support Jews in need, especially in Israel and the former Soviet Union, faced competition from other causes inspiring American Jews. Peoplehood represented new language to reinforce philanthropic objectives of the Federation system. This connection between fundraising objectives and peoplehood can be seen in studies funded by the Federation world such as *The Power of Peoplehood: How Commitment to the Jewish People Undergirds Tzedakah for Jewish Causes*. The study concluded: "Jewish Peoplehood commitment is strongly linked with Jewish philanthropic generosity."[26] The vocabulary for galvanizing Jewish support of centralized philanthropy shifted, but the objective of promoting solidarity for fundraising remains a key goal of the peoplehood initiative.

The effort to raise the visibility and importance of peoplehood has produced dissenters, especially those who fall outside dominant structures and personalities in the peoplehood program. The conveners of the peoplehood movement, to their credit, include dissenting voices. For example, author and activist Jay Michaelson has attacked the peoplehood literature by arguing that its amorphous statements say nothing; for Michaelson, "There is no there there."[27] Instead, in his view, generalizations about shared solidarity serve as little more than a cover for ethnocentrism. Others, like Daniel Septimus, editor-in-chief at My Jewish Learning.com, and Ruth Messinger, executive director of American Jewish World Service, have criticized the emphasis on the language of peoplehood, which seems to ignore "Jewish values, practices, rituals, and learning."[28] A much louder expression of dissent can be heard simply in the deafening silence with which many Jews respond to peoplehood rhetoric. Especially considering that this is a concept with powerful resources backing its development, it is noteworthy that few younger, grassroots Jewish leaders have embraced the term.[29]

My intention in briefly comparing and contrasting contemporary discourse on peoplehood with its earlier formulation as a critique of Zionism is not to suggest that one is more authentic or correct. Instead, the comparison illuminates what is missing in recent peoplehood rhetoric. A term that in the hands of one its most important proponents was once wielded to critique the statist focus of Zionism and to promote a vision of Jewish collectivity that includes religio-cultural practice and outlook—and that further evolved in the incubator of social theory to explain ethnic and national solidarity utterly unrelated to state politics—is now being deployed in ways that diverge significantly from these previous uses.

Even as the recent trajectory of peoplehood claims to mitigate classical Zionist critiques of the diaspora, it extends the construction of the Jewish people in the modern era on the foundation of the nationalist paradigm, whether the secularized and ethnic notions of the late twentieth century or the more religio-cultural versions developed in the mid-twentieth century. Indeed, the evolution of the contemporary discourse of peoplehood from a diaspora critique of statist-oriented Zionism to the official position of the Jewish Agency for Israel has only strengthened the relationship between nationalism and peoplehood as the language of Jewish collectivity.

While recent historical developments have generated a renewed interest in peoplehood as a reaffirmation of Jewish solidarity, essential ties, and connection to the homeland, we see in the next section the ways in which contemporary articulations of Jewish peoplehood stand in direct opposition to the contributions of recent scholarship on collectivity and parallel sociological realities, both of which reflect an increasing fluidity and complexity in group self-understanding and individual identity. While there are a few references here and there to imagined communities or hybrid identity in the peoplehood conversation, the full implications for the Jewish people of critical readings and emerging realities of groupness are not reflected in the contemporary literature of Jewish peoplehood. Consequently, wider scholarly critiques of key categories of collectivity—critiques with which some aspects of Jewish studies, at least, are implicitly in dialogue—have not been fully understood, brought to bear upon, or responded to in the contemporary communal conversation on Jewish peoplehood. An appreciation of the significant shift in how scholars think about those categories of collectivity and an understanding of where Jewish studies scholarship stands in relationship to these wider scholarly trends, as well as to the Jewish communal peoplehood discourse, are necessary before proceeding to a constructive proposal for conceiving of Jewish peoplehood in the twenty-first century.

Nationalism, Globalization, and the Limits of Peoplehood

"Why do we simplify and reify people into essentialized categories of modern peoplehood? Even more bizarre, why do people identify principally with one or another category of modern peoplehood?"[30] Sociologist John Lie asks these deceptively simple questions in his 2003 study *Modern Peoplehood*—questions that exemplify how trends in Jewish communal discourse increasingly clash with changing scholarly and popular understandings of peoplehood. In the same decade that Jewish communal conversations experienced a renewed dedication to affirming the unique, enduring, and unquestionable nature of Jewish peoplehood (2000–2010), peoplehood emerged as the subject of new scholarship analyzing the very recent roots of the concept of peoplehood. Despite the overlapping timeframe and interest in the same key word, these two conversations remain completely isolated from one another. This section explores the deep tension between the increasingly divergent visions of peoplehood in the Jewish communal and broader intellectual contexts.

Lie's question cuts to the heart of an epistemological transformation that has characterized scholarship since the 1980s, pushing readers to question the very proverbial conception of group self-definition. Building on the work of other scholars such as Anderson, Lie challenges the idea that modern groups have a clear-cut correlation with the premodern communities they claim, and more profoundly, that the very composition of modern peoplehood has anything to do with the categories that premodern communities used to differentiate groups from one another. This challenge carries with it the implication not only that specific group identities are constructions, but even more fundamentally that the very idea of aligning individuals across time and space with a singular group (whether national, ethnic, or religious) is itself a modern innovation that obscures very different prior categories, taxonomies, and ideas about groups. The emerging academic arena of what we might call the field of peoplehood studies builds on changing conceptions of nationality, ethnicity, and race during the last two to three decades—confronting the modern concept of peoplehood, especially (if indirectly) Jewish peoplehood, given its deep roots in the nationalist paradigm as well as its links to ethnicity and descent.

But contemporary discourse in academia and social movements as well as sociological realities do not merely change the language of group identity—they disrupt notions of a people's very existence as such. Recent scholarship on nationalism, ethnicity, and race ultimately restricts claims that groups can make about themselves. At the same time, changing social forces encourage individuals to be part of multiple groups and freely mix various cultures, and often replace broader territorial and/or national allegiances with contingent local commitments.

This shift is already confounding many of the basic categorical assumptions in modern definitions of the Jewish people. Does an Israeli living in Los Angeles and telecommuting to work in Haifa fit into a homeland or diaspora community? What about the progressive cheeseburger-eating twenty-year-old who studies Talmud at an egalitarian yeshiva but avoids attending synagogue—is he secular, cultural, or religious? Where do college kids with names like Avi Cohen, whose mothers are not Jewish (but may serve as the education chairs of their campus Jewish community), fit on the map of discrete categories and hierarchies? The blurring of boundaries between expected dualities creates problems for those interested in evaluating precisely the state of Jewish life. Applying outdated categories and decreasingly coherent dualities—homeland versus diaspora, secular versus religious, Jewish versus not-Jewish/of Jewish heritage—measures Jewishness against benchmarks that tell us far more about the limits of old paradigms than the richness of new possibilities.

This does not mean that group identity is disappearing, but that we will inevitably need to adjust our expectations of its meaning and impact. Before considering possible conceptions of Jewish peoplehood in a new key in this volume's final chapter, we need to gain a clearer understanding of the changing meaning of the categories of collectivity that have served as the theoretical building blocks of Jewish peoplehood, specifically nationality, ethnicity, and race—as well as the questioning of the very category of peoplehood itself.

The study of nationalism, and with it the existence of discrete and delineated peoples, has been one of the areas of study most profoundly reshaped by the shift in scholarship from analyzing the behavior and structure of groups to tracing the emergence of group identity. Until about thirty years ago, scholarship on nationalism created the intellectual and historical foundation for legitimizing and articulating peoplehood claims in general, and Zionism in particular. For instance, Hans Kohn, one of the fathers of modern nationalism scholarship, not only viewed Jews as a national group but also saw ancient Israel as the blueprint of the national idea and exemplar of modern ethical nationalism.[31] Kohn, like other leading scholars of nationalism before the 1980s, studied the link between modern nations and their historical antecedents. In other words, they largely continued a nineteenth-century tradition of nationalist historians whose goal was to document the evolution of national groups by highlighting major events, ideas, and leaders over time. This approach secured the key role that Jewish historians, such as Abraham Geiger, Heinrich Graetz, and Simon Dubnow, had played in creating narratives of the Jewish people that assumed continuity over time of ethnic, religious, cultural, political, and/or moral values.[32]

So, for example, Kaplan could argue for significant historical changes within Judaism without questioning the existence of a unifying Jewish national ideal that connected Jewish thought and practice through various historical epochs. While Kaplan's dedication to modern thought compelled him to reject the existence and thus the idea of a supernatural God, he did not perceive any need to apply the same critique to the very concept of the Jewish people. Instead, Kaplan could build a theory of Jewish peoplehood on the most cutting-edge social theory of his day. In addition, the second half of the twentieth century saw the ascendance of the categories of ethnicity and religion in modern social theory, providing another strong set of paradigms for translating Judaism into modern politics and societies.

Early twentieth-century social theory offered a theoretical basis for groups as fundamental units who behaved according to certain generalizable principles, explaining how they structured themselves and functioned. Indeed, the two major streams of twentieth-century social thought—structuralism and functionalism—debated whether the key to understanding groups involved locating underlying structures that govern social relationships or identifying functional needs and benefits of group practices.[33] By making social relations, and even their deeper patterns that transcend place and time, into objects of academic study, social theory legitimated group solidarity as a social fact and historical reality.

It was the critical turn in historical scholarship in the 1980s that transformed the study of nationalism from discovering stable characteristics of specific nations to underscoring the constructed nature of national identity. Scholars delegitimized the practice of tracing characteristics in national groups across time as primordialist for attempting to link national origins with modern collectivities. Instead, most scholars came to argue for a modernist perspective on nationalism that views national groups as distinctly modern innovations, with either no or very limited connections to premodern antecedents. Historians largely shifted their focus toward understanding the impact of not only modern political processes, but technological, cultural, and economic ones as well, on the invention of national communities. From the modernist vantage point, nations are not real collective groups; instead, nationalism is completely rooted in the historical fabric of modernity, and national ideologies construct histories to support present-day agendas. Not only are historical antecedents for modern nations invented, but the creation of national history is a means for achieving political ends.[34]

Some scholars of nationalism have tried to identify links between modern and premodern collective groups without embracing the primordialist position that overlooks any modern influences on group definition. These scholars, identified in the literature as perennialists, modify claims of a primordial national essence by exploring the perpetual and permanent bases of collective claims that manifested themselves as nationalism in the modern period. Anthony Smith, the scholar most closely identified with this camp, acknowledges the transformative impact of modernity, but contends that national ties are modern variations on persistent (or perennial) types of solidarity that have premodern origins. While Smith challenges nationalist claims that groups are unchanging, he attempts to locate the ethnic origins of modern national groups: "We must trace [nations] them back to their underlying ethnic and territorial contexts; we must set them in the wider historical intersection between cultural ties and political communities, as these were influenced by, and influenced, the processes of administrative centralization, economic transformation, mass communications and the disintegration of traditions which we associate with modernity."[35]

However, the scholarship of nationalism continues to drift toward the modernist camp, resulting in a dramatic rupture in concepts of collectivity, even in those cases where there are premodern precursors to modern nations. Even Smith has moved away from his earlier support for a perennialist position; in more recent essays, he has taken a firm position on the need to appreciate the rupture that distinguishes premodern ethnic groups from modern nations, and has sharply countered contentions that modern national groups arise directly from premodern ethnic communities. Premodern ethnics, Smith argues, understand the nature of group identity in a fundamentally different way than modern nations do. Several key breaks must be taken into account, he says, including a shift from elite groups to mass nations, the emphasis on territory and political organization as the primary markers of collective groups, and the way in which modern nations "are legitimated through a universally applicable ideology, nationalism."[36]

Indeed, the modernist and perennialist debate in scholarship no longer has much currency; the modernist point of view has, in the main, achieved supremacy. With debates on the origins of nationalism decided in favor of modernists, scholarly focus has shifted in the direction of understanding the ongoing forces shaping collective claims. For example, Rogers Brubaker argues for the study of ethnic or national groupness without validating their actual or enduring existence as groups. The question of real or imagined is not even relevant. Rather, scholars should focus on such practical questions as how conceptions of group identity, whether called ethnicity or nationalism, exist without any necessary reference to an actual group, instead viewing the language and concepts for collective groups as novel constructions that emerge to mobilize individuals for a variety of political, economic, or social objectives.

The approach Brubaker champions does not dwell upon the evolution of processes over time, but instead explores rapid fluctuations and myriad possibilities for group claims at any particular place and time.[37] Brubaker suggests that the modernist approach does not go far enough in focusing on the specific elements that generated nationalism. For him, the historical approach should be expanded to study the ways in which a variety of collective identities, including ethnicity and nationalism, are regularly invented and reinvented to justify highly local agendas with absolutely no connection to the existence of actual groups. Politicians, leaders, and skilled ethnic entrepreneurs manipulate group definitions and boundaries to support their agendas. The rhetoric, vocabulary, and claims of groupness, in this view, tell us far more about current issues, competing concerns, and power dynamics than about the groups themselves.

The question of how these trends influence understandings of the Jewish people, interestingly, appears front and center in the scholarly literature on nationalism. Many key works on the topic consider if the Jewish people are an exception to the invented nature of modern nationalism. Among other things, at stake in this question is whether or not the claims of a Jewish people united around a 3,000-year history with roots in the Land of Israel—that is, modern Zionism—is or is not an exception to the modernist hypothesis of invented groupness.

For most modernists, Jewish nationalism fits the paradigm of the invention of nationalism. For example, for the historian and scholar of nationalism Eric Hobsbawm, Zionism emerges precisely as a paradigmatic example of the rupture between premodern and modernist notions of collectivity: "There is no historical continuity whatever between Jewish proto-nationalism and modern Zionism."[38] While Hobsbawm emphasizes Zionism, rather than broader claims of Jewish peoplehood, the implications of his thinking extend beyond that modern political movement. The severing of Zionism from the Jewish past also suggests a broader rupture in the conception of the Jewish people, since fundamental claims of Jewish peoplehood are shared with Zionism (e.g., historical continuity, origins in the Land of Israel, Jewish solidarity that transcends cultural and geographic divisions).

In contrast, Smith, the scholar most sensitive to modern national links with premodern ethnic groups, identifies Jews as representing an exceptional case. He writes, "Some ethnies, because of their strong alternative modes of transmission (usually through decentralized or itinerant religious and cultural personnel), have been able to preserve and transmit their heritages and ethno-histories from generation to generation—one thinks of diaspora people like the Jews."[39] In Smith's view, the concept of the Jewish people thus has a more substantial link to a premodern group than other national groups. Jews emerge in his work as exemplars of the perennialist category. The modern form of Jewish nationalism is a completely new variation of the Jewish people, but one that continues a history of collective consciousness.

In a later publication, however, even Smith qualifies the extent to which one can find continuities between ancient Israel and modern Israel.[40] The idea that the nature of national solidarity was the same, Smith warns, fails to appreciate the ways in which modernity has "affected the basic structures of human association."[41] The conflation of ancient Israel with modern Israel (a link consciously reinforced by the decision to name the state Israel, as we see below) fails to recognize that the two paradigms of collectivity are fundamentally different. Scholar of nationalism Elie Kedourie highlights the rupture in understandings of Jewish collective solidarity by illustrating his claim that "nationalist historiography operates, in fact, a subtle but unmistakable change in traditional conceptions," with his contention that "in Zionism, Judaism ceases to be the raison d'être of the Jew, and becomes, instead, a product of Jewish national consciousness."[42]

The centrality of Jews, and the case of modern Jewish nationalism, in this scholarship is significant for a few reasons. First, the politics around the premodern roots of nationalism have incredibly high stakes in the contemporary political context of the State of Israel. In fact, popular conversations about the role of Israel in Jewish collectivity at a moment of greater global integration can easily break down around the question of the impact of the historical significance of nationalism on modern Israel. Indeed, debates about the claims of Zionism rely indirectly on these two readings of the relationship between premodern and modern conceptions of Jewish collectivity. Smith's earlier position on ethnies has been crucial for some Zionist historians, such as Gideon Shimoni, author of *The Zionist Ideology*, to demonstrate the historical continuity of Zionism.[43] Smith provides the most promising theoretical basis among modernist historians for supporting Zionist claims that it is a modern version of a group with historical antecedents in the Land of Israel. On the other hand, the intellectual groundwork laid by modernists such as Hobsbawm offers a means through which other scholars raise fundamental questions about the Zionist narrative.[44]

Second, debates in the scholarship of nationalism about the nature of Jewish collectivity have a yet unfulfilled role to play in contemporary discourse about the Jewish people in Jewish studies. The spotlight on Jews as a test case in general scholarship of nationalism contrasts with the field of Jewish studies, which has demonstrated a hesitance to think about Jewish collectivity in relationship to changing notions of nationalism. The state of nationalism studies, then, represents a multifaceted challenge for Jewish studies, which remains deeply invested in nineteenth-century historical scholarship and twentieth-century Zionist historiography. Both of these approaches for thinking about Jewish collectivity assume the endurance of a national group that fits the criteria of the nationalist paradigm, while modernist scholarship on the history of nationalism undermines essentialist claims to the Jewish past, shared Jewish present, and collective ties to the Land of Israel. With some exceptions, Jewish studies scholars have yet to engage with the implications of scholarship on nationalism for claims about Jewish collectivity. Nor, certainly, have Jewish communal conversations done so.

There is, however, a rich modern Jewish conversation about the relationship between conceptions of Jewish peoplehood and the study of nationalism—just not within the field of Jewish studies. The general scholarship on nationalism would not be the most obvious place to understand changing interpretations of the Jewish people by Jews themselves—yet a disproportionate number of scholars of nationalism are Jews, whose own lives as émigrés were deeply touched by the forces of nationalism in the twentieth century. For the most prominent theorists in the field of nationalism studies, including Kohn, Kedourie, Smith, and Hobsbawn, as well as Gellner, the question of Jewish identity assumed centrality in their own biographies. While all of them drew clear distinctions between their personal experiences and their academic work, the prominence of the Jewish case in their writings provides one clue that the question of Jewish collectivity was paramount in their broader thinking on the topic. The study of nationalism in academic scholarship, as shaped largely by Jewish scholars, emerged in the late twentieth century as an important terrain for debates about the nature of the Jewish people. The field of Jewish studies might expand its research agenda to think more systematically about the place that scholarship on nationalism plays as a site of Jewish debate about collectivity and identity, in the hands of many individual Jewish scholars.[45]

The erosion of the nationalist paradigm is not only an abstract scholarly issue for scholars of nationalism to debate. There is another, far more practical and day-to-day challenge to contemporary conversations about Jewish peoplehood as it relates to the changing realities of the relationship between nation and state. The process of economic globalization, transnational migration, and digital communication has affected the state's role in defining national identity. Within states, privatization further diminishes the state's role in the economic life of its citizens. Migration patterns, often driven by economic opportunities in other countries, make it increasingly difficult for democratic states to privilege ethnic majorities. Digital technology allows culture to flow easily across political and territorial boundaries. Local contexts often now transplant larger spatial contexts in defining individual identities.

According to many theorists, globalization has transformed how social groups interact with one another and define their boundaries.[46] The impact on social relationships caused by the increased flow of people, communication technology, and transnational economic ties requires rethinking the meaning of group identity.[47] Ulrich Beck, a German sociologist, calls out not only several methodological assumptions and myths of the nationalist outlook—such as the nation-state as the "self-evident point of departure" and the historical association of ethno-national groups with a particular territory—but its failure to recognize that political, cultural, and economic forces have no borders.[48] The key, he says, to appreciating the dynamic of greater levels of interchange between groups formerly identified as distinct national communities is the "mixing of cultures, and its self-conscious political formation, its reflection and recognition before a global public via the mass media."[49]

Beck details this changing reality in his book *Cosmopolitan Vision*. He contends that the process which he calls "cosmopolitanization" is "the defining feature of a new era . . . in which national borders and differences are dissolving and must be renegotiated."[50] Beck acknowledges that these processes often take place behind the symbols and structures of national claims. Nevertheless, the day-to-day process of dissolving the state's authority to control and enforce political, economic, and social authority is proceeding and is an "irreversible process."[51] Bounded groups limited by territorial, cultural, and racial borders cannot be preserved given economic, technological, and communication revolutions.

As described by theorists of globalization, the shifts it effects call into question—on a practical as well as a theoretical level—the core principles that shape definitions of Jewish peoplehood. Scholars such as Anthony Giddens, one of the foremost global social theorists, argues that the defined boundaries of the nationalist paradigm applied for a relatively brief period in the nineteenth and twentieth centuries, but are not applicable either to premodern societies or contemporary social interactions. He characterizes the rupture of the twenty-first century as the shift from "emancipation politics" focused on class, inequality, and exclusion, to a "life politics" that focuses on the possibility of individual self-actualization and self-discovery in multiple contexts.[52] The fundamental question of identity has changed from defining collective boundaries to local engagement and global concerns.[53] The national is both too large a concept and too small a group to speak to either individual or global concerns; the primary unit of social, cultural, and political interest has at the same time moved away from the collective in these two opposite directions, and the most important issues are those that affect the entire globe, not just particular national interests. These developments—which will only accelerate as the organizing power of states over economic, social, cultural, and political factors further diminishes—are not conducive to the articulation of robust, unambiguous, and particularist visions of collectivity, especially so for conceptions of the Jewish people, constructed on a nationalist paradigm of collectivity.

A variety of theoretical scholarly shifts and on-the ground developments render the pillars of a Jewish national identity far less stable, resting as they do on the shifting sands of global processes and the fluidity of individual identity. Nevertheless, while lamenting the growing disinterest in peoplehood, communal leaders and theorists of peoplehood have been unwilling to assess critically the internalized assumptions about Jewish collectivity that have been shaped largely by Zionist ideology during the last several decades. Polemical debates between supporters and detractors of Israel—a political debate often marked by competing claims about the legitimacy of Jewish nationalism—and the perception of the high stakes involved have translated into little tolerance in discussions of Jewish peoplehood, let alone recognition, of the erosion of the nationalist paradigm or a consideration of that erosion's impact. Other than circumscribed and distorted references to scholars such as Anderson, Jewish leaders and public thinkers have shied away from addressing the impact of new approaches to collectivity in a global era.

As a result, discussions of Jewish collectivity have yet to come to terms with realities that last century's theorists of Zionism, living in a world organized by the logic of the nation-state, could not have imagined—and so the reality of permeable borders, transnational networks, and geographic mobility have yet to make significant inroads in foundational assumptions about Jewish collectivity.

We can see the deep discomfort in engaging with changing interpretations and realities of national identity in the reactions to a highly controversial article published in the *New York Review of Books* in 2004 by the European historian Tony Judt, "Israel: The Alternative."[54] Judt claimed that "Israel is an anachronism" because it was envisioned against the backdrop of nineteenth-century nationalism. With the radical changes affecting the nature of nationalism in a global era, expectations of Jewish nationalism no longer reflect political realities of the twenty-first century.

Judt's conclusion, which obscured for many readers his important argument, was his call for a bi-national state for Jews and Palestinians.

Various and justified critiques of Judt's conclusion failed to address the historical observation that drove his article.[55] Because he linked his historical analysis with a polemical political position, consideration of Judt's perspective on the impact of denationalization on Zionism and Jewish identity was completely drowned out by the deeply felt need to reject his call for a bi-national state. Judt touched the third rail of modern Jewish thought by historicizing rather than essentializing the relationship between Jewish collectivity and nationalism. As the response to the Judt article illustrates, the conflict between pro-state and anti-state voices has obscured the space to consider seriously how notions of Jewish collectivity have to change in the face of new historical realities. Linking people and state was once an innovation in Jewish thought that allowed Judaism to fit itself into the most important identity paradigm of the modern era. But what was originally a creative innovation in Jewish identity formation has become a conservative force, in a world where new models of identity redefine what it means to be part of a group today, and is increasingly alien to Jewish populations around the globe (including in Israel) who live in a world in which a neat delineation into nation-states, ethnic groups, and the like is far less relevant—and also raises ethical concerns.

Ben-Gurion and other early Zionist thinkers could not have imagined a need, for example, for hundreds of thousands of guest workers or Muslim refugees walking around Tel Aviv. A state dedicated to the preservation and promotion of one ethno-national group will have an increasingly difficult time preserving its democratic nature in a global era characterized by an increasingly heterogeneous population and fueled by transnational economic pressures, regional conflicts, and demographic shifts.

Over sixty years after the founding of the state, the Jewish people are too dispersed and diverse to fit comfortably into a statist or other nationalist identity, yet too statist in orientation to imagine a robust set of identity criteria for Jewish peoplehood that are not linked to the state. Instead, a messy hybrid of Jewish peoplehood ignores the difficulty of simultaneously continuing to assert nationalist claims and living a postnational reality. It is not simply the case that the actors on the peoplehood scene are not open to or cultivating conversations about the implications of these shifting realities. The peoplehood discourse itself is based on assumptions that are at odds with consideration of these new realities, and its place in communal advocacy work for Israel makes that consideration difficult and unlikely.

The logic of peoplehood not only leaves key questions unanswered, but even declares the discussion of new political, sociological, and demographic realities outside the very definition of the term itself. The language of unity within peoplehood discourse—including being one with Israel—makes it difficult to focus on a variety of kinds of diversity, including a diversity of thinking about Israel, leading to the rejection of critiques and proposals that are more modest than Judt's and often still framed in the terminology of Zionism. Taboo questions include whether support for the State of Israel is an inherent underpinning of Jewish peoplehood around the globe, whether local Jewish practices contribute as much to Jewish peoplehood as collective political solidarity, and whether the affirmation of unity has lost its relevance in the face of tremendous internal fragmentation of Jewish life.

The process of globalization and denationalization has introduced a transformative collective logic that has yet to make a dent in the meaning of peoplehood. As we see below, recent shifts in attitudes toward ethnicity, race, and religion in the United States have destabilized other historical pillars of peoplehood imagined through a nationalist paradigm. These enlarge the disconnect between the ingrained assumptions of Jewish peoplehood and rapidly evolving conceptions of—and lived relationships to—American pluralism, group identity, and collective membership.

Race, Ethnicity, and Peoplehood Studies

What does Barack Hussein Obama's narrative as the first African American U.S. president illuminate about the contemporary conversation on Jewish peoplehood? Obama's own family history of racial integration, geographic mobility, and multiple faiths resonates with many emerging narratives of identity and collectivity (both academic and popular) dedicated to reconciling, integrating, and celebrating the coexistence of previously incompatible allegiances. In his speeches such as "A More Perfect Union" and in his autobiography, *Dreams from My Father,* Obama underscores his journey across national boundaries, racial groups, and religious communities, weaving his narrative of identity by highlighting group boundary crossing.[56] Indeed, his transnational attachments, multiethnic commitments, and exposures to multiple religious communities emphasize the post-condition that has become an integral part of understanding group and individual identity formation. Phrases such as post-national, post-ethnic or post-racial, and even post-religious have emerged as shorthand to reflect the deconstruction of stable collective categories and trends toward piecing together various identities in ways that transcend historical boundaries. No single public figure better represents or articulates this transition from a fixed identity as a member of a descent group to the dissolution of rigid group boundary markers.

A 2011 *New York Times* article, "Black? White? Asian? More Young Americans Choose All of the Above," reported that the current population of college students includes the "largest number of mixed-race students ever to come of age"; that trend is only increasing.[57] Dramatic changes in fundamental group categories illustrated by rising numbers of multiracial and multiethnic Americans does not mean that race or other modern categories of nation, ethnicity, religion, or people simply no longer shape individual and group practices and boundaries. Moreover, many of these categories, especially race, remain influential in day-to-day power relationships and social hierarchies. Nevertheless, the notion that individuals are linked throughout their lives with one or two primary collective groups has been severely eroded by both scholarly research and social trends. The emergence of shifting understandings of ethnicity and race—and thus peoplehood—serves as a crucial counterpoint to contemporary communal conversations about Jewish peoplehood—and interferes with the effectiveness of the peoplehood narrative in the post-ethnic period.

Obama's narrative does illustrate the enduring role that groups and group identity continue to play, despite the various forces eroding their relevance and claims; it is a story of a radically new way of thinking about descent in the shaping of self-understanding and group politics. Obama's autobiography struck a chord because it resonates with a popular concept of Americanization that emerged in the early twentieth century, the melting pot—also the title of an American play about a Jew and a non-Jew falling in love, written and staged by Jewish nationalist Israel Zangwill in 1908. But Obama's story also demonstrates how far concepts of what it means to be an American have changed since 1908. Zangwill's cauldron of American identity contained only white European groups. Obviously, Obama's concept of race integrates, as it were, black and white, and his geographical journey is transnational and global in nature. Even more, it is a vision informed by trends of pluralism and multiculturalism that fuse such previously antithetical identities as white and black without erasing the sense of obligation, attachment, and particularity in each collective story.

Obama's life story, and his telling of it, celebrates diversity and multiplicity as enriching rather than threatening. He succeeded in becoming the first black president—and the first biracial president as well. While this is not some facile evidence of a post-racial America, it does illustrate the dissolution of the rigid boundaries of group identity that remained firmly in place for much of the twentieth century, despite the melting pot language and imagery. This changing understanding of ethnicity and race in the United States clashes with the nationalist paradigm's historical focus on shared ancestry and blood ties.

For many readers, any association of Jews with racial categories is not only strange but problematic, given the history of antisemitism with its racial basis for planned genocide against Jews. It is important to note here that race per se is a social construction, with no scientific validity. Racial categories and their logics develop in societies and cultures to produce and facilitate group hierarchies. Even though racial ideas do not correspond to scientific reality, they do have enormous power to shape how groups view themselves. Indeed, even groups who are victims of racial persecution often internalize and assume the very racial boundaries that are used to marginalize and categorize them.

My interest here in opening up the question of the relationship between notions of Jewish peoplehood and racialized definitions of groups is not to suggest by any means that Jews are a racial group, or should be categorized as one—or even that Jews have conceived of themselves as a race per se—but to consider the enduring influence of racial logic on the discourse of Jewish peoplehood. While the view of Jewish membership as an involuntary but essential act of birth resonates with racial logic, the term *race* has not itself been used—at least by Jews—to articulate a category of Jewish membership for many decades. This ambiguous relationship with racial thinking in modern definitions of Judaism can then be too easily overlooked for three reasons. First, the need to (re)consider the relationship between the critique of racial categories and Jewish collectivity is not obvious, because the discourse of Jewishness has largely expunged race from the vocabulary of what is meant by the Jewish people; the language of race is no longer considered a viable or appropriate vocabulary for articulating Jewish collectivity. Second, Jews' desire to delegitimize both the United Nations' 1975 equation of Zionism with racism and enduring claims that Israel's policies have racist underpinnings has further contributed to a context in which there is no room to question the problematic nature of the racial overtones in definitions of Jewishness—and also of Israeliness, in the Law of Return. Third, while matrilineal descent as a traditional pillar of the definition of Jewish status means that there is a basis for focusing on bloodlines as a model of Jewish membership, in the contemporary context this *halakhic* (Jewish legal) definition has provided a kind of cover for and obfuscation of racially based definitions. The emphasis on descent criteria, trumping other ways of determining Jewish membership—individual choice, engagement with culture, social relationships, political affiliations, and religious practice—reflects the influence of racial thinking in its definition of identity, despite the factors that obscure that influence.

But there are signs that Jewish communities will have to consciously address an underlying double standard of claiming religious or cultural cohesion when the actual determinant is deeply shaped by the logic of race. In 2009, the British Supreme Court ruled that the London Jewish Free School violated racial discrimination laws by allowing only children of Jewish mothers to attend the school.[58] The court ruled that this traditional indicator of Jewish membership, the matrilineal line of descent, was a racial rather than religious distinction that violated the British Racial Discrimination Act. The ruling provoked consternation in the Jewish community. For our purposes here, the ruling has two significant implications.

First, it indicates that concepts of Jewish collectivity inevitably exist in relationship to and in the context of wider and changing ideas of group identity. Definitions of Jewish peoplehood are not determined, practiced, and theorized in isolation. Indeed, this recent example demonstrates the critical role that changing social norms and identity categories play in shaping Jewish acculturation and adaptation. Second, the decision implicates Jews in a growing moral critique of forms of collective membership rooted in racial or descent-based characteristics. The decision in this case illustrates the importance of considering the relevance of changing notions of race and ascriptive categories of identity for the construction of the Jewish people. Making group distinctions based on racial criteria (construed broadly as any type of characterization based on biological lineage, established at birth, and essentially unchangeable) has become problematic from both a practical and moral perspective. Western societies' increasing attempts to neutralize deeply embedded prejudices based on race and descent now make any biological standards for group membership morally suspect.

The study of changing historical and contemporary definitions of Jewishness, then, cannot ignore the impact of racial logic on twentieth-century definitions of membership in the Jewish collective. In the establishment of the Law of Return, which, it must be noted, parallels Nazi racial logic in granting any person with one Jewish grandparent automatic citizenship in the State of Israel, Jews have enacted and formalized the very blood basis of membership used by antisemites. And even in situations where a direct relationship to racial thinking is not as obvious, the language of modern Jewish peoplehood is inflected with what are essentially quasi-racial concepts, in its focus on a shared essence inherited through descent, blood, and birth.

Traditionally, there have been two ways to become part of the Jewish people—matrilineal descent or conversion. While conversion is possible, descent informs a rhetoric of Jewishness that is binary in nature—one is either in or out; a simple standard can be applied that eliminates any confusion. Boundaries based on descent serve a valuable function as status markers. Even the customs of conversion hint at the importance of genealogy, with immersion in the mikveh symbolizing rebirth, and the practice of giving converts a new Hebrew name with Abraham and Sarah as their symbolic parents assimilating them into racial logic. Cultural integration into U.S. society has had little impact on the internal logic of descent for articulating a secular, overarching definition of Jewish collectivity in American Jewish and Israeli expressions of Jewishness. Political developments in Israel, as well as the growth of ultra-Orthodoxy in the United States, have only strengthened the emphasis on descent. While conversion exists, the criteria for gaining full Jewish status in the State of Israel have (in the context of the Orthodox rabbinate) become increasingly difficult to meet, and limited to avenues controlled by centralized religious authorities.

Quasi-racial thinking is also reflected in articulations of Jewish peoplehood today in the link between peoplehood and in-marriage. "Unquestionably, one of the great challenges of boundary setting for Judaism and peoplehood generally is the issue of intermarriage."[59] This quotation from *The Case for Jewish Peoplehood: Can We Be One?* indicates the intimate relationship between kinship and contemporary understandings of the Jewish people. The discourse on Jewish peoplehood has continued the emphasis on continuity, as defined by in-marriage, that characterized Jewish communal conversations in the 1980s and 1990s.

Almost a century after Kallen, his grandfather thesis endures. A strong Jewish cultural emphasis on genealogy and genetics has provided this thesis with new life.[60] Books on the genetic make-up of Jews abound, as do the stories of secret Jews who have come forth to claim their membership in the Jewish people on the basis of long-lost ancestors in New Mexico and other locales in the United States, South America, and elsewhere. Scientific studies and best-selling books claim genetic evidence of biological descent from specific groups of ancestors. This fascination with Jewish genes supports an understanding of Jewish identity as an inherited characteristic.

While Kallen's conception of Jewish status in some ways endures in practice, it is clearly outdated in others. His grandfather thesis as the basis for Jewish collectivity could not make sense of an important shift toward a more open logic of familial connection. While these newer expressions of membership in the Jewish people depend on some genetic or descent-based criteria, they have also internalized a rejection of racial exclusivism. Unlike racial models that classify members of a minority population with a kind of one-drop logic, Jewish genetic ideas popular today allow for, and even encourage, individuals to identify with multiple descent-based identities. A calculus of fractional membership has emerged that views genetic identities as additive rather than mutually exclusive.

The shift from a one-drop model of exclusive membership to an acknowledgment of a fractional Jewishness is exhibited, for example, in pop culture. Adam Sandler's "Chanukah Song" humorously tracks Jews, partial and otherwise, in movies, TV, and music. It exemplifies the endurance of a kind of racial thinking even in cultural expressions that acknowledge the fragmentary, fractional nature of contemporary identities. The idea of "half-Jewish" doesn't fit into a halakhic framework; conversely, in a world of hybridity, the fact that one also has other identities doesn't have to diminish one's claim to Jewishness. While those with ties to particular groups may, playfully or seriously, acknowledge the role of descent, the partial erosion of racial and other descent boundaries delineates a shift in how the current generation thinks about groups. Emphasizing difference based on inherited characteristics now possesses a negative normative valence. While racial politics beginning in the 1960s affirmed the importance and positive, enduring relevance of group identity based on descent, current attitudes reflect a negative association with rigid social distinctions based on biology.

Jewish peoplehood as an organizing principle for Jewish collectivity distracts from a difficult process of rethinking the relationship between modern Jewish concepts of solidarity and changing racialized notions of inclusion and exclusion. Adoption of language to discuss Jewish collectivity that is not fundamentally descent-oriented would more easily represent the fact that Jewish concepts of membership include practices such as conversion that fail to fit racialized notions of difference. The seeming invisibility of racial logic in the peoplehood paradigm, juxtaposed with powerful motivations for distancing thoughts about Jewish collectivity from racial categories, complicates an important task that challenges Jewish leaders (that is, which both presents itself to them, and is difficult for them): reconsidering the rhetoric of Jewish peoplehood in both the United States and Israel, and in particular its emphasis on descent.

A growing number of public intellectuals are attempting to usher in— that is, to both acknowledge and to contribute to the development of—a post-ethnic and post-racial zeitgeist. Both the reality of mixed-race individuals and others with more complex relationships to descent and the moral critique attacking group descent-based distinctions undermine the moral legitimacy of racially construed identity politics. The contemporary world is, of course, not entirely post-racial, but—for example—U.S. historian David Hollinger emphasizes that changing assumptions about racial allegiances raise a new set of questions on how to think about solidarity beyond "the problem of color"[61]—or about descent more generally. Hollinger's advocacy of a post-ethnic approach to group identity argues that liberal paradigms of group membership must erase the close link between descent and identity central to ethnic and racial models of collectivity. The increasingly sharp critique of descent, and the challenge of defining group identity at a moment when post-ethnicity rejects markers of descent as determinative, inevitably has implications for the language and conceptualization of Jewish groupness, and specifically for the use of categories like the Jewish people and Jewish peoplehood.

Another scholarly shift, in the field of ethnic studies, also—although differently—undercuts the notion of stable collective categories. For example, Norwegian sociologist Fredrik Barth, who in 1969 published *Ethnic Groups and Boundaries,* shaped scholarship on ethnicity by emphasizing the need to stop analyzing ethnic groups with respect to how they preserve continuous sets of traits that mark difference based on enduring characteristics.[62] Barth's influential work shifted the study of groups from the specific content that defined the group as unique, to the process of the creation and preservation of boundaries between groups. In this approach, group definitions are relative and constructed in opposition to other groups—as we have seen in recent scholarship on nationalism as well, which often especially emphasizes the historical context of that construction—rather than based on enduring and essential characteristics.

Influential sociologist Mary Waters echoes Barth's work in her classic volume *Ethnic Options: Choosing Identities in America.* Like Barth, Waters questions popular assumptions that "ethnic groups are stable categories and that one is a member of a particular ethnic group because one's ancestors were members of that group."[63] Indeed, as the title suggests, Waters claims that ethnic identity is, for white Americans, a choice; individuals can decide whether to opt in to an ethnic group, and even which ethnicity to join. As a result of this freedom, both identity and membership—linked to the shifting norms of one's peer group and the individual's relationship to them—fluctuate over the course of a lifetime; changes in social situation, for example through conversion or emigration, affect membership in place-based formal and informal groups. A sense of group membership not only involves a static feeling of belonging, but also varies with the relative physical proximity of an individual to others in the group. Closer proximity often correlates with more intensive socialization to a group's identity norms.

Despite the voluntary nature of ethnicity and its lack of day-to-day impact, Waters still concludes that a passionate desire to preserve ethnic connections remains. Conflicting urges and opposing forces coexist within the logic and reality of collectivity; membership is completely voluntary, but members often articulate a language of ethnic solidarity through the involuntary criteria of race and descent. The explicit rejection of racial categories alongside the simultaneous influence of racial logic in the current rhetoric of Jewish peoplehood, in de facto code words for descent such as continuity and birthright, mirrors that broader tension in the study of ethnicity. Rhetorics of communal solidarity based on allegiances inherited at birth clash with realities of individual choice, fluid group identifications, and variable external forces on an individual at specific times and places.

The gap between ascriptive Jewish rhetorical assumptions about solidarity and contemporary scholarship grows even larger as scholars critique the very idea of identity itself. One of the terms central in marking collectivity, identity, highlights the marked difference between modern and premodern notions of groupness. For instance, social theorist Zygmunt Bauman views identity as a modern term that emerges "only when human beings begin to be disembedded from traditional spaces and relationships, long accepted rhythms of time and well-established activities of survival."[64] Ironically, when viewed through the lens of scholarship, identity destabilizes the nature of these collective groups; identities, scholars suggest, are malleable, dependent on external circumstances. Thus, the building blocks of groups, often defined by ascribed characteristics such as nationality, race, or ethnicity, are themselves constructed and thus contingent rather than essential. The focus on identity, then—whether individual or group—has emerged precisely as organic ties have dissipated and a need for theoretical constructs to replace lived connections has become pressing.

The broad reach of cultural studies has also challenged the notion of a core identity that defines an individual as part of one particular group. Cultural studies encourages a shift toward viewing identity through such terms as fractured self, hybridity, and disparate identities.[65] For instance, cultural theorist Stuart Hall, an influential voice critiquing identity as a fixed entity, disabuses us of the assumption that individuals have long-term and relatively stable associations with particular groups. Instead, as one scholar describes Hall's definition of identity: "Identity is not a fixed and permanent entity existing continuously through time but an always unfinished suturing together of fragments. Identity is never a neat and singular whole, but always plural, always fluid, more both/and than either/or, and therefore there is no authentic core, no stable point of origin that will guarantee the rightness or wrongness of any decision."[66] This passage reflects a pendulum swing in the opposite direction from paradigms of stable group boundaries implied by national and racial categories. Those models emphasized rigid boundaries, clear insider/outsider division, and a dominant, overriding ethno-national identity; contemporary social theory explicitly undermines each of these claims. Modern Jewish claims about the Jewish people thus face erosion from two sides: historians of nationalism replacing the idea of primordial origins with historically situated constructions of group boundaries, and social theories demonstrating the fictitious nature of identity itself. The clear collective boundaries and pure, authentic identities imagined in modern notions of nationalism and ethnic cohesion of the nineteenth and twentieth centuries have been replaced by assumptions that severely limit claims that any group can make on, or about, individuals within its orbit.

A growing appreciation for the value of preserving group identities in the literature on multiculturalism has generated a variety of scholarly works sensitive to the value and enduring reality of particular groups and difference, but even this literature supporting the value of group difference aligns itself with a moral critique of differentiating based on descent per se. The theme of voluntary choice as a basic criterion for a liberal paradigm of collective membership runs through the work of a variety of leading multicultural scholars.[67] These scholars set clear limits on the claims of group membership and challenge the rigid hierarchies of privilege inscribed by differences set by birth, based on their conception of individual freedom to choose as the foundation of political liberalism. Groups have a right to preserve culture and encourage solidarity, but they do not have a right to coerce individuals into membership. The individual's right to choose trumps the group's ability to claim individuals as members based on descent. The legacy of race and colonialism has generated little tolerance for coercing membership by automatically assigning individuals to groups based on any inherited criteria (even among fellow/sister group members).

In addition to rapidly changing understandings of nations and nationalism, race, and ethnicity in scholarship and contemporary life, the growing study of peoplehood itself has important implications for discussions of Jewish collectivity. Once a term limited to Jewish discourse, peoplehood has now become a mainstream academic term, but—as we have seen with studies of nationalism—scholarly investigations contrast with the contemporary discourse of Jewish peoplehood. Indeed, the field of what might be called peoplehood studies questions peoplehood's baseline assumptions.

Academic studies of peoplehood view all of the above terms for group categories—even peoplehood itself—as essentialist and outmoded, against a backdrop of the recognition of transnational networks, religious ties that transcend family history, and the hybridity of biological characteristics. While early twentieth-century Jewish theorists anticipated such a reconceptualization of identity categories, contemporary Jewish theorists and communal leaders have ignored this parallel field of investigation that could provide important conversation partners for rethinking what Jewish collectivity might mean today. Outside of Jewish discussions, an investigation of peoplehood has become associated with a critique of the state as the central address of a group's collective identity, and of the various essentialist categories that are embedded within or overlap meaningfully with Jewish peoplehood. Thus Jewish communal and scholarly thinking that links peoplehood with the centrality of Israel and with those categories keeps the Jewish conversation in direct opposition to the potentially relevant emerging academic field of peoplehood studies.

John Lie's *Modern Peoplehood* is not the only prominent scholarly work to turn to peoplehood as a broader theoretical framework to critique the modes of categorization that have defined modern culture and politics. Yale political theorist Rogers M. Smith published *Stories of Peoplehood: The Politics and Morals of Political Membership* a year earlier in 2003. For both Lie and Smith, peoplehood is at best a modern construction that theorists must take into account in analyzing political and social trends—and at worst, a troubling one that can be used by leaders to promote political objectives at the expense of others who are actively excluded from their definition of the particular people. Smith defines peoplehood in opposition to "chauvinistic political narratives" that promote exclusive, descent-based, or coerced conceptions of collectivity.[68] Instead, he views collective bonds as particular, ideally voluntary, attachments that engender a greater appreciation of multiplicity, diversity, and equality.

Peoplehood's evolving role in the scholarship of groups and identity categories appeared as early as 1970 in sociologist Immanuel Wallerstein's "The Construction of Peoplehood in Race, Nation, Class."[69] Wallerstein notes how the use of peoplehood allows groups to fashion an imagined idea of a shared past to serve a contemporary agenda. Wallerstein urges his readers to "try to understand peoplehood for what it is—in no sense a primordial stable social reality, but a complex, clay-like historical product of the capitalist world-economy through which antagonistic forces struggle with each other."[70] An articulation of peoplehood is an enduring aspect of human society, not because peoplehood describes a common type of essential bond that links various societies, but rather because economic and social factors demand the narration of particular stories of the past to make present-day political claims.

Peoplehood, or people-making, has become a convenient term for scholars to examine how modern categories of difference—specifically nationalism, ethnicity, and race—share a common need to create narratives that explain the existence of group with a distinct identity and clear boundaries. As Wallerstein wrote, "It makes little difference whether we define pastness in terms of genetically continuous groups (races), historical socio-political groups (nations) or cultural groups (ethnic groups). They are all peoplehood constructs, all inventions of pastness, all contemporary political phenomena."[71] His conclusion is particularly damaging for the claims of Jewish peoplehood, because it undermines the argument of Jewish peoplehood as an exceptional category, unaffected by modern critiques of national, ethnic, or racial groups.

Lie argues that the very "basis of peoplehood is a modern enterprise."[72] The particular criteria that modern groups use to differentiate themselves, which he defines as ascriptive characteristics that are unchanging, contrast directly with premodern groups whose identities emerged from evolving definitions of religion, culture, and language.[73] In other words, the effort of modern groups to link themselves to premodern groups belies the fact that premodern groups themselves related to groupness very differently! Lie's description of the modern tendency to classify by involuntary associations, to define a homogenous collective through essentialist descriptions, and to link groups to territorial areas renders peoplehood a kind of uber-category for similarities across various modern modes of group creation. Peoplehood studies now view claims of peoplehood as no less than the common theme in the construction of a variety of modern categories of identity—the most constructed group terminology of all.

Peoplehood, then, has moved far from its origins in American identity scholarship, in the work of Milton Gordon, to becoming the defining essence that all major modern groups share. For Gordon, peoplehood established the "common social-psychological core" of a broad range of categories, including religion, race, and nation,[74] an essential set of bonds that characterized a variety of types of group identity. Gordon's theoretical support for a core set of membership criteria for a particular people supported Jewish peoplehood claims that an essential set of criteria unified Jews to one another. In contrast, scholars such as Lie and Smith use peoplehood as a vehicle for demonstrating how a variety of different identity constructions have generated similar types of stories of peoplehood to justify their claims that there is an intrinsic bond linking members of their group across space and time. Yet no peoples in the words of Smith (and echoed in Lie's arguments) are in fact really "natural or primordial."[75]

Peoplehood as a scholarly term has swung, then, from being viewed as justifying and grounding a variety of collective identities to being used to demonstrate and sum up the constructed, contingent, and potentially chauvinistic quality of a variety of modern forms of group categorization. Peoplehood studies today undermines the understanding of a stable ideal of Jewish collectivity as an intrinsic, and unquestionable, component of Jewish identity. And this most recent conceptualization of peoplehood is certainly also a far cry from Kaplan's peoplehood, which—rooted in a different intellectual moment and outside of academia—presented an enduring ethical principle embedded within the Jewish tradition.

Scholars of peoplehood studies argue that collective stories of peoplehood are perceived as "somehow intrinsic to the core identities of potential constituents."[76] The assumptions behind those claims about the relationship of individuals to the group and its nature are portrayed as so incontestable that individuals cannot question them; the construction of peoplehood inoculates itself from critique by insisting on its own eternal validity (as I have been claiming about Jewish peoplehood specifically). This makes peoplehood claims particularly powerful tools for politicians and communal leaders to galvanize widespread support for their policies or objectives. It also helps explain the gap between communal articulations of peoplehood and those of scholarship.

Affirmations of the core characteristics of any people raise serious questions about morality and intergroup relations. Racism, Lie argues, comes from the need to differentiate groups from one another through essentialist claims. Peoplehood studies looks at peoplehood as an enduring part of this problem that must be mitigated, rather than its solution. Any emphasis on an abiding essence ignores the emergence of an understanding of social constructs and its critique of collective essential claims. Peoplehood studies' emphasis on understanding the present-day political agendas of peoplehood claims make it difficult to avoid, for example, the association between Jews and commitments to social justice with critiques of Israel's policies toward Palestinians and the occupation of the West Bank. For peoplehood studies theorists, the way forward would be to open up boundaries and stop affirming parochial attachments over universal ones, so that individuals could choose their allegiances without being influenced by peoplehood narratives that generate the hierarchies and particular stories that inevitably marginalize others. Jewish peoplehood affirms the preservation of robust boundaries between groups and collective narratives as a path to ensuring humanistic interactions between individuals and communities; peoplehood studies points out both the constructed nature of those groups and collective attachments, as well as the dangers inherent in allegiance to them.

Can Jewish peoplehood face the critical challenges of peoplehood studies? One response to Lie and Smith et al. might be to argue that Jewish peoplehood represents an exception to this problematic model of peoplehood. Indeed, Jewish peoplehood emerged as a partial challenge to precisely the narrative that Smith and Lie want to call into question. Lie, for example, draws a sharp distinction between premodern cultural definitions of civilization and modern peoplehood notions that reject fluid understandings of religion, culture, and language to focus on ascriptive criteria, essentialist characteristics, and territorial attachments. Kaplan's turn to peoplehood as a critique of Zionism attempted to use religion, culture, and language as a way of translating premodern Jewish collective categories into a modern framework. He also eschewed racial definitions, railed against chauvinistic assumptions, and shied away from making political claims in the name of a collective people. Neither Lie nor Smith seem aware that a Jewish thinker introduced peoplehood in a way that challenges the theoretical premise they view as both integral to the term and problematic.

Yet even if they were aware of at least one Jewish intellectual's pioneering use of the term peoplehood almost a century ago, the similarities between Jewish peoplehood as it functions today and modern peoplehood more generally are too obvious to ignore. Even Kaplan's vision of peoplehood, his critique of Zionism and emphasis on religion notwithstanding, would have been impossible without Jewish nationalism and its attendant ideas of an essential and unified past and a future collective mission. Despite challenging the secular and territorial notion of Zionism, Kaplan's peoplehood emerged largely in line with the trends highlighted in Lie's study of modern peoplehood.

Parallels with the academic model of peoplehood presented by Lie and Smith are even more evident in the versions of Jewish peoplehood that have served as a code word for Zionism. From its earliest expression in Rabbi Stephen Wise's call to political unity, to its most recent mobilization by state institutions such as the Museum of the Jewish People, this formulation of peoplehood reflects many of the specific attributes in Lie's work. While advocates of peoplehood articulate the category as a unique attribute of Jews, scholars of peoplehood would simply consider Jewish expressions largely in line with other groups who rely on ethnic, national, and racial conceptions of solidarity.

Why is the tension between Jewish peoplehood and the scholarship of race, ethnicity, and peoplehood never seriously confronted? The dissonance between the scholarly critique of essentialist claims and Jewish peoplehood's insistence on precisely the unchanging and incontrovertible nature of peoplehood likely represents a perceived threat, a largely unarticulated concern that any serious recognition of the former critique would undermine the legitimacy of the latter claims. There is too much energy, not to mention capital, already invested in peoplehood. It is too big to fail; the peoplehood paradigm as it has developed permeates the ideological and political underpinnings of Israeli and American Jewish institutions.

In Israel's case, the state relies on the existence of the Jewish people and its continuous attachment to the Land of Israel as a pillar in its internal definition. Moreover, attacks on Israel's legitimacy often come through direct hits on the authenticity of peoplehood claims. But American Jews also have their own investment in the peoplehood narrative. American

Jewish life has organized over the past century around the principle of solidarity for Jews in need and support for the Jewish homeland. The ideals of unity and solidarity have heavily shaped Jewish organizational life and identity construction over the last several decades.

The major American Jewish organizations of the twentieth century—Jewish Federations, the American Jewish Committee, the Joint Distribution Committee, Hadassah, and many other Zionist organizations—arose to express solidarity with other Jews and support them in a time and place of need. The ideal of unity and shared responsibility underscored the position that Jews across vastly different political, cultural, and social contexts should prioritize each other's needs. In addition, these organizations gained political strength by creating a unified voice to defend common interests. As a result of the need to rescue persecuted Jews and to bolster Jewish life in various host countries, Jews developed coordinating organizations to centralize and unify Jews, from the emergence of a state to the creation of federated philanthropic organizations. Articulations of Jewish peoplehood reflect the ways in which institutions and identity have evolved to place unity and solidarity at the center. In addition, peoplehood provides a secular identity vocabulary that mitigates tensions between American Jews' self-definition as a religious minority and their discomfort with the theological commitments that characterize other communities defined as religious.

However, given the broader intellectual and cultural context of identity construction, it is no wonder that many Jews are now—and increasingly—shying away from (or just being left cold by) a discourse of peoplehood that espouses unquestionable allegiance to other Jews regardless of their worldviews, that privileges particular over universal concerns, and that maintains rigid boundaries between Jews and non-Jews. The effectiveness of peoplehood as an organizing principle will likely be increasingly limited, and conceptions of peoplehood that merely repackage old assumptions about Jewish identity will find that these premises clash with the political and ethical commitments and the world experiences of those its advocates are most anxious to mobilize, or at least retain within the fold. Imagining the Jewish people through the lens of a bounded nation marked by descent and territory has little theoretical room to encourage local expressions of Judaism, to address global concerns, and to recognize radically shifting identity paradigms. Contemporary conversations about the Jewish people must recognize changing assumptions in social theory as well as shifting sociological realities; viable theoretical categories of Jewish collectivity in an age of *post*-thinking will have to rely to a significant degree on defining Jewish membership in language that reflects fluidity rather than essence.

Tensions between scholarly notions of peoplehood's constructedness and Jewish communal understandings do not, of course, render moribund the idea of Jewish collectivity. The publication of two recent books on the topic indicates that the recognition of the enduring nature of group identities remains as important as ever. In many ways, the post–Cold War era, new technologies, and demographic shifts are reminiscent of the interwar period, when a need for new terminologies was essential to respond to the destabilization of existing categories. Once again, typologies of groups—religious, national, ethnic, and racial—are under intense scrutiny. Yet even scholars and critics of peoplehood still recognize the importance of stories that individuals feel are intrinsic to who they are and how they define their obligations and commitments. Despite significant trends toward hybridity, post-nationalism, and post-ethnicity, and a scholarly critique of peoplehood itself, peoplehood (along with related concepts of collectivity) remains a crucial and understudied force in politics. Within the Jewish communal context, a conceptual vocabulary is needed that could provide a substantial alternative to twentieth-century models of nation, race, ethnicity, and religion that have crumbled under the stress of global, political, and cultural transformation.

A potential resource for bridging the divide between the divergent paths of the discourse of Jewish peoplehood and the study of nationalism, ethnicity, race, and peoplehood would seem to be the scholarly field of Jewish studies, in which a number of scholars already integrate critical scholarship with the study of Jewish collective life. Why has Jewish studies not yet pointed toward an alternative vision of Jewish peoplehood for the twenty-first century?

Jewish Studies and Jewish Peoplehood

In 1976, Hebrew University historian Hayim Ben-Sasson published an English translation of a comprehensive Jewish history textbook called *A History of the Jewish People.*[77] The narrative, written collectively by Ben-Sasson's Hebrew University colleagues, traces the story of the Jewish people from ancient Israel to the 1970s. The book begins with chapters entitled "Canaan" and "A Dawn of Israel" and ends with a chapter entitled "Consolidation of the State of Israel." The narrative from ancient Israel to modern Israel parallels the architectural and thematic layout of the Museum of the Jewish People, then known as the Museum of the Jewish Diaspora, which would open two years later in 1978. Like the museum, this book reflected and shaped understandings of the Jewish people as a collectivity whose story could be traced from ancient Israel, through the diaspora, and back to the modern land of Israel.

However, just as Jewish peoplehood reached the status of representation by a major museum and appearance in an English-language textbook in history, a counter-critique in Jewish studies, especially in the fields of history and feminism, began to challenge its major epistemological assumptions. A review of *A History of the Jewish People* by rabbinic scholar Jacob Neusner articulated this new perspective. "The volume," Neusner pronounced, "brings to ultimate expression the 'peoplehood-and-history' theory of Jewish historiography. The theory presupposes that a single, clearly defined entity, 'the Jewish people,' has produced a unitary and linear history."[78] Neusner, already a critic of Zionism's claims about Jewish history and diaspora life, now developed a bias against any scholarship that attempted to make general arguments about Jews' beliefs, practices, and worldviews. But Neusner's sharp critique of a narration of all Jewish history as a unified progression reflects the wider scholarly transformation that soon shifted the role of historians from supporters to critics of nationalist positions.

That shift has also taken place within Jewish studies over the past three decades, from actively supporting claims of Jewish collectivity to raising critical questions reflecting new scholarly directions. As we have seen, until the last third of the twentieth century, modern scholarship had helped justify group categories and collective identities. Historians created singular narratives with clear national traits, sociologists used the nation as the basis of their analysis, and political scientists defined the nation-state as the building block of international relations. Jewish studies scholars participated in these trends, especially in the field of history. Then the emphasis in the historical and contemporary study of national groups shifted in the direction of understanding those groups' cultural constructedness rather than their essential defining characteristics over time. Jewish studies scholars who were neither immersed in larger communal conversations or invested in the peoplehood discourse were part of that shift. Consequently, there remains a significant divide between scholars who fundamentally critique visions of a singular unified Jewish people and those who use their training to demonstrate the existence of the Jewish people. Indeed, the interest in studying peoplehood among scholars of Jewish studies is now divided into two distinct camps. On one side is a small number of thinkers, often directly associated with communally funded projects, who explicitly use the term peoplehood and participate in its discourse; and, on the other, a larger number whose work has contributed to radical reinterpretations of the meaning of Jewish collectivity yet rarely use the language of peoplehood, and whose work—like that of their scholarly counterparts outside of Jewish studies (both those who study peoplehood per se and those whose work takes up other collective categories), and for many of the same reasons—is not brought to bear on peoplehood in the broader Jewish communal context.

It may be that the Jewish studies and peoplehood conversations have been segregated because they have become so different not only in their assumptions, but also in their fundamentally different scholarly tasks and terminologies. For example, those engaged in the peoplehood discussions measure it, whereas those whose scholarship is not part of those communal discussions take approaches that are critical of collective identity construction. The absence of so much of Jewish studies scholarship from the peoplehood conversations means that participants in that conversation can largely ignore scholarly advances in thinking about group identity and fail to integrate even the scholarship within Jewish studies on nationalism, ethnicity, globalization, and peoplehood that represents innovative and potentially important ideas for understanding and shaping Jewish collectivity.

In a few fields, specifically the social sciences and the study of Zionism, some Jewish studies scholars still help to articulate the meanings of Jewish peoplehood. Often funded by the same foundations promoting peoplehood, Jewish social scientists measure levels of peoplehood in various Jewish communities throughout the world. These studies tend to affirm existing paradigms.

For example, a collection of essays published in 2009, with the assistance of the Jewish Agency for Israel and UJA-Federation of New York, includes a number of scholarly perspectives on peoplehood that demonstrate the limited nature of academic contributions to the communal peoplehood discussion. These scholars, sensitive to the ways that Jewish collectivity defies easy categorization, define peoplehood as a strategy for navigating the relationship of Jewish identity to the major group categories of our time—nationalism, ethnicity, and religion. Peoplehood in their hands becomes a more flexible and appropriate term, rendering Judaism and Jewishness compatible with Western categories, yet standing for a unique blend of elements and a sui generis model of collectivity that does not fit into already existing categories. For example, the volume's introduction explains, "'Peoplehood' is probably the *only* concept that suits the present situation and meets present needs. 'Nation' and 'religion' are each in their way too all-encompassing."[79] The depiction of Jewish peoplehood as a unique intervention into the conceptual vocabulary of nation, ethnicity, or religion still clings to the logic of these categories even as it asserts that they were never individually adequate to the task of capturing Jewish collectivity. While at one time peoplehood as a conception of Jewish collectivity was in the forefront of new identity paradigms, it is now a relatively conservative conception, one that positions Jews as slightly unique in their ability to somehow transcend the categories of nation, religion, and ethnicity, without coming to terms with the fundamental challenge that shifting understandings of those categories have for Jewish peoplehood.[80]

Another area where the theoretical basis for an enduring Jewish collective is articulated in Jewish studies is in the work of some scholars of Zionism and Jewish nationalism, who are invested in refining the language of Jewish collectivity because of the importance of the link between people, land, and sovereignty. This Zionist narrative reflects the ongoing influence of Ahad Ha-am's cultural Zionism. The work of historian Gideon Shimoni provides a good illustration of this perspective. Shimoni assumes that Jews constitute a national group, based on his reading of historian Anthony Smith's theory of premodern ethnics that emerged as national movements in the modern period. In this view, Judaism's primary identity is most closely connected to the secular national category, and the Jewish people, like other modern national groups, should have a political center in their homeland. In a brief article he wrote about peoplehood, he argues that the key term is "essentially quite the same as the Zionist idea in regard to the basic proposition: Jews are a distinctive entity possessing attributes associated with the modern concepts of ethnicity and nation, not just attributes associated with religion." This scholarship follows a long Zionist historiography that views the emergence of secular Jewish nationalism as the teleology of Jewish history and the state as political redemption after centuries of exile.

This particular scholarly approach to the history of Zionism has the most in common with the Jewish communal peoplehood discourse. Two other areas of scholarship that explicitly deal with Israel-diaspora questions—positions one could call multicentered collectivist and diasporist perspective—bring critical scholarly trends more firmly into conversation with Jewish peoplehood.

Several Jewish studies scholars implicitly critique the discourse of Jewish peoplehood by arguing for multiple centers, taking account of divergent kinds of solidarity, and integrating religious definitions of Judaism into the conversation of ties that bind Jews. Arnold Eisen's extensive writing on modern Jewish thought, specifically the meaning of exile and Zionism, offers an excellent illustration of this perspective. For Eisen, the religious concept of covenant stands at the core of what unites the Jewish people. His approach challenges the homeland-diaspora hierarchy of the statist-Zionist position. "Statehood," Eisen argues, "has immense advantages in that respect, for the calendar is Jewish, the media are Jewish, etc. but it also means dependence upon force of arms and allies. Neither option is without risks. Such are the ground rules of life in the modern world."[81] This presents a more measured analysis of the advantages and benefits of multiple approaches to Jewish life between living as a Jew in the Jewish state and a Jew as a minority citizen of another country. Historians Deborah Dash Moore and Ilan Troen published a collection of essays called *Divergent Jewish Cultures: Israel and America*, which similarly highlights the importance of recognizing the cultural and political diversity that has emerged between the two current population centers of world Jewry. David Myers's work on the mid-twentieth-century thinker Simon Rawidowicz has also emphasized the concept of a dual center for the Jewish nation that views homeland and diaspora on equal footing.[82]

The multicentered collectivists who most closely follow Kaplan's vision of Zionism as a model of ethical nationalism are Israeli scholars such as Chaim Gans and Yuli Tamir. These political thinkers use such terms as liberal nationalism and just Zionism to emphasize that national claims have very specific moral commitments to minority populations, and that national groups—especially those with political power—must acknowledge the limits of their particular claims in order to meet the individual and even collective rights of minority populations. However, a liberal or just Zionism remains rooted in the nationalist identity paradigm, including a focus on the homeland and political sovereignty as the defining element of modern peoplehood.[83]

A growing body of scholarly research focuses on the ways in which the diaspora, and not the homeland, in fact have the keys to understanding Jewish peoplehood. This challenge to the centrality of the state can be seen, for instance, in the Boyarin brothers' book *The Power of Diaspora*, which insists that the contribution of Judaism is actually its ability to preserve a collective sense of identity without territory or political power.[84]

As the quotation earlier in this section on Jewish studies indicates, in the 1970s the role of the historian began to shift from telling *the* story of *the* Jewish people to tracing a plurality of expressions of what has been considered Jewish in various times and places. Jewish studies, inspired by paradigms of studying individual and collectivity boundaries as porous, began to introduce a new set of challenges to a singular collective Jewish narrative. These new ways of thinking about how to tell the story of the Jewish past are well represented by an edited volume published in 2002, *The Cultures of the Jews*, an example of historical scholarship that reflects these important shifts in historiography.[85] That work, with contributions primarily from a group of American scholars (as opposed to the Israeli scholars responsible for the earlier volume *A History of the Jewish People*), draws attention to the decline of the national narrative of the Jewish collective past so central to nationalist paradigms of Jewish collectivity.

Put most simply, cultural history provides an overview of a particular aspect of Jewish history: the history of Jewish collective self-understandings. This approach begins from the assumption that the self-understanding of Jewish groupness is subjective and socially constructed; has changed over time; and has been multilayered at any given point in history. It shifts the focus away from any assumed essence or timeless attributes of Jewish membership and collective boundaries, and instead emphasizes how historical forces have created these concepts of Jewish collectivity, which have varied dramatically over time and space. Contemporary discussions of Jewish peoplehood often try to trace or vaguely refer to how Judaism relates to biblical or rabbinic definitions, and how historical sources support the alignment of the Jewish people with this contemporary vocabulary of difference. Jewish sources thus become used as proof texts to demonstrate answers to the question of whether Judaism is a religion, ethnicity, nation, or peoplehood fusion of these categories—and more than a few scholars participate in efforts to superimpose anachronistic modern definitions of groupness on historical texts and practices.[86]

The largely communally driven overlay of modern categories onto a textured and diverse Jewish history clashes with current scholarly approaches that seek to understand and articulate an evolving, non-teleological construction of Jewish identity within its local cultural, political, social, and economic milieus. Such studies also expose the disconnect between any singular definition of groupness and the variety of terms for the Jewish people in classic sources and practices. The most consistent characteristic of the history of Jewish conceptions of collectivity may actually be the apparent complete lack of interest in systematically, and consistently, defining the rules of membership.

This resistance to conceiving of the Jewish people as a fixed category of identity contrasts with communal and ideologically driven desires to categorize Jews and Judaism within a clear taxonomy of groups. For example, recent scholarship on the biblical era argues that the Israelite nation was in the main not itself an object of focus, nor does the biblical text reflect an end goal of identifying that collectivity within then-existing group paradigms. Moreover, even when the people Israel existed distinct from other groups, the boundaries of insider and outsider appear far less relevant to the texts that document the story of that collective. Those who are invested in peoplehood within communal conversations and institutions would have to do much to catch up—if they could afford to do so—with the move within Jewish studies (and the wider trends in academia more generally) toward a post-nationalist scholarship that highlights diversity, fragmentation, and external influences on the shaping of Jewish life.

Finally, perhaps the most important Jewish studies challenge to the idea of a unified Jewish past and a united commitment to a common mission derives from Jewish feminism. How can a story of a unified people claim to encompass and represent all of its constituents when half of the purported group has been marginalized from the sources and historical narratives that defining that collective essence? Conceptions of Jewish collectivity—from classical sources to modern nationalism—have in fact reflected gendered perspectives that privilege male (and generally elite male) ideas about group membership, historical experiences, and collective characteristics. Since the 1970s, feminist scholarship and activism have brought new interpretations to the construction of Jewish peoplehood that pinpoint the limitations of twentieth-century narratives rooted in sources, both ancient and modern, which privilege men's voices and experiences in articulating the history and meaning of the Jewish people.[87] This rich body of scholarship has reshaped Jewish studies, and scholarship more broadly, in its demonstration of male biases that direct communal and scholarly interpretations. Feminist scholarship has not only emphasized recovering the largely ignored role of half of the Jewish people, but more significantly has raised fundamental questions about maintaining the canonical status of texts with their various depictions, articulations, and expressions of Jewish collectivity, without fundamentally reshaping those texts' messages and ideals.

Theologian Judith Plaskow put forth the fundamental limitations of Jewish sources as core texts for defining the Jewish people in *Standing Again at Sinai*.[88] By focusing on the absence of women at this founding moment of Jewish collectivity in religious sources, the revelation at Sinai, Plaskow illustrates the extent to which Jewish sources and rituals are defined by the experience of men. There is also a fundamental problem, she insists, in the biblical image of God as male, one that cannot be overlooked in all subsequent definitions of Jews and Judaism. In attempting to reconstruct Jewish belief and practice to integrate women's experiences, Plaskow argues for new interpretations (*midrashim*) and rituals to reimagine and actively reshape the past, present, and future of Jewish life and community.

With notions of peoplehood so deeply rooted in the asserted memory of the past, a feminist approach demands a significant reevaluation of the historical significance and future mission of the collective. More fundamentally, feminism challenges the very idea that there could be one static essence that defines the Jewish people. Instead, articulating peoplehood itself must be an ongoing process of rediscovery and explanation that constantly seeks to overcome hierarchies and biases by giving voice to historically marginalized members of the collective.

Feminist historians also argue that modern definitions of Jewish nationality, like ancient conceptions of Judaism, often reflect a masculine perspective that distorts the narrative of the Jewish people by imposing gendered values on what merits inclusion in the collective narrative. For example, historian Naomi Seidman illustrates the gendered construction of national identity used in language debates between Hebraists and Yiddishists in the early twentieth century. Hebrew authors marked Yiddish as an effeminate language in order to elevate the status of Hebrew as the national tongue.[89] One of the pioneers of Jewish feminist scholarship, Paula Hyman, asked historians to reconsider who they counted as Jews in analyzing the historical experiences of Jewish acculturation in modernity. By focusing on the public sphere, historians only considered male patterns of Jewish integration, which differed significantly from the picture that emerged from tracing women's experiences.[90] Seen through the lens of a feminist critique, modern nationalism (the underpinnings of peoplehood) also embodies a number of gendered biases about the nature of modern progress.

In looking at Jewish sources and discovering new ones, feminist scholars offer alternate visions of the defining characteristics of Jewish peoplehood. Scholar Ilana Pardes notes that, while the dominant biblical terms for defining the Jewish people are masculine nouns (*yisrael, am, ivrim, yehudim*), there are also several feminine terms that represent the collective—and that reflect a counter-narrative. Focusing on Israel as the name of the male God-wrestler gives a theological connotation to Israel and one that passes on membership in a genealogical fashion based on the idea of a holy seed.[91] A broader gender lens illuminates other visions of the Jewish people. For example, the prophets offer a different set of gender associations by referring to Israel as female, with terms such as Jerusalem and Zion rounding out the panoply of collective names.[92] Pardes suggests that these feminine nouns deemphasize divine commandments, military dominance, and sovereignty and instead introduce ideals of shared universal morality and actions.

A similar interpretive revolution is taking place with regard to rabbinic sources. For example, scholars underscore the problem with rabbinic literature's emphasis on interpretation as the basis for community formation, in that it applies only to the male elite.[93] The models of collectivity that emerge from this rabbinic material leave a paradigm limited to privileged males engaged in interpretation and tell its readers too little about social or cultural difference. Nevertheless, rabbinic engagement with a wide set of legal issues does provide some insight into the nature of boundaries. For instance, Seder Nashim (the talmudic tractate "Women") focuses on women and households and reflects a crucial alternate space for understanding the building of solidarity through realms of ritual and family rather than textual interpretation.

In struggling to uncover women's voices in Jewish tradition, feminist scholars have forged an implicit critique of conceptions of Jewish peoplehood as first imagined by the male rabbinic leadership of the early twentieth century. Feminist scholars emphasize the importance of relationship building, communal process, and sensitivity to the other. The contrast appears, for example, in Jewish feminists' activism in pushing the American Jewish community to be critical of Israel's attitude toward its minorities. The project of peoplehood is a fitting object of the critique that feminism has introduced toward monolithic allegiances that often marginalize concerns of women for the sake of affirming a greater degree of unity.

Divergent approaches to Jewish peoplehood today—Jewish communal conversations; studies of nationalism, ethnicity, race, and peoplehood itself; and Jewish studies—leave us with two fundamentally different views of Jewish collectivity in the past, present, and future. On one side, Jewish communal conversation (in which a small but prolific group of scholars are involved) emphasizes an unchanging understanding of Jewish collectivity with a strong emphasis on boundary preservation and support for the state. On the other side, academic approaches to Jewish peoplehood historicize the concept and question the practical possibility and moral validity of any group identity steeped in the nationalist paradigm and/or fixed collective boundaries. There is a fundamental divide between essentialists and constructivists, particularists and universalists, and statists and diasporists, and there are good reasons why Jewish peoplehood as it is currently conceived does not provide a comfortable meeting ground for the two camps. But Jewish peoplehood—or something like it—will remain an important idea, albeit one that needs to be redefined. Is there a way to bridge the gap between these camps, or at least draw from both—the peoplehood proponents and the cultural constructivists—in order to rehabilitate Jewish peoplehood in a new key?

3 In a New Key

CAN PEOPLEHOOD SPEAK TO A GLOBAL ERA?

We have examined here the evolution over the last century of the key word Jewish peoplehood, from its emergence as a neologism with few precedents in the English language to its position as the conceptual vocabulary at the heart of contemporary rhetoric on Jewish identity formation, Jewish communal institutions, and the State of Israel. Looking forward, two major questions about the term emerge: First, since the distinctly modern character of Jewish peoplehood represents a rupture from premodern paradigms of Jewish collectivity, is peoplehood worth preserving in some fashion? Second, given the clash between communal assumptions about the meaning of Jewish peoplehood and changing understandings and experiences of group identity more broadly, can Jewish peoplehood be revitalized in a new key? Or, to put the question another way: can it speak to twenty-first-century Jews sensitive to cosmopolitan critiques of collectivity and open to new paradigms of global connectivity?

It is certainly easy to imagine how a conclusion to this volume might be dedicated chiefly to arguing for the abandonment of Jewish peoplehood. The historical evidence, as well as contemporary scholarly trends interpreting peoplehood (like other vocabulary of groups) as inspired by the modern project to support specific political agendas, renders peoplehood merely a construction—at best a misleading myth, and at worse a concept easily manipulated to bolster ethnocentric claims. But even if the specific paradigm of Jewish peoplehood developed in the modern period, conceptions of Jewish collectivity have existed in Jewish sources, institutions, and daily life from the earliest days of Jewish history. Furthermore, understanding the historical invention of concepts for collective communities or nations does not destroy either the experience or the importance of what have become key cultural, political, and social categories in the world. While various processes of denationalization and globalization have eroded the dominance of the nationalist paradigm, nationalism—with its assumptions about groups and membership—continues to shape polities.

As such, acknowledging national group invention should not be equated with rejecting the reality, and even the value, of community and collectivity. A critical view of the past should make national and other collective claims more humble, and tolerant, but will not eliminate the practical necessity and moral possibilities of articulating collective solidarity and recognizing the realities of group identity and experience. Indeed, the invented nature of the term illustrates the strength of modern Jewish peoplehood—the key word's success in molding itself to meet the changing circumstances of Jewish life in radically new geographical, political, and social settings actually demonstrates the power of this conceptual adaptation to reshape fundamental ideas of group identity in a relatively short period of time. However, the invention of new concepts and terms to meet specific historical needs also accounts for the temporary nature of their utility. What is created in one context will inevitably have limitations as that context changes.

The historical influence of nationalism on the emergence of Jewish peoplehood is the latest chapter in the ongoing evolution of Jewish conceptions of collectivity, always defined to a greater or lesser extent in conversation with non-Jewish interlocutors and peer communities. The emergence of Jewish peoplehood in the 1930s signified an opportunity to rethink the existing paradigms of Jewishness in the diaspora, but the conversation sparked by tectonic shifts in Jewish demographics, ideology, and global politics quickly lost its openness and willingness to explore new models of and vocabulary for Jewish collectivity. Exploring peoplehood's evolution from experimental vocabulary to communal dogma inevitably invites the question of whether the terminology used to express the commitments and agendas of American rabbis facing opposition to Zionism in the Jewish community, as well as Nazism in Europe, can be sufficiently reframed to define Jewish collectivity almost a century later.

In considering the possibility of such a reframing, we must note that it is difficult to challenge the internal logic of a concept that presents itself as timeless and irrefutable. Yet one advantage of this book's critical analysis of our term is that the process can also empower. Understanding the historical context of peoplehood's introduction and evolution demystifies the aura of a supposedly unchanging notion of collectivity. Key words are much easier to imagine in new ways when their origins in particular places and times are known. While Jewish intellectuals introduced and popularized this term, the Jewish conversation, which for some time pushed the limits of available language for understanding collectivity, now lags significantly behind current intellectual and sociological developments.

The opportunity here is not just for some academic exercise. There is a practical need for an English-language concept and a vocabulary for

Jewish identity and collectivity that overcomes the dichotomy of religious versus secular modes of identifying as Jewish and being part of the Jewish people. The results of the recent Pew survey with which we began this volume portray an increasing number of Jews who don't feel comfortable identifying themselves in religious categories. Alternate categories will increasingly become far more central in defining Jewish collectivity. As the existing default category, peoplehood—but only a significantly reimagined peoplehood—has the potential to meet this emerging need for new ways of thinking about that collectivity.

But Jewish peoplehood as it is currently defined is ultimately inadequate to fill this important function. The role it has long assumed as the catch-all term to define expressions of Jewish belonging that are not religious is vulnerable to the same *post-* trends that have increasingly battered ethnicity's effectiveness as a viable category for describing highly fluid patterns of group attachment and identity formation. Unbound by the perceived need to make a case for unity, religious definitions of Judaism have at least recognized denominational differences and included a variety of metrics to capture various modes of engagement. In contrast, the inherent lack of theoretical sophistication in defining a peoplehood-based identity was evident in the Pew survey.

As historian Ari Kelman has pointed out, the survey instrument continued to ask those who did not identify as religious a host of questions related to religious practice. He wryly observed that this focus on asking *all* Jewish respondents about their religious practices is like asking lactose-intolerant people to select their own cheese.[1] While the survey might have asked better questions related to identification with the Jewish people, Kelman's joke illuminates peoplehood's popularity as a concept without the theoretical sophistication to describe fully contemporary Jewish identity patterns. One of the reasons that survey instruments have a hard time addressing questions to Jews who do not label themselves as religious is because the vocabulary for describing other modes of identifying as Jewish is impoverished. The problem is not so much fewer affiliated Jews, but rather the inadequacy of the primary model for analyzing, measuring, and describing Jewish identity—that is, in terms of religious belief and practice and denominational affiliation—and the need for new ways of articulating connections to a Jewish collective enterprise. But peoplehood advocates, consciously or not, have held off from developing a more varied vocabulary for measuring, describing, and promoting particular types of peoplehood practices and allegiances, because peoplehood's primary goal has been to include as broad a range of constituents as possible emphasizing unity over diversity. Ambiguity and lack of specificity has had a clear advantage for affirming unity.

What possible directions might be taken to craft Jewish peoplehood in a new key, in order to capitalize on the decline of religious categories as the prominent mode of Jewish identification in the United States and to reinvigorate the role of collectivity in contemporary Jewish life?

Those who theorize Jewish peoplehood today need to take into account that only an understanding of the Jewish people which rejects an essentialized definition of groupness grounded in nationalism; that works with the theoretical models and emerging realities of globalization, hybridity, and choice; and that recognizes that the essence of the Jewish people has always been its openness to multiple and even conflicting constellations of meaning will provide an enduring basis for Jewish collectivity in the twenty-first century. Disentangling Jewish peoplehood from the modern nationalist logic of groups is an increasingly difficult proposition. The term, which began with a critique of many of statist nationalism's core principles, has resisted efforts to challenge the dominance of nationalism in shaping Jewish group identity construction. Indeed, in short, the term has been largely co-opted by the nationalist paradigm it was introduced to counter. There is no doubt that the Jewish state, with over half of the global Jewish population, will need to be part of any theory of peoplehood that remains identifiable as a serious attempt to define Jewish collectivity. But retaining the homeland/diaspora axis of Zionist ideology, even in its more diaspora-friendly versions, as the basis for peoplehood leaves it unable to respond to intellectual, political, and sociological currents, with its limited ability to mobilize for the collective enterprise Jews whose worldview is increasingly shaped by the processes of denationalization, globalization, and localization.

In order to break free from assumptions embedded in the peoplehood discourse, peoplehood proponents need to talk about new terms and concepts that will ensure that expressions of Jewish collectivity remain compatible with changing norms and expressions. Peoplehood as a concept deeply rooted in nationhood has become too ingrained with a particular set of assumptions to survive unscathed the necessary transformation. In the spirit of pushing the currently narrow vocabulary for defining the Jewish collective category, I introduce several new terms and concepts in this conclusion. My goal is to propose language to provide a starting point for a radical reenvisioning of the thinking about and articulation of what links Jews to one another. It might, in fact, be more continuous with the sweep of Jewish history—and in that sense, more authentic—to embrace post-ethnic trends rather than to reject them.

Peoplehood in a new key will directly challenge core aspects of the phrase Jewish peoplehood that are reflected in each of its linguistic constituent parts. The three elements of the term—*Jewish, people,* and *-hood*—contain a set of linguistic assumptions that I propose to recalibrate and redefine in reimagining the key term in this chapter. First, *Jewish* plays a secondary role in the key word, as an adjective indicating the specific name of the people. *Jewish* should not merely describe who is included in the collectivity, but define and refer to the content that characterizes the collective enterprise. Second, the rootedness of *-hood* in peoplehood's conceptual relationship with nationhood connotes a shared essential set of characteristics that unifies a group's members and collective status as an end unto itself; as a suffix creating an abstract noun, *-hood* underscores the assumed existence of a specific condition. *-Hood* needs reimagining to reflect the plurality of Jewish communities and expressions, rather than an assumed, enduring, and unifying collective Jewish spirit. Finally, the adequacy of the very language for a people must be called into question, shifting our focus from the timeless nature of the collectivity to an active, collaborative Jewish enterprise.

My vision for peoplehood in a new key, then, revolves around three pillars: a greater stress on *Jewish,* a shift from nationhood to neighborhood networks, and an emphasis on project rather than people. My objective is to unseat the essentialist foundations of modern Jewish peoplehood, with the hope of shifting the core emphasis in Jewish collectivity from being to doing. The paradigm of Jewish collectivity discussed in this concluding section departs so significantly from current models of peoplehood that I also consider the possibility of a new key phrase to represent peoplehood in this new key.

Jewish: From Periphery to Center, from Describing to Defining

One of the most searing and prescient critiques of modern Jewish peoplehood came in 1959 from Rabbi Abraham Joshua Heschel, a leading Jewish thinker of the twentieth century. When Mordecai Kaplan championed a proposal at that year's United Synagogue meeting for the Conservative movement to affiliate officially with the World Zionist Organization, Heschel sardonically responded, "I should have preferred to discuss the idea of whether the World Zionist Organization should not join a synagogue."[2] This provocative remark demonstrates Heschel's belief that Kaplan's Zionist platform represented a shift from the "one place where we meet as Jews: the synagogue, by which I mean the House of Prayer, House of Study, and House of Assembly."[3] The largely secular nationalist assumptions that fueled Kaplan's peoplehood offered, Heschel believed, a dead end for American Jewish life. He countered: "The supreme need of the hour is neither a definition or a world organization of the Jewish people but a renewed personal attachment to Jewish thinking and living."[4]

Heschel's speech questioned the emerging dominance of Jewish peoplehood as the most strategic path for American Jewish life. At the core of his position was a critique of the replacement of individual religious experience with secular collective commitment as the basis of Jewish collective consciousness. Remembering his powerful yet now all-but-forgotten rebuttal underscores the relative newness of the peoplehood discourse and its secularizing impulses. As a modern mystic, Heschel located Jewish collectivity within its spirituality, not its secular collective values. While Kaplan did emphasize the religious nature of Jewish peoplehood, his critique of theology and his close connection to secular Zionist culture positioned peoplehood as a relatively secularized alternative to religious ideas of Jewishness.

A half-century later, the trajectory Heschel identified has only intensified. Peoplehood has become a broad term, serving as a catch-all for a variety of nonreligious definitions of Judaism. The tension Heschel raised between two models—Judaism as spirituality and Jewish peoplehood—has been obscured, but his observation that peoplehood threatens to shift the emphasis away from Jewish "living and thinking" remains as relevant as ever.

Peoplehood in a new key would reopen the Heschel/Kaplan debate about whether Jewish identity is fundamentally reflected in secular nationalism or religious individualism. The success of both of these paradigms means that few Jews would even recognize that this debate ever took place, or that it remains an unarticulated internal tension today. Indeed, Heschel's critique of Kaplan on this issue is far less well remembered than their respective legacies as representatives of the mystical and rational sides of American Jewish thought. By focusing on either Jews or Judaism since the 1950s, peoplehood and religion have internalized a secular/religious split (but largely sidelined the accompanying tension within it) that reflects two very distinct paths of fitting into Western nation-states: as a nation and as a religious minority.

The unreconciled relationship between the two paradigms—nationalist and religious—that has divided up avenues for engaging Judaism into distinct categories has left little organizational structure, communal support, or language for a Judaism that combines advocating for Jews in need and praying to God. American Judaism is, in the main, divided into secular organizations—such as Federations, advocacy organizations, and Jewish Community Centers—and religious organizations, like synagogues and other congregations. The two categories—nationalism and liberal American religious denominationalism—work side by side, in two increasingly outdated and thus impaired modes for articulating Jewish identity, with an implicit shared agreement to avoid facing the competing nature of their claims and emphases. Jewish peoplehood and Judaism as a religion have developed as two parallel modes of Jewish identification that coexist, partner, and share participants, but are not integrated; they play together by splitting the deck. Jewish peoplehood has left Judaism to other ventures.

The prominence of *Jewish* in the existing phrase Jewish peoplehood should not be confused with bridging between secular and religious paradigms. Jewish peoplehood first developed as a vision of Jewish nationalism that recognized the importance of integrating religious models of Jewish identification (albeit in a relatively secularized mode, as we have discussed), but as Kaplan's initial emphasis on peoplehood as the term for a "religious civilization" was eclipsed by even more secular definitions, peoplehood came to function chiefly as a secular category. Despite the rhetoric of "We are one" from the State of Israel and American Jewish organizations, too rarely have they sought to engage Judaism—those experiences, sources, and traditions that could possibly create some shared, even unifying conversations. Instead, *Jewish* in Jewish peoplehood functions as an adjective used to describe the noun *people,* referring to the who, not the what, of peoplehood. By moving the meaning of Jewish from describing what Jews do to who Jews are—a move which I advocate reversing—Jewish peoplehood established an alternative vision to Judaism as a religion, with Jewish peoplehood and Judaism as a religion as two dominant—and distinct—paradigms of Jewish identity.

A tacit agreement to support two parallel paths, for a time, worked well for American Jews, who could separate their interests into articulating a nationalist connection to the State of Israel and maintaining a religious identity as a minority community in the United States, with their respective parallel organizing principles of homeland/diaspora and religious denominationalism. But by coexisting so well (with any competition siphoned off into compartmentalization), the two paths have failed to see how each could benefit from—and in light of changing sociological realities, must shift to include—the other's approach to defining Jewish identity.

Religion has long been a central category for Jewish collective self-definition, but the changing landscape of religious life is eroding possibilities for articulating Jewish solidarity through facile religious categories in a postmodern age. Religion is both more important to individuals in the twenty-first century and less central in defining their identity and allegiances. As sociologist and religious studies scholar Robert Wuthnow observes, interest in religion has shifted from an emphasis on a sense of group connection to individual searching, a renewed interest in spirituality and religious practice without any necessary collective allegiance or identification. This overall trend has largely severed the link between a particular creed, belief, or commitment associated with a religious tradition and a given individual's relationship to that tradition.[5] Instead, religion is understood as increasingly about individual searching for spirituality that may bring them in contact with different traditions throughout their lifetimes (even if their primary allegiance is to one). Religions today are developing along a trajectory that clashes with, rather than supports, collective claims; postmodern trends in religion have disrupted the close association between ethnic and religious identities as described by Will Herberg.[6]

For example, in 2007, an exhibit called "The New Authentics: Artists of the Post-Jewish Generations" opened at the Spertus Museum in Chicago. The introduction to the exhibit describes post-Jewish Jews as "free to choose their affiliations; they are Jewish culturally, religiously, spiritually, intellectually, emotionally, partially, biologically, or invisibly."[7] At a moment when *post-* everything is au courant, it is not surprising that the term has entered into the popular lexicon of Jewish life. Like the emergence of post-nationalism and post-ethnicity, the language of post-Judaism introduces a fundamental shift in the conceptualization of Judaism.

The concept of post-Jewish relies upon recent theoretical currents in sociology of religion as well as empirical observations about changing patterns in religious engagement. Polls indicate that Americans change religious affiliations regularly (about half of American adults have changed religious affiliation at least once in their lives), mix multiple faiths in their practices, and increasingly marry spouses from other religious communities.[8] The language of the Spertus Museum exhibit reflects a scholarly emphasis on choice, and an ability to fit together individual religious narratives that do not necessarily reflect traditional sets of practices or beliefs. Wuthnow calls this "patchwork religion"; religious studies scholar Nancy Ammerman agrees that concepts like "tinkering" and "bricolage" best describe today's fluid religious identities. She concludes, "Religious practices and affiliations change over a complicated lifetime, and the array of religious groups in a voluntary society shifts in equally complex ways. If religious identity ever was a given, it certainly is no longer."[9] Religion is increasingly a highly individual experience whose authenticity clashes with obligation to collective categories that might dictate specific religious doctrines, practices, and collective allegiances.

Another important trend in the United States disrupts a division between secular and religious conceptions of identity. Ammerman sees "religious identity as constructed in the intersection between 'public narratives' and individual 'autobiographies.'"[10] It is increasingly difficult to separate secular and religious conceptions of Jewish identity, because individuals create their narratives in ways that don't necessarily reflect a distinction between public secular selves and private religious personalities. This marks a significant shift in thinking about models of collectivity that emphasize or embody public versus private spheres. While nationalism largely highlighted secular aspects of Judaism, like nation and culture, and religious notions—from Reform to Modern Orthodox—have stressed creed and practice as primary criteria of collectivity, neither has conceptualized public and private Jewish selves. In recent decades, this dichotomy between secular and religious so central to defining paths of modern Jewish life and collectivity has become increasingly blurred. Ammerman concludes at the end of her study of religion in everyday life that "few people in these pages have absorbed an all-encompassing religious way of life. But few have eliminated religion entirely, either."[11]

In sum, then, separating Jewishness into an adjective for Jewish peoplehood and a noun of Judaism as a religion has allowed two distinct, and theoretically conflicting, approaches to modern Jewish groupness to coexist—but at the cost of integrating a full range of Jewishness into Jewish collective self-understanding across the secular-versus-religious divide.

The first goal of peoplehood in a new key should be to muddle the false distinction between secular and religious expressions of Judaism by placing Jewish at the core of the conversation about Jewish collectivity. Only Judaism—and by that I mean the exploration of Jewish tradition and Jewish life in its manifold expressions—can inspire a global sense of interconnectedness. A vision for peoplehood in a new key would make Jewishness as the defining noun (and Jewish the defining adjective) that serves not just to label the members of the group or to refer vaguely to their shared values, but as the basis for the collective, active enterprise itself. Placing Jewish as the unifying, varied, and active content at the center of peoplehood in a new key cuts across the Jews-versus-Judaism split, between peoplehood and the parallel category of Judaism as a religion—a split that has left peoplehood in the main bereft of the ability to articulate the importance of Judaism in the cultural, social, and political identity of Jews and relegating serious engagement with textual sources, practices, and ideas to religion.

Putting Jewish at the center would mean defining what links Jews to one another as the active engagement with Jewish ideas, communities of practice, and other forms of intentional engagement. From this perspective, measures of connections to what we now call peoplehood would be just as strong for someone studying the weekly Torah portion as it would be for someone who regularly participates in organizations such as

AIPAC, J Street, the American Jewish Committee, and others explicitly dedicated to advocating on behalf of collective Jewish interests. In this model, Jewish peoplehood would be seen as building from individual experiences with Jewishness both public and private, rather than establishing peoplehood as an absolute foundation of Jewish identity. In other words, instead of a sense of Jewish peoplehood being necessary for Jewish identity, Jewish engagement would shape and benefit peoplehood.

Emphasizing the importance of Judaism in Jewish peoplehood also requires a serious evaluation of the role that Judaism plays in the State of Israel. Israeli nationhood has put religion at the center of its national definition and has succeeded in fusing the national and religious. But it has done so at the expense of an open and dynamic Judaism that can speak to audiences beyond Orthodox and ultra-Orthodox communities. The lack of separation between church and state in Israel and between Jewish peoplehood and Israeli citizenship must be addressed for a variety of reasons—the most important, in the context of the issues highlighted in this volume, being to address the conflation of historical definitions of the Jewish people with modern notions of citizenship, a confusion that fails to make sense in either a nationalist or global paradigm. But it is also from the perspective of creating an equal playing field for a variety of religious expressions that would create a shared interest in Judaism. The ties necessary to connect Israel and American Jews will need to include an attachment to Judaism. As long as there is a monolithic definition of Judaism supported by the State of Israel, the connection between the two centers of global Jewry will lack the most important potential bridge connecting increasingly divergent populations.

On one level, this desire to put Jewish back into Jewish peoplehood and to separate Judaism from statist nationhood invites a return to Kaplan's initial formulation of the concept. He saw the integration of religion and nation as central to his vision. His efforts to create institutions such as the Kehillah in New York City, the precursor to the Jewish community center, underscore his interest in bridging divides between secular nationalism and Judaism as a religion. However, placing Jewish at the center of peoplehood actually represents a rupture from Kaplan's historical model, because he remained largely invested in the secular/religious dichotomy. Even as he tried to integrate Judaism into Jewish nationalism, he insisted on making very clear statements limiting the religious aspect of Judaism to non-creedal expressions of folkways. Kaplan's conception of religion was restricted and limited to practices that fit within the intellectual bounds of a secular scientific worldview.[12]

In addition, religion served primarily to support Kaplan's idea of Jewish nationhood. Embedded in the Jewish religion were the fundamental characteristics of Judaism that served as the collective basis for the group. Kaplan substituted principles of nationhood found in Jewish folkways and beliefs for territory and political sovereignty, in differentiating Jewish nationhood from other models. In his view, Judaism as a religious tradition justified national collectivity by demonstrating the importance of certain ethical principles that differentiated Jewish nationhood from dominant forms of exclusivist and intolerant nationalisms. In his articulations of nationhood and peoplehood Kaplan gave lip service to religion, but in doing so he highly circumscribed its role by employing it in the service of national claims. The link Kaplan provided between peoplehood and religious civilization may even have helped obscure an emerging secular/religious dichotomy, by making the religious tradition the textual and historical basis for defining a unique vision of Jewish peoplehood.[13]

What Jewish means has devolved into so many possibilities that it seems to lack any potential to unite Jews, undoubtedly one of the reasons it has been functionally excised from peoplehood. In order to integrate Jewishness, peoplehood in a new key must recognize a diversity of Judaisms not as a problem that must be overcome, but as the basis for building a sustainable alternate model of collectivity.

Neighborhood: From National to Local, from Core to Cohort

The second pillar of peoplehood in a new key is a shift from nationhood to neighborhood. Echoes of nationhood remain fundamental to the concept of peoplehood and how it is explained, analyzed, and evaluated. In order to neutralize the nationalist paradigm when peoplehood is voiced in a new key, I propose a different *-hood* with different connotations.

A neighborhood approach to Jewish peoplehood underscores, rather than erases, not only the diversity in Jewish life, but even the fragmented and irreconcilable differences that characterize local expressions of Jewish identity around the globe. Contemporary calls for Jewish peoplehood recognize diversity; indeed, there are clearly accepted categories of difference among Jews around the world. For instance, peoplehood conversations talk about "Israel versus diaspora" and recognize denominational differences in Jewish observance. But peoplehood advocates seek to surmount differences, for example, by developing programs that allow Jews from Israel and diaspora communities to have encounters that build people-to-people relationships in order to overcome their different cultural backgrounds. A paradigmatic peoplehood program is the *mifgash* (meeting) model of people-to-people connections. In addition, peoplehood language is often the rhetoric of shared values that Jews from across religious denominations (particularly Reform, Conservative, and Orthodox) articulate when they come together in various contexts.

Peoplehood's goal today, then, is to help make the case for Jewish unity in the face of acknowledged diversity. But the focus on unity and articulating a shared mission dilutes the particular logic of each individual or communal Judaism. The goal of finding common ground puts pressure on proponents of peoplehood to seek the lowest common denominator, built on mostly abstract claims about Jews and Judaism that often rely on general slogans, external threats, or ambiguity rather than specific and meaningful content.[14] Peoplehood is stuck in a race to the bottom, or the watered-down middle; unity is achieved at the expense of failing to fully reflect the particular passions that individuals and their local communities identify.

Is Jewish collectivity fundamentally about unity? Modern notions of Jewish peoplehood certainly have insisted that the answer is yes. Peoplehood assumes that Jews are unified and have a common mission that transcends their apparent differences. This is a fundamental characteristic of modern peoplehood—to have a shared core past, present, and future. For many readers, the idea that peoplehood's primary goal need not be the promotion of unity will undermine the very idea of peoplehood. This makes complete sense as long as Jewish peoplehood defines itself according to the logic of nationhood, which concentrated on unity and shared characteristics to create (rather than merely describe) a political, cultural, and economic entity. But a historical awareness of the emergence of Jewish peoplehood in the last century is crucial to overcoming the circular logic that defines Jewish peoplehood as transhistorical, sharing criteria of Jewish life across time and space. By adopting the ideology of nationhood as models, Jewish peoplehood internalized the priority of unity and downplayed the de facto decentralized model of Jewish collectivity, articulated in highly divergent manners in specific cultural contexts across the global Jewish population. Overturning the modern nationalist paradigm, constructed by political entities to facilitate the development of the modern nation-state, as the basis of Jewish collectivity opens up the question of whether unity is a necessary building block of collectivity. Peoplehood in a new key presents a paradigm shift that reverses the ascendency of understanding collectivity as analogous to unity across diversity.

Neighborhood offers a number of advantages over nationhood as the basis for imagining the nature of Jewish collectivity. The idea of a neighborhood offers a less systematic and more elastic set of guidelines for organizing the diversity of Jewish community. And while neighborhoods can exist in specific geographical spaces, the neighborhood concept is not primarily a spatial definition; neighborhoods understood figuratively capture Jewish networks that develop across shared interests, social groups, religious practices, cultural commitments, and age cohorts. Connections do not only literally take place locally in the geographic sense ("in the hood"), although they can. Neighborhood-like networks, especially with an increasing shift toward virtual conversations and easy possibilities for long-distance travel, develop more in line with interests than fixed geographies.

A neighborhood model approaches Jewish collectivity through an opposite perspective from that of the nationhood model. While nationhood seeks to identify the most broadly shared common denominator, neighborhoods seek to build collective consciousness by recognizing the organizing power of specific groups to develop different, and sometimes even mutually incompatible, visions of what it means to be part of the Jewish people. A sense of connection to a larger entity is generated most authentically—and thus enduringly—from the bottom up. Grassroots communities provide open spaces to raise questions about Jewish identity and what, if anything, binds Jews to one another. It is the very act of facing these issues that engages individuals in the meaning of peoplehood. Small, individuated communities are not the final straw that will break the back of peoplehood. Instead, the emergence of group differentiation around interest, location, or age cohort creates the building blocks of the Jewish people.

A shift to a neighborhood approach deemphasizes the ideal of unity and promotes disaggregation of Jewish institutions and communities. The breakdown of centralized states and non-state institutions is a reality that, if ignored, will continue to result in the offering of models of community and collectivity based on outdated assumptions. The emphasis on size and centralization privileges numbers and power over individual meaning-making and grassroots organization. The neighborhood approach promotes local informal expressions of collectivity, rather than overarching institutional centers. Micro-communities will emerge as the creators and perpetuators of the ongoing Jewish enterprise. Divergent and grassroots expressions of Jewish involvement are not signs of the end of Jewish peoplehood, but the very basis for its future.

Vibrant collective life cannot rely on one center to disseminate the meaning of identity. The legacy of Ahad Ha-am's vision of a cultural center, a vestige of cultural nationalism, has little relevance for global models of collectivity. As Simon Rawidowicz pointed out decades ago, the meaning of Jewish engagement and membership is a localized phenomenon that cannot be exported from one context to another.[15]

There is also a moral imperative in acknowledging irreconcilable and fundamentally different neighborhood visions of Judaism as a goal for a vibrant peoplehood in a new key. Rogers Smith's *Stories of Peoplehood* concludes with an affirmation that peoplehood will continue to thrive as an important aspect of global politics. His concern is that certain forms of peoplehood, especially those that have "an unduly 'strong' chauvinistic sense of peoplehood," can be potentially quite threatening to promoting intergroup cooperation and intragroup dedication to individual human rights. A centralized, top-down vision of peoplehood that attempts to define the nature of all members of the group has a much greater likelihood of affirming extreme visions of particularism, which can easily disregard the internal diversity of voices, pursue ethnocentric communal policies vis-à-vis other ethnic groups, and undermine democratic values by privileging the collective over the individual.

Smith envisions the following blueprint for building diverse visions of peoplehood that create an internal check on the claims of the collective group vision: "We should instead seek to multiply and diversify them and set them against one another. We might then foster a politics in which individuals, groups, parties, and movements often are compelled to rethink their most extreme positions, so that they can form coalitions broad enough to gain power and advance their most valued goals."[16] Acknowledging competing visions within the discourse of Jewish collectivity (as opposed to just diversity, or differences only across denominations and the Israel-diaspora divide) would foster a level of humility within conversations about Jewish membership, and erode a singular, potentially coercive narrative of Jewish collectivity. Inevitably, the call to unity is also a call to fall in behind the voice calling for unity, and the language of unity as the basic shared assumption can easily be co-opted in the service of the political gains of a very particular set of goals. A neighborhood model ensures that no single centralized voice can either claim to be speaking for the collective or ignore equally valid counter-expressions. And a neighborhood paradigm fosters a democratic nature in Jewish collectivity, in which no single voice can arise to claim to represent the entire people through a singular paradigm of peoplehood.

The map of Jewish collectivity will certainly become more fragmented in a neighborhood model. But a neighborhood model holds the possibility of expanding the relevance of Jewish identity and collectivity by acknowledging that desires for identity as part of something broader flow from local engagements with something particularly relevant and personally meaningful.

Moreover, the Jewish nationalism that developed against the backdrop of European antisemitism and as a moral response to it in the nineteenth and twentieth centuries has led to very different consequences in the era of Jewish sovereignty. Conceptions of the Jewish people—often experienced or depicted as benign and harmless or wholly positive—too easily normalize particularist assumptions that clash with humanitarian and universalist principles. Pressures to preserve peoplehood and its commitments justify prioritizing ethnocentric concerns over universal principles. For example, the motto of the American Jewish Committee is "to enhance the well-being of the Jewish people and Israel, and to advance human rights and democratic values."[17] The idea that those ideals could be in tension was a foreign one in the 1940s, but in the twenty-first century and in the context of a sovereign Jewish state, a confrontation between claims of Jewish nationalism and those of human rights cannot be avoided.

The positive fragmentation of peoplehood expands the reach of Jewish collectivity. Conversely, unifying attempts that emphasize common ground alienate parts of the Jewish constituency, and focus on a tired definition of peoplehood at the expense of speaking to a larger group of people linked by a diversity of connected commitments. Rather than getting stuck on what abstractly unites Jews, we should focus on how Jewish neighborhoods can—by addressing and embracing very individual and particular expressions of Jewish identity and Jewish life—in fact generate a sense of membership in something much larger than the local.

Having focused on Jewish content, at local levels, the question shifts to how to determine what actually constitutes Jewish and what a new model might be for how Jews can in fact produce shared membership across fragmented neighborhoods.

Project: From Being to Doing, from Essence to Action

The final pillar of peoplehood in a new key shifts the logic of peoplehood from identifying a characteristic essence shared by all members of the Jewish people to defining the Jewish collective as that which Jews do out of a sense of connection to the Jewish enterprise. In order to emphasize the open-ended, non-essentialist concept of Jewish collectivity, I propose the use of the term *project* to define how an individual gains membership in the collective, and the term *family* to talk about group boundaries.[18] These terms attempt to answer a fundamental question left by moving away from the centrality of unity and essence in concepts of modern Jewish peoplehood: What are the criteria of membership and collective boundaries for a group defined by individuals engaging in various ways in the Jewish enterprise?

While peoplehood seeks a unifying essence, the Jewish project emphasizes fluidity, change, and an unfinished state of development. In this approach to Jewish collectivity, the accent shifts from what the Jewish people *is* to what Jews do. Instead of attempting to measure a peoplehood index with metrics about the group's numbers and commitment to unity, a focus on the Jewish project would explore the individual's sense of meaning and personal engagement. Another non-instinctive part of the shift to a project would be the celebration of diversity and fragmentation. The fear of relinquishing the notion of a Jewish communal glue has privileged relatively recent historical models of Jewish collectivity over the evolving process that has consistently throughout history demonstrated many kinds of bonds and even eschewed the elevation of any one kind of glue above all others. The Jewish project shifts the emphasis away from the slogan "We are one" toward a greater appreciation for fragmentation and multiple nodes of Jewish collective existence. Further, the lack of systematic explanation of the Jewish people in premodern Jewish texts and thought would seem to demonstrate that the Jewish people has always been a project, and only recently became described as a static condition.

The language of project emphasizes the gathering together of groups committed to particular agendas, ideals, and interest in creating specific communities—building experiences in local communities even when those efforts do not directly contribute to the unity of the Jewish people. Instead of a top-down definition of what unites Jews, this approach builds on individual experiences and neighborhood-like interactions to generate conversations about what connects people who call themselves Jewish across time and space.

A Jewish project does not seek to realize political ends or to police boundaries. The Jewish people would not be viewed as an instrument to blunt the forces of assimilation, galvanize Jews to advocate politically for Israel (even as Israel is a clear and important component of the Jewish project), or generate litmus tests for Jewish involvement. Developing language around a project would emphasize the increasing importance of engaged choice in the construction of individual and group identity. But engaged choice differs from the idea of voluntary association so central to modern notions of collective membership in liberal democratic societies. Joining a project demands action and active participation. The growing interest in American culture in discovering and recapturing lost traditions may symbolize a shift in conceptualizing ties—a shift from the low bar of entry suggested by voluntary association toward a far greater emphasis on finding authentic and meaningful connections to something larger and older than one's self. Perhaps counterintuitively, one key to invigorating peoplehood is to promote far broader criteria of what might constitute membership in the Jewish people, with shift in emphasis from predefined benchmarks to diverse forms of engagement with Jews and Judaism.

As a thought experiment: What would it look like if the diaspora museum decided to rename itself the Museum of the Jewish Project rather than the Museum of the Jewish People? A museum of a people tells a narrative story that suggests a clear link between people, place, and time, while a museum of a project highlights experiences and expressions, moments and phenomena, that demonstrate diverse engagements, without an overarching narrative or an attempt to demonstrate the logic linking one element to another. The unreflective use of Benedict Anderson by museum curators and leaders of the peoplehood movement illustrates an ongoing attempt to tell a larger story about the meaning of peoplehood, but a deeper engagement with Anderson and other contemporary scholars of nationalism and ethnicity or museum studies would acknowledge the role of museums in inculcating specific ideologies and would seriously question the possibility of building a museum around the organizing principle of peoplehood at all.[19] A museum of the Jewish project, on the other hand, would foreground diversity and the challenges of categorizing Jewish experiences into an evolving story with a beginning, middle, and end.

The subjectivity of defining Jewish collectivity through the terminology of individual projects has a clear weakness: How can group membership be established across networks of people and neighborhood experiences? One option would be to approach boundaries through the concept of family. By family I do not mean to propose its use at the simplistic rhetorical level of "in the end, we're all family"—or certainly, as a biological metaphor. Indeed, the use of family to suggest connections based on blood relationships between human family members would conflict with a central argument in this book. I have demonstrated the emergence of descent, a concept closely connected to racial definitions of ethnic groups, as a powerful trope in the contemporary rhetoric of Jewish peoplehood—one which supports essentialist arguments, by providing a clear marker of Jewishness to circumscribe unity and homogeneity across the many Judaisms practiced around the globe. Yet such markers have less relevance as Jewish families increasingly include non-Jewish parents and other blood relatives. Moreover, a definition of group boundaries based on descent often appears blatantly racist to a generation raised on the idea that group identities should not be inherited or ascribed but chosen. Instead, my different use of family intends to parallel changes in its definition in contemporary American life. As a recent *New York Times* article, "The Changing American Family," reports, "Families are more ethnically, racially, religiously and stylistically diverse than half a generation ago."[20] Jewish families reflect these changes, leaving descent models of peoplehood unable to accommodate dramatic social transformations taking place.

For an alternate way in which the term *family* can be used, to define groups with constantly shifting and permeable boundaries, I turn to the linguistic philosopher and assimilated Jew Ludwig Wittgenstein. He suggests a more complex understanding of the concept of family in his work on categorizing language groups.[21] Families have common features, but no one feature defines all members of a family. This model offers a crucial difference from dominant models for defining Jewish collectivity (genetic Judaism, statist Zionism, or potential victimhood) that stress unity around a singular bloodline. In addition, Wittgenstein's conception of family resemblance possesses another key advantage for defining Jewish collectivity without grounding claims in any essential criteria of membership, as the boundaries of inclusion within families are constantly shifting and evolving. In Wittgenstein's application of his family metaphor to languages, no set of fixed boundaries permanently marks borderlines between language families. This prevents a focus on boundary preservation and instead recognizes the fluid nature of inclusion and exclusion, with membership and participation not limited by a preordained axiom or static marker.

A family model also reflects the intellectual and social realities of the twenty-first century. Families get together for certain purposes at particular times and in particular ways. Yet some relationships are stronger than others, and there is no automatic assumption that various members within families share all of the same values, or even the same vision. The language of family both recognizes the centrality of descent in defining Jewish membership historically and reflects the reality that today's families rarely define inclusion by descent alone. A reshaped use of the Jewish family as a collective model shifts talk about collectivity from unity to diversity, static boundaries to fluid membership, and enduring traits to evolving norms.

The conception of a Jewish family that encompasses individual and neighborhood projects seeks to create a platform for engagement, meaning creation, and innovation, with Jewish communities looking to develop what the software community calls open-source standards. Open-source software is nonproprietary, open to customization, and readily interchangeable. This paradigm meets the demands of Jews who no longer find specific identity packages relevant. An open-source model promotes multiple entry-points, recognizes diverse interests, and allows creative self-expression.

Open-source does not, however, mean no boundaries or that anything goes. Any open-source community works together to decide on parameters. Yet the nature of open-source also means that these parameters are constantly in flux and in need of reshaping in response to various environmental changes. Moreover, the consensus on parameters remains humble. As one scholar of religion writes in another context, "We can give reasons for preferring one interpretation over another—including by appealing to professional obligations and pragmatic criteria—though we cannot claim that our account exhausts all significations or corresponds to 'external reality.'"[22]

The language of family is often used to define a fundamental commitment to the State of Israel as a defining feature of Jewish peoplehood. But my proposal for a new use of the family metaphor argues for a paradigm of peoplehood calibrated to acknowledge multiple loyalties, promote local networks, and reflect cosmopolitan objectives—including meaningful relationships with Israeli Jews and the State of Israel. Preserving a sense of shared past and future—across such starkly different realities as nationality in a political homeland and minority religious community in the diaspora—demands that both communities acknowledge and debate fundamental differences. Paradoxically, only by distinguishing but not disconnecting peoplehood from Zionism, and from survivalist fears of Jewish continuity and a romantic premise of Jewish unity, will future generations of American Jews view group identity and connection to the State of Israel as integral aspects of their Jewish self-definition.

Of course, a family or open-source approach to collectivity, as opposed to more concrete criteria like descent, territorial attachment, or shared essence, will raise complicated and provocative questions. As the pendulum swings away from descent and toward consent, what will define groupness? *New York Magazine* recently published a cover with the headline "The First Jewish President," depicting Barack Obama wearing a kippah.[23] Could/should a biracial Christian man with a Muslim father who was schooled in politics by Jews and hosts an annual seder be somehow considered part of the larger Jewish collective—that is, of the Jewish project? What key words we could use for articulating the shift from peoplehood to project is a complicated question that raises important challenges for defining peoplehood in a new key.

Jewishhood Project(s)

Reformulating peoplehood in a new key around the pillars of *Jewish, -hood,* and *project* pushes against core assumptions of modern Jewish peoplehood as it has evolved over the past century, shifting the emphasis from Jews to Jewishness, from a unified and homogenous nation to fragmented neighborhoods, and from clear ascriptive boundaries to engagement in a Jewish enterprise and participation in the Jewish family (as conceived above). This all requires more than a tweak of terminology. The very paradigm upon which peoplehood developed will need to be reconsidered as peoplehood responds to contemporary shifts in the political, social, and religious landscape. Current academic trends—and perhaps in part in reaction against them, in response to the perceived threat of the delegitimization of peoplehood—complicate this endeavor. The legacy of the term peoplehood (including its assumption of its own reality) may well be too ingrained and too entrenched in Jewish communal discourse to merely reinvigorate the term with a new set of expectations and institutional support.

I offer *Jewishhood* as a new term to serve as a touchstone for conceptions of Jewish collectivity in a new key. In hopes of sparking a productive conversation about the meaning of Jewish collectivity, rather than offer the new key word I propose to explore the term as one alternate model to peoplehood—one that respects the critical nature of groupness within Jewish tradition and Jewish life, without privileging the nationalist paradigm as the default and outdated model for the ties that bind Jews to one another.

Jewishhood is a self-consciously constructed term intended to highlight the three key elements of peoplehood in a new key. The *Jewish* in *Jewishhood* makes the study of Jewish collectivity a reflection on an evolving story of what Jews do, rather than an affirmation that Jews exist as a discrete group. The conceptual vocabulary of *Jewishhood* is not positioned to make essentialist claims about the nature of the collective; instead, the term *Jewishhood* acknowledges family resemblances in Jewish expressions without erecting rigid boundary markers. *-Hood* (decoupled from the nouns *people* and *nation*) signifies here a shift from nationhood to neighborhood, underscoring local, diverse, and multiple natures of community building and a sense of group solidarity, and drawing our attention to local aspects of Jewish interaction and belonging that together constitute global Jewish collectivity. Most radically, peoplehood in a new key will not necessarily include people at all. Instead, a robust conception of Jewish collectivity can be imagined in the vocabulary of project—again, reflecting a fundamental modification in the vision of Jewish collectivity from who Jews are to what Jews do.

The Jewishhood project is not proposed here as the replacement term for Jewish peoplehood, but as the basis for a new conversation that acknowledges the extent to which a very limited and singular definition of Jewish collectivity has come to both dominate communal vocabulary and eclipse the potential evolution of new concepts reflecting contemporary trends—concepts that might even more closely resemble premodern visions of how Jews are linked to one another. Jewishhood certainly sounds jarring, without any clear precedent in English. But peoplehood must have sounded quite strange to the ears of English speakers during its formative years in the beginning of the previous century. Playing with the language of Jewish collectivity in English is, in a sense, itself an important part of the legacy of the peoplehood innovation in American Jewish life. The pioneers of peoplehood recognized that only a new vocabulary of collective Jewish identity could change people's thinking; new key words reshape how individuals imagine their own sense of self and their relationship to broader groups. A process of generating new key words, then, is not only about terminology; the conscious and unconscious shaping of new key terms allows communities to imagine collective connections in radically new ways.

The consideration of peoplehood in a new key, by proposing alternative language, also fulfills the intention of the major progenitor of the term. Kaplan was quite hesitant about the use of peoplehood in any long-term way without a more serious evaluation of its implications. Certainly, Kaplan would be surprised, and I imagine even disappointed, by the ascendency of this one particular term—one that he adopted rather quickly and without much consideration—as the rarely questioned conceptual terminology for defining the Jewish collective, decades after he urged a more thorough conversation about the term and its meaning. New language for articulating peoplehood should preserve peoplehood's early adapters' sensitivity to navigating radical changes in group definitions and their awareness of the constant need to reevaluate the position of Jews as both apart from and a part of the modern societies in which they live.

Unlike Kaplan's situation, however, our own challenge involves not only finding the right key word but, more fundamentally, facing the very question of whether we can identify a single term or concept to categorize and name this collective group, one that fully comes to terms with scholarly critiques of groups as invented or imagined communities and sociological trends which parallel that critique. In some ways, the very need to consider the case for any given singular organizing principle reflects the modern nationalist project far more than it does the plural approach to articulating collectivity that has long dominated Judaism's classical sources. That diversity of names for the group has both expressed the importance of viewing Jews as connected to one another and embodied an appreciation of the multiple ways of articulating the nature of the bonds between them.

In thinking about peoplehood in a new key, I am keenly aware of a tension. There is a need for a new key term to challenge the hegemony of an existing key word for describing the criteria and boundaries of Jewish collectivity. How can a new key word be introduced that also challenges the very idea of a singular all-encompassing term articulating a specific set of assumptions about collectivity? Indeed, one open question is whether the Jewishhood project is itself too singular. Including the definite article carries over the supposition from the Jewish people and the Jewish nation that there is one set of unifying and shared boundaries. Jewishhood projects would more profoundly break from the nationalist paradigm by emphasizing the inherently plural and often incompatible visions of Jews' primary goals, practices, politics, and allegiances.

My hope is that whatever language we use going forward moves beyond unity, solidarity, and rigid boundaries to integrate fragmentation, conflicting visions of Judaism, and permeable boundaries of Jewishness into definitions of the Jewish people past, present, and future. Such a shift in conceptualizing the meaning of the Jewish people would address the limitations of the term as it was defined in the modern period and preserve the possibility of reclaiming the ability of some term to reinvent itself in conversation with shifting paradigms of individual and group identities.[24] It is my hope that this shift will also help address the polarization that has developed between peoplehood advocates, who view their role as making a case for Jewish unity, and peoplehood critics, who question the historical validity of collective claims and treat group solidarity with suspicion. Jewishhood is thus an idea meant to bridge oppositional thinking about Jewish peoplehood between those threatened by critical scholarship and those driven by critical scholarship to make interventions by discrediting the theoretical basis of particular group loyalties.

Will Jewishhood serve the important function that Jewish peoplehood has served in American Jewish life—to articulate the value, obligation, and Jewish roots of preserving a strong sense of Jewish collectivity and connection? Jewishhood (and the fuller term, Jewishhood projects) is meant to change the conversation, not to declare Jewish collectivity a dead concept. The analysis in this book suggests that peoplehood was consciously constructed to reflect certain assumptions—including an idea that certain definitions inherently violate peoplehood's internal boundaries and go beyond the acceptable meanings of the term. As a result, the term is not neutral. The escape velocity needed to redefine peoplehood may be too great to salvage that terminology. However, it is not too late to salvage Jewish collectivity itself.

Jewishhood provides a terminological and conceptual model potentially more effective and more consistent with contemporary realities than peoplehood. Jewish communal policy shaped by Jewishhood projects, rather than peoplehood, might undermine some specific strategies for galvanizing peoplehood currently supported by American and Israeli institutions, but placing pressures on institutions to change is not the same as advocating the end of everything that we currently know as peoplehood. The ultimate goal of building a sense of shared connection and co-membership in a group that transcends time and place remains the aim; the optimal path, however, and the institutions necessary to reach toward that objective, may look quite different than the contemporary Jewish communal landscape. Jewishhood would likely not, in fact, immediately bolster support for the Federation movement or positively transform attitudes among American Jews toward Israel. But refocusing the conversation with new terminology and emphases might spark a revitalization of Jewish collective life and institutions—perhaps even to the level of creativity, growth, and innovation that accompanied the emergence of Jewish peoplehood in the last century. It is only in the context of the acknowledgment that Jewish peoplehood is indeed a relatively new and thus negotiable concept—open to reinvention and transformation—that a workable vision of collectivity can emerge and function as an essential part of the wide expanse of Jewishness.

Jewish studies as a field has a potentially significant role to play in shaping the direction of Jewish peoplehood on both a theoretical and practical dimension. The role of scholars in what is now called Jewish studies has historically focused on establishing the study of Jews and Judaism within academia more generally. Jewish studies emerged as its own field on American college campuses in the second half of the twentieth century, successfully making the case that it deserved a place in academia alongside the study of other ancient cultures and modern ethnicities. Jewish studies, like other academic fields, did not conceive of its role as directly contributing to the communal conversation about Jewish identity in America.[25] Although the field, especially its professorships, centers, and training programs, has long enjoyed the financial support of philanthropic individuals and entities committed in one way or another to the Jewish future, an applied model of Jewish studies would have threatened the academic prestige of Jewish studies and risked marginalizing scholars from their broader disciplines and areas of interest.

Today, the relationship between scholarship and community is evolving. Changes in higher education, especially for large public universities whose state funding has been cut significantly, have lead to new challenges such as less funding for the humanities and reduced resources for small programs like Jewish studies. But one of the interesting changes has been the shift toward public engagement as an acceptable, and even encouraged, aspect of academic scholarship and of the service responsibilities of professors. The application of scholarship to pressing communal needs, in areas such as K–12 education, cultural programming, and public discourse, has become an increasingly important facet of many universities' mission. These changed circumstances create an opening for a wider range of Jewish studies academics—especially those whose work is relevant to, but has been largely or entirely absent from, the peoplehood conversation—to integrate their role as scholars with that of community researchers, public intellectuals, and engaged participants in Jewish communal life.

This opening for rethinking and invigorating the role of Jewish studies vis-à-vis the Jewish community and the landscape of Jewish peoplehood could not come at a more important moment. The Jewish community in America faces an unprecedented degree of polarization and internal tension over attitudes toward Israel, religious practice, and philanthropic priorities. Peoplehood serves to tape together the various factions to maintain the ideal of unity. But the factions are only spinning further apart, often propelled by longstanding institutions with a vested interest in preserving their economic stability, political agenda, and relevance against a rapidly changing American Jewish landscape. Obviously, the greater involvement of Jewish studies scholars in communal conversations will not alone overcome the increasingly conflicting Jewish visions splintering the Jewish communities. But Jewish studies academics and the programs of which they are part, at hundreds of universities across North America and globally, have a unique contribution to make by addressing key areas of fragmentation in a sophisticated and informed way rather than simply buttressing the rhetoric of peoplehood by any means.

First, as discussed earlier, Jewish studies has made significant contributions to providing a more critical appreciation for the historical and contemporary expressions of Jewish collectivity. In particular, the study of Jewish nationalism, cultural history, and feminism has provided a fundamentally different view of Jewish collectivity that is historically contextual, critically researched, and nonessentialist in its claims. This scholarship will be crucial to help bridge the divide I suggested in the previous chapter between those concerned with metrics, boundaries, and political unity and those critical of the claims of national or ethnic claims. Many Jewish studies scholars can translate between the divergent perspectives on group articulated by communal supporters of peoplehood and academic critiques of their claims.

Second, Jewish studies programs have the ability, and indeed the mission, to bring diverse voices into conversations about complex issues without drawing red lines between views that are inside or outside the comfort zone of particular religious, political, or communal institutions. Academics and our work can help foster and be part of civil discourse between Jewish positions, a discourse that at times has been eclipsed by the desire to hear only those whose views fall within a predefined spectrum. The academic setting in which many of us find ourselves provides a kind of freedom and financial stability not often enjoyed by other Jewish professionals. This is particularly important as, increasingly, a small number of philanthropists and communal leaders have a disproportionate say about what is, and is not, acceptable in Jewish public discourse. In the contemporary context, attempting a sense of unity (or achieving it for a smaller subsection of the community) by preventing voices outside the tent from entering will need give way to an appreciation of the broad range of Jewish opinions that make up the very diverse Jewish community around the world. While campuses and Jewish studies programs also have to keep communal opinions in mind, the university remains one of the few places dedicated, at least in theory, to the value of an open exchange of ideas precisely as the basis for building community.

Third, Jewish studies scholarship contains one of the most important concentrations of knowledge about Jews and Judaism in the landscape of the Jewish people. The tremendous growth of Jewish studies over the last four decades has both concentrated and multiplied the intellectual resources of American Jewish life. This could be the first time in Jewish history when such a large cadre of Jewish scholars is disconnected from the community whose texts, practices, language, and history it studies. The success of Jewish studies has taken some of the most knowledgeable voices—with training in a wide variety of fields and disciplines, both classically Jewish and unquestionably academic—outside of Jewish professional roles or leadership positions. The concentration of their knowledge in an ivory tower takes these voices outside of the communal conversation. As a result, so many with a vested interest in critical understandings that might challenge simplistic visions of the past and present are structurally removed from, keep themselves removed from, are excluded from communal conversations among the very population with which we are concerned, and separated from the public intellectuals (including a small subset of Jewish studies academics) who are part of those conversations.

Finally, Jewish studies is on the frontline of each wave of the new generation of young adults engaging with individual and group identity in new ways. Working with students in our classrooms provides regular reminders of that engagement and opportunities to observe and participate in it, and to explore with them new directions and frontiers in thinking about Jews and Judaism. That encounter is a source of valuable information. In the classroom and in our offices, we see the questions young Jewish adults ask, the issues they bring to their learning—and often the frustrations with the institutions and programs that currently serve (or don't serve) young Jews. Few other Jewish professionals have the chance to work with them so intensively over such a long period of time while they think about and work on their connection to Jewishness, past, present, and future.

Certainly there are Jewish studies scholars, both Jewish and non-Jewish, who don't see their role as contributing their expertise, scholarly perspective, and insider/outsider role in the Jewish communal space to shaping peoplehood in thought and practice. I make no assumption here about any individual's level of interest, and no judgment about any lack thereof; an academic career is perfectly valid—and sufficiently demanding—unto itself. But where there is a communal desire to engage with it, the work of any scholar can be brought to bear on the Jewish communal conversation, even if she isn't interested in speaking at the General Assembly of Jewish Federations of North America or going on the circuit of synagogue adult education programs. More importantly, the changing landscape of higher education, especially an increasing interest in demonstrating its applied value beyond campus, will allow those scholars who are interested in making a more explicit communal impact to see that doing so is not antithetical to but part of their role within Jewish studies. If the Jewish peoplehood conversation is able to widen and even transform its own mission, and to make a place for the full range of Jewish studies scholarship as part of that conversation, the field's alternative (and highly relevant) view of peoplehood's ongoing evolution (rather than its timeless nature) will immeasurably enrich both the Jewish present and future itself, and the ability of that conversation to meet the challenges of the global era.

Notes

INTRODUCTION: A DECEPTIVELY SIMPLE KEY WORD

1. "A Portrait of Jewish Americans," Pew Research Center, 2013, http://www.pewforum.org/2013/10/01/jewish-american-beliefs-attitudes-culture-survey/.

2. Jewish peoplehood, peoplehood, and Jewish people are not italicized in the book. The key words' meaning, and their status as words, are too closely linked to distinguish uniformly.

3. See Susan M. Kardos, "Jewish Day Schools and Their Future Place in American Jewish Life," *Journal of Jewish Communal Service* 85 (2010): 84–87.

4. There was even a proposal to rename the Jewish Agency for Israel as the Foundation of the Jewish People. See Stephen G. Donshik, "The Foundation for the Jewish People," *Journal of Jewish Communal Service* 88 (2013): 57–62.

5. Jerold S. Auerbach makes the point that these popular slogans illustrate the shift in American Jewish life from defining the shared content of Judaism as a religious tradition to unity grounded in non-religious principles. See Jerold S. Auerbach, *Are We One? Jewish Identity in the United States and Israel* (New Brunswick, NJ: Rutgers University Press, 2001). Other literature on these popular Jewish communal terms includes Melvin Urofsky, *We Are One! American Jewry and Israel* (Garden City, NY: Anchor Press 1978); Judith Elizur, "The Fracturing of the Jewish Self Image: The End of 'We Are One'?," *Israel Affairs* 8 (2001): 14–30; Jonathan D. Sarna, "The Secret of Jewish Continuity," *Commentary* 98 (1994): 55–58; Zvi Bekerman and Marc Silverman, "The Corruption of Culture and Education by the Nation State: The Case of Liberal Jews' Discourse on Jewish Continuity," *Journal of Modern Jewish Studies* 2 (2003): 19–34.

6. An overview of various responses to the Pew survey can be found in Jonathan Tobin, "Special Report: American Jews Respond to Pew," *Commentary* 136:5 (2013): 4–5. See also "After #Jewish America Survey, What Do We Do?," *Jewish Daily Forward*, October 3, 2013, http://forward.com/articles/184954/after-jewishamerica-survey-what-do-we-do/?p=all, accessed May 13, 2014; Theodore Sasson, "New Analysis of Pew Data: Children of Intermarriage Increasingly Identify as Jews," *Tablet Magazine*, November 11, 2013, http://www.tabletmag.com/jewish-news-and-politics/151506/young-jews-opt-in, accessed April 16, 2014.

7. See Sergio Della Pergola, *Jewish Demography and Peoplehood* (Jerusalem: Jewish People Policy Planning Institute, 2008); Daniel Gordis, "From a Jewish People to a

Jewish Religion: A Shifting American Jewish Weltanschauung and Its Implications for Israel," *Israel Studies* 17 (2012): 102–110; Steven Cohen and Jack Wertheimer, "Whatever Happened to the Jewish People?," *Commentary Magazine* 121 (2006): 33; Alan Hoffman, "Jewish Peoplehood: From Vision to Reality," *Journal of Jewish Communal Service* 85 (2010): 15–19.

8. Some of the recent scholarship on Jewish peoplehood includes Menachem Revivi and Ezra Kopelowitz, eds., *Jewish Peoplehood: Change and Challenges* (Boston: Academic Studies Press, 2009); Shlomi Ravid and Varda Rafaeli, *Jewish Peoplehood Education: Framing the Field* (Israel: Center for Peoplehood Education, 2011); Alexander Yakobson, "Jewish Peoplehood and the Jewish State, How Unique?—A Comparative Perspective," *Israel Studies* 13 (2008): 1–27. See also the collection of essays in Shlomi Ravid, ed., *Jewish Peoplehood Papers*, vol. 1 (New York: United Jewish Communities, 2007); Shlomi Ravid, ed., *Jewish Peoplehood Papers*, vol. 3 (Israel: School for Jewish Peoplehood Research, 2008); Shlomi Ravid, ed., *Jewish Peoplehood Papers*, vols. 4–6 (Israel: Jewish Peoplehood–The HUB, 2009–2010); Shlomi Ravid, ed., *Jewish Peoplehood Papers*, vols. 7–14 (Israel: Center for Jewish Peoplehood Education, 2012–2014).

9. Leonid Nevzlin, *Jewish Peoplehood Papers* 4 (Israel: Jewish Peoplehood–The HUB, 2009), 4–5. Nevzlin is founder of the Nadav Fund (an Israeli foundation dedicated to Jewish peoplehood) and the chairman of the board and major supporter of the Museum of the Jewish Diaspora in Tel Aviv.

10. Academic Raymond Williams popularized the study of key words as a tool for social and cultural analysis. See Raymond Williams, *Keywords: A Vocabulary of Culture and Society* (Oxford: Oxford University Press, 1985).

11. See, for example, Naomi W. Cohen, *The Americanization of Zionism, 1897–1948* (Hanover, NH: Brandeis University Press, 2003).

12. My argument challenges the scholarly assumption that views Jewish peoplehood as "replacing 'nationhood' with 'peoplehood.'" See, for example, Barry Chazan et al., "The Connection of Israel Education to Jewish Education," *Israel Education Research Briefs* (Stanford, CA: Consortium for Applied Studies in Jewish Education, 2013). The argument that progenitors of peoplehood in the United States, such as Mordecai Kaplan, represent a break from European Zionism can be traced to Arthur Goren's work. See Arthur Goren, *New York Jews and the Quest for Community* (New York: Columbia University Press, 1979).

13. John Lie, *Modern Peoplehood* (Cambridge, MA: Harvard University Press, 2004); Rogers Smith, *Stories of Peoplehood* (Cambridge: Cambridge University Press, 2003).

14. Lie, *Modern Peoplehood*, 49.

15. See, for example, Arnold Eisen, "Four Questions Concerning Peoplehood—And Just as Many Answers," in *Jewish Peoplehood: Change and Challenge*, ed. Ezra Kopelowitz (Boston: Academic Studies Press, 2008).

16. Paul Mendes-Flohr and Arthur Cohen, *Contemporary Jewish Religious Thought* (New York: Free Press, 1988).

17. One exception is Shlomo Sand, *The Invention of the Jewish People* (London: Verso, 2009).

18. See David Aberbach, "Zionist Patriotism in Europe, 1897–1942: Ambiguities in Jewish Nationalism," *International History Review* 31 (2009): 268; Irving M. Zeitlin, *Jews: The Making of a Diaspora People* (Cambridge: Polity Press, 2012). See chapter 2 for a further discussion of scholarly approaches to Jewish peoplehood.

19. See Cohen, *Americanization*; Ezra Mendelsohn, *On Modern Jewish Politics* (Oxford: Oxford University Press, 1993).

CHAPTER 1 — TERMS OF DEBATE: JEWISH NATIONHOOD AND AMERICAN PEOPLEHOOD

1. For a recent analysis of the Soviet Jewry movement, and its impact on American Jewish life, see Gal Bekerman, *When They Come for Us We'll Be Gone: The Epic Struggle to Save Soviet Jewry* (New York: Mariner Books, 2010). See also Shaul Kelner, "The Bureaucratization of Ritual Innovation: The Festive Cycle of the American Soviet Jewry Movement," *Jewish Cultural Studies* 3 (2011): 360–391.

2. Steven Cohen and Jack Wertheimer, "Whatever Happened to the Jewish People?" *Commentary* 121 (2006): 33–37.

3. Ibid., 33. Emphasis mine.

4. Cohen and Wertheimer use the term "Jewish people" rather than "peoplehood" in their title, but—as I have argued in the introduction to this volume—these terms are so intimately connected that notions of peoplehood inevitably shape understandings of the Jewish people in this article and elsewhere.

5. Cohen and Wertheimer, "Whatever Happened," 33.

6. See Introduction, note 1.

7. For a discussion of the proposal, which was rejected, to obtain official recognition of *amiyut* from the Academy of the Hebrew Language, see Menachem Revivi and Ezra Kopelowitz, eds., *Jewish Peoplehood: Change and Challenge* (Brighton, MA: Academic Studies Press, 2008), xvi.

8. *Even Shoshan Hebrew-Hebrew Dictionary* (Jerusalem: Hamilon Hechadash, 2009).

9. Francis Brown et al., *Brown-Driver-Briggs Hebrew and English Lexicon* (New York: Snowball Publishing, 2010).

10. See Eric Goldstein, *The Price of Whiteness: Jews, Race, and American Identity* (Princeton, NJ: Princeton University Press, 2007).

11. See chapter 3 for a full discussion of the decision to name the Jewish state "Israel" in 1948. The doctrine of Christian supersessionism also used the name "New Israel" to refer to the Christian church.

12. For an analysis of the language of Jewish collectivity in the Zionist context, see Yosef Gorny, "Between Center and Centrality: The Zionist Perception of Klal Yisrael," in *Identities in an Era of Globalization and Multiculturalism*, ed. Eliezer Ben Rafael (Leiden: Brill, 2008), 25–35.

13. "Hood," *Merriam-Webster.com*, http://www.merriam-webster.com/dictionary/hood, accessed July 10, 2014.

14. Recent Jewish studies scholarship highlights a cultural matrix that demonstrates how closely connected biblical culture was to its surrounding neighbors. See David Biale, ed., *The Cultures of the Jews* (New York: Schocken Books, 2002); Shaye Cohen, "Was Judaism in Antiquity a Missionary Religion?," in *Jewish Assimilation, Acculturation and Accommodation*, ed. Menachem Mor (Lanham, MD: University Press of America, 1991), 14–23; Christine Hayes, *Gentile Impurities and Jewish Identities: Intermarriage and Conversion from the Bible to the Talmud* (Oxford: Oxford University Press, 2002), 188; Shaye Cohen, *The Beginnings of Jewishness* (Berkeley: University of California Press, 2001); Moshe Halbertal, "Coexisting with the Enemy: Jews and Pagans in the Mishnah," in *Tolerance and Intolerance in Early Judaism and Christianity*, ed. G. N. Stanton and G. G. Stroumsa (New York: Cambridge University Press, 1998), 159–172; Francesca Trivellato, *Familiarity with Strangers: The Sephardic Diaspora, Livorno, and Cross-Cultural Trade in the Early Modern Period* (New Haven, CT: Yale University Press, 2012); Gershon Hundert, *Jews in Poland-Lithuania in the Eighteenth Century: A Genealogy of Modernity* (Berkeley: University of California Press, 2006); Mark Cohen, *Under Crescent and Cross: The Jews in the Middle Ages* (Princeton, NJ: Princeton University Press, 2008).

15. The primary boundary marker in the Hebrew Bible, Talmud scholar Christine Hayes argues, is not ethnic in nature, but reflects certain theological criteria to shore up monotheist belief and practice. Christine Hayes, "The 'Other' in Rabbinic Literature," in *The Cambridge Companion to the Talmud and Rabbinic Literature*, ed. Charlotte Fonrobert and Martin Jaffee (Cambridge: Cambridge University Press, 2007), 251.

16. Scholar Richard Wright argues that the Bible, unlike other Near Eastern sources, is not written to emphasize the role of political institutions or land in defining the collective group. Instead, he writes, it makes a "clear distinction between the nation and the state." Richard Wright, "The Commemoration of Defeat and the Formation of a Nation in the Hebrew Bible," *Prooftexts* 29 (2009): 433–473.

17. The most comprehensive overview of the varieties of modern Jewish political ideologies and movements can be found in Ezra Mendelsohn, *On Modern Jewish Politics* (Oxford: Oxford University Press, 1993).

18. For an in-depth analysis of the process of emancipation, and its impact on Jewish history, see Jacob Katz, *Out of the Ghetto: The Social Background* (Syracuse: Syracuse University Press, 1998); Pierre Birnbaum and Ira Katznelson, eds., *Paths*

of Emancipation: Jews, States, and Citizenship (Princeton, NJ: Princeton University Press, 1995).

19. The role of nationalism on modern Jewish political ideologies in general is well documented. See Mendelssohn, *On Modern Jewish Politics*. However, nationalism's impact on Jewish thought, especially by religious thinkers committed to disconnecting Judaism and nationalism, is not underscored. For example, Leora Batnitzky convincingly traces the emergence of Judaism as a religion in the context of European religious thought, but does not consider the impact of ideas of nationalism on definitions of Judaism as a religion. See Leora Batnitzky, *How Judaism Became a Religion* (Princeton, NJ: Princeton University Press, 2013).

20. Integrating the study of peoplehood into the national paradigm reflects an important trend in recent Jewish historiography to trace the influence of Jewish nationalism to diasporic and non-statist expressions of Jewish collectivity. Several recent books have highlighted the roll of nationalism in diaspora Jewish politics. See David Myers, *Between Jew and Arab: The Lost Voice of Simon Rawidowicz* (Waltham, MA: Brandeis University Press, 2009); Joshua Shanes, *Diaspora Nationalism and Jewish Identity in Habsburg Galicia* (Cambridge: Cambridge University Press, 2012); Joshua M. Karlip, *The Tragedy of a Generation* (Cambridge, MA: Harvard University Press, 2013); Jess Olson, *Nathan Birnbaum and Jewish Modernity* (Stanford, CA: Stanford University Press, 2013); Simon Rabinovitch, ed., *Jews & Diaspora Nationalism: Writings on Jewish Peoplehood in Europe and the United States* (Waltham, MA: Brandeis University Press, 2012).

21. See Noam Pianko, *Zionism and the Roads Not Taken* (Bloomington: Indiana University Press, 2010), 26–60; Erez Manela, *The Wilsonian Moment: Self-Determination and the International Origins of Anticolonial Nationalism* (Oxford: Oxford University Press, 2009).

22. For example, scholar of nationalism Ernest Gellner defines nationalism as "primarily a political principle, which holds that the political and the national unit should be congruent." Ernest Gellner, *Nations and Nationalism* (Ithaca, NY: Cornell University Press, 1983), 1.

23. Ernest Renan, "What Is a Nation?," in Becoming National: A Reader, ed. Geoff Eley and Ronald Suny (Oxford: Oxford University Press, 1996), 41–55.

24. See Karlip, *The Tragedy of a Generation*. For a discussion of *Stamm* in the German Jewish context, see Till van Rahden, "Germans of the Jewish Stamm: Visions of Community between Nationalism and Particularism, 1850 to 1933," in *German History from the Margins*, ed. Neil Gregor et al. (Bloomington: Indiana University Press, 2006), 27–48.

25. Uriel Weinreich defines *folk* as "ethnic group" or "people." Uriel Weinreich, *Modern English-Yiddish Yiddish-English Dictionary* (New York: Schocken, 1987), 309. The *Langenscheidt German-English English-German Dictionary* (New York: Pocket Books, 2009), 312, defines *Volk* as "people" or "nation." For a detailed description

of the meanings of the Russian *narod*, see Alexey Miller, "Natsiia, Narod, Narodnost," in "Russia in the 19th Century: Some Introductory Remarks to the History of Concepts," *Jahrbücher für Geschichte Oseuropas* 56 (2008): 379–390.

26. Van Rahden, "Germans of the Jewish Stamm."

27. Ibid., 31.

28. Original source: Adolf Jellinek, *Der Judische Stamm: Ethnographische Studien* (Vienna: Herzfeld and Bauer, 1869), 66. Quoted in Marsha L. Rozenblit, "Jewish Identity and the Modern Rabbi: The Cases of Isak Noa Mannheimer, Adolf Jellinek, and Moritz Güdermann in Nineteenth-Century Vienna," *Leo Baeck Institute Year Book* 35 (1990): 116.

29. Van Rahden, "Germans of the Jewish Stamm," 31.

30. Dubnow's essays on Jewish nationalism can be found in Simon Dubnow, *Nationalism and History Essays on Old and New Judaism*, trans. Koppel S. Pinson (New York: World Publishing Company, 1961).

31. See Nathaniel Deutsch, *The Jewish Dark Continent* (Cambridge, MA: Harvard University Press, 2011).

32. Miller, "Natsiia, Narod, Narodnost," 380.

33. Yiddish intellectuals adapted *yidntum* (Jewishness) as a parallel term for the German *Deutschtum* (Germanness); just as Germans had certain cultural values, historical attachments, and ethical ideals, so too did the Jews.

34. See, for example, Benedict Anderson, *Imagined Communities* (London: Verso, 2006); Eric Hobsbawm, *Nations and Nationalism since 1780* (Cambridge: Cambridge University Press, 1990); Anthony D. Smith, *The Ethnic Origins of Nationalism* (Hoboken, NJ: Wiley-Blackwell, 1991).

35. Anderson, *Imagined Communities*, 16. See also Anthony Giddens, *The Consequence of Modernity* (Stanford, CA: Stanford University Press, 1991), 38.

36. See David Kertzer and Dominique Arel, eds., *Census and Identity: The Politics of Race, Ethnicity, and Language in National Censuses* (Cambridge: Cambridge University Press, 2002), 2; James Scott, *Seeing like a State* (New Haven, CT: Yale University Press, 1999), 81–82.

37. For a description of the relationship between nationalism and the politics of race, ethnicity, and language, see Kertzer and Arel, *Census and Identity*, 6.

38. Rogers Brubaker, *Ethnicity without Groups* (Cambridge, MA: Harvard University Press, 2008), 8.

39. The role of racial distinctions in modern Jewish thought and life has been documented by several scholars. See Mitchell Hart, ed., *Jews and Race: Writings on Identity and Difference, 1880–1940* (Waltham, MA: Brandeis University Press, 2011); John M. Efron, *Defenders of the Race: Jewish Doctors and Race Science in Fin-de-Siecle Europe* (New Haven, CT: Yale University Press, 1994); Goldstein, *The Price of Whiteness*.

40. Renan, "What Is a Nation?"

41. See Pianko, *Zionism*, 26–60, for a detailed discussion of the concept of spirit or cultural essence in European Jewish nationalism.

42. Anderson, *Imagined Communities*, 22.

43. Ibid., 13.

44. Ibid., 26.

45. Defining the national essence as the shared bond linking the Jewish people through time and space also accompanied a corollary shift toward secular history in Jewish thinking, as detailed by historian Yosef Hayim Yerushalmi in his influential book *Zakhor: Jewish History and Jewish Memory* (Seattle: University of Washington Press, 1982). See also Ismar Schorsch, *From Text to Context: The Turn to History in Modern Judaism* (Waltham, MA: Brandeis University Press, 2003).

46. See Rabinovitch, *Jews and Diaspora Nationalism*; Karlip, *The Tragedy of a Generation*; Myers, *Between Jew and Arab*.

47. For more on the varieties of early twentieth-century Zionisms, see Pianko, *Zionism*.

48. Dmitri Shumsky, "Medina b'toch medina? Tziyonut, Hagdara Aztmait, v'imperia rav-leumit," unpublished lecture delivered on December 29, 2013, Hebrew University of Jerusalem.

49. Eugene Kohn, "The Reconstructionist Summer Conference," *Reconstructionist* 8:11 (October 2, 1942): 16–17.

50. Ibid.

51. Mordecai Kaplan, "In Reply to Dr. Gordis," *Reconstructionist* 8:14 (November 27, 1942): 15.

52. Mordecai Kaplan, *The Future of the American Jew* (New York: Macmillan, 1948).

53. While "peoplehood" did not appear in the third edition (1961) of *Webster's New International Dictionary*, it did appear in the 1969 edition, demonstrating the emergence in the American mainstream of a new English-language term.

54. For example, Rabbi Isaac Mayer Wise called his paper the *Israelite* when it was founded in 1854 (it was later renamed the *American Israelite*), and called the effort to create a centralized organization for American Jewish congregations in 1873 the "Union of American Hebrew Congregations."

55. Moses Seixas refers to Jews as "the children of the Stock of Abraham" in his letter of welcome to George Washington. "Correspondence Between Washington and Jewish Citizens," *Proceedings of the American Jewish Historical Society* 3 (1895): 90–91.

56. For an excellent account of the role that race played in American Jewish history, see Goldstein, *The Price of Whiteness*.

57. This contrasted with the connotations of genetics and descent that were reflected, for example, in restrictive immigration legislation of the 1920s that viewed Jewish immigrants as a problematic racial group.

58. Horace Kallen, "Democracy versus the Melting Pot: A Study of American Nationality: Part I and Part II," *Nation* 100 (February 18, 1915): 190–194, and (February 25, 1915): 217–220. For an analysis of Kallen's thought, see Daniel Greene, *The Jewish Origins of Cultural Pluralism* (Bloomington: Indiana University Press, 2011); Noam Pianko, "'The True Liberalism of Zionism': Horace Kallen, Jewish Nationalism, and the Limits of American Pluralism," *American Jewish History* 94 (2008): 299–329.

59. Arthur Goren, *New York Jews and the Quest for Community* (New York: Columbia University Press, 1979), 48.

60. Kallen, "Democracy versus the Melting Pot," 220.

61. See Greene, *Jewish Origins*; Werner Sollors, *The Invention of Ethnicity* (New York: Oxford University Press, 1989).

62. Mordecai Kaplan, *Judaism as a Civilization* (New York: Macmillan, 1934).

63. Mordecai Kaplan, "Judaism and Nationality," *Maccabean* (August 1909): 61–63; Mordecai Kaplan, *The Religion of Ethical Nationhood: Judaism's Contribution to World Peace* (New York: Macmillan, 1970). For an analysis of Kaplan's early interest in nationalism, see Noam Pianko, "Reconstructing Judaism, Reconstructing America: The Sources and Functions of Mordecai Kaplan's 'Civilization,'" *Jewish Social Studies* 12 (2006): 39–55.

64. Kaplan, *Future of the American Jew*, 125.

65. See, for example, Kaplan, *Judaism as a Civilization*, 232, 234, 239.

66. See, for example, Kaplan's diary entry, February 15, 1939, Mordecai Menahem Kaplan, 1881, File ARC 65, Kaplan Diaries and Papers, Jewish Theological Seminary, New York City, box 3, volume 8.

67. See Manela, *Wilsonian Moment*.

68. "World Jewish Congress Inevitable: Will Appeal to Masses for Support Says Wise," JTA News, September 27, 1932, http://www.jta.org/1932/09/27/archive/world-jewish-congress-inevitable-will-appeal-to-masses-for-support-says-wise, accessed September 6, 2013.

69. "Jewish Congress Hailed by Leaders," *New York Times*, September 26, 1932, 15.

70. Theodore Herzl, *The Jewish State* (Minneapolis: Filiquarian Publishing, 2006), 11.

71. For more about Wise's biography, see Mark A. Raider. "The Aristocrat and the Democrat: Louis Marshall, Stephen S. Wise, and the Challenge of American Jewish Leadership," *American Jewish History* 94 (2008): 91–113.

72. "Jewish Congress Hailed by Leaders," 15. Wise himself had been at the Second Zionist Congress in nearby Basel in 1898.

73. Morris Lazaron, "The American Jew: His Problems and His Psychology," *Journal of Religion* 1 (1921): 378–390. Lazaron later founded the American Council for Judaism, a non-Zionist organization.

74. Ibid., 383.

75. Ibid., 384.

76. Ibid., 383.

77. Ibid., 384.

78. Kallen, "Democracy."

79. Lazaron, "The American Jew," 390.

80. Ibid., 385.

81. For a detailed history of the American Council for Judaism, see Thomas Kolsky, *Jews against Zionism* (Philadelphia: Temple University Press, 1992).

82. "Judaism Message Held World Force," *New York Times*, June 17, 1934, 8N.

83. Kaplan, "Judaism and Nationality."

84. An anonymous 1941 editorial in the *Reconstructionst*, a journal that Kaplan edited, argued, "The Jewish people is one . . . as expressed by Theodor Herzl, 'Wir sind ein Volk, *Ein Volk*.'" "Who Should Call the Conference on Post-War Problems?" *Reconstructionist* 14 (1941): 4.

85. Mordecai Kaplan, *Judaism as a Civilization*, 2nd ed. (New York: Macmillan, 1957), ix.

86. Eugene Kohn, "The Reconstructionist Summer Conference," *Reconstructionist* 8 (1942): 16–17.

87. Samuel Dinin, "The Jewish Commonwealth," *Reconstructionist* 10 (1944): 15.

88. See Allan C. Brownfield, "An Early Council Leader's Previously Unpublished Work," http://www.acjna.org/acjna/articles_detail.aspx?id=549, accessed September 11, 2013.

89. For example, Morris Waldman, executive secretary to the American Jewish Committee, opposed Jewish nationalism. Thanks to James Loeffler for pointing this out.

90. See Elmer Berger, *The Jewish Dilemma* (New York: Devin-Adair Company, 1945).

91. Milton Steinberg, "The Statement of the Non-Zionist Rabbis: A Critique," *Reconstructionist* 8 (1942): 13.

92. Ibid.

93. "Jewish State Held a World Problem," *New York Times*, October 17, 1942, 13.

94. Kaplan, "In Reply," 15.

95. Mordecai Kaplan and Samuel Dinin, "Reconstructionism as Both a Challenging and Unifying Influence," *Reconstructionist* 10 (1944): 16–22.

96. Mel Scult argues that Kaplan did indeed put God at the center of his religious worldview. See Mel Scult, *The Radical American Judaism of Mordecai Kaplan* (Bloomington: Indiana University Press, 2014).

97. Gary Gerstle, *The American Crucible: Race and Nation in the Twentieth Century* (Princeton, NJ: Princeton University Press, 2002).

98. Elihu Burritt, *The Western and Eastern Questions of Europe* (Hartford, CT: Hamersly & Co., 1871), 41.

99. See Arnold Eisen, *The Chosen People in America: A Study in Religious Ideology* (Bloomington: Indiana University Press, 1983).

100. See ibid.

101. Mordecai Kaplan, *The New Zionism* (New York: Theodore Herzl Foundation, 1955), 107.

102. Kaplan, *Judaism as a Civilization*, ix.

103. Kaplan, *New Zionism*, 108.

104. Simon Rawidowicz, *State of Israel, Diaspora and Jewish Continuity* (Waltham, MA: Brandeis University Press, 1998).

105. An analysis of the terms "Jewish people" and "Jewish nation" in Google's Ngram of English-language publications reveals a wider switch from the language of Jewish nation to that of Jewish people beginning in the 1880s. The gap in the frequencies of these two terms in published references to the Jewish collective grows significantly during the 1930s and 1940s. By 1947, references to the Jewish people far exceed those to the Jewish nation—a trend that remains steady into the twenty-first century. Google Ngram with the parameters "Jewish People" and "Jewish Nation" between the years 1800 and 2000, accessed January 11, 2014. Jean-Baptiste Michel, Yuan Kui Shen, Aviva Presser Aiden, Adrian Veres, Matthew K. Gray, William Brockman, The Google Books Team, Joseph P. Pickett, Dale Hoiberg, Dan Clancy, Peter Norvig, Jon Orwant, Steven Pinker, Martin A. Nowak, and Erez Lieberman Aiden, "Quantitative Analysis of Culture Using Millions of Digitized Books," *Science* 331:6014 (January 14, 2011): 176–182; published online December 16, 2010, http://www.sciencemag.org/content/331/6014/176.

106. The number of references to Jewish peoplehood in English-language books in Google's sample grows from .0000000220 percent to .0000080021788 percent. Google Ngram with the parameters "Jewish peoplehood" between the years 1940 and 1959, accessed December 4, 2014, https://books.google.com/ngrams.

107. See, for example, R. E. Gilmore, "'Peoplehood' and Process,' Review of Mordecai M. Kaplan," *Christian Century* 69 (1952): 1031.

108. Jack Cohen, "New Emphases in Jewish Education," *Journal of Jewish Education* 26 (1955); Mortimer Cohen, "A Layman's Guide to Modern Religions," review of *The Great Religions of the Modern World*, ed. Edward J. Jurji, *Jewish Quarterly Review* 38 (1947): 104.

109. Kaplan, *New Zionism*, 112.

110. Mordecai Kaplan, "The Future of Zionism and Its Role in Judaism," *Proceedings: Biennial Convention of the United Synagogue of America*, 1959 (New York: United Synagogue, 1959), 55.

111. Jerome Kohn and Ron H. Feldman, eds., *The Jewish Writings of Hannah Arendt* (New York: Schocken Books, 2007), 347. Special thanks to Ron Feldman for pointing out this reference to me.

112. Ibid., 466.

113. Ibid., 467.

114. Ibid.

115. Irving Spiegel, "Council Attacks 'Jewish Vote' Idea," *New York Times*, April 7, 1952, 22.

116. "Zionism's 4-Year Plan," American Council for Judaism, http://www.bjpa.org/Publications/downloadFile.cfm?FileID=16822, accessed February 14, 2014.

117. "America-Israel: Common Frontier of Democracy," Zionist Organization of America Report, 1964. http://www.bjpa.org/Publications/downloadFile.cfm?FileID=16837, accessed February 14, 2014.

118. Ibid., 17.

119. *Aliyah* literally means "ascent" and serves in the Jewish liturgical tradition as a term linked to the honor of blessing the Torah reading. While aliyah does have precedent in Jewish history as the term for pilgrimage to the Land of Israel, the adoption of this value-laden term in Modern Hebrew to refer to Jewish immigrants emphasized Zionism's belief that moving to the Land of Israel was a social, cultural, and political elevation.

120. "Rabbis Criticize Foes of Zionism," *New York Times*, May 5, 1963, 62.

121. "Zionists Publish Brochure on 'Persecution' in Soviet Union," *New York Times*, May 8, 1966, 42.

122. The relative frequency of "peoplehood" and "Jewish peoplehood" in the corpus of English-language books digitized by Google remains quite consistent from the 1920s until 1965. Google Ngram with the parameters "peoplehood" and "Jewish peoplehood" between the years 1920 and 2010, accessed January 11, 2014, https://books.google.com/ngrams. From that point onward the frequency of peoplehood as a distinct English word dramatically increases, while the use of Jewish peoplehood remains quite consistent. Below I argue that this indicates a notable rise in the currency of peoplehood as a general term in the English language immediately following the publication of Milton Gordon, *Assimilation in American Life: The Role of Race, Religion, and National Origins* (New York: Oxford University Press, 1964).

123. Julius Drachsler, *Democracy and Assimilation: The Blending of Immigrant Heritages in America* (New York: Macmillan, 1920); Oscar Handlin, *The Uprooted*

(New York: Little, Brown, 1951); Nathan Glazer, *Beyond the Melting Pot* (Cambridge, MA: MIT Press, 1963); Will Herberg, *Protestant-Catholic-Jew* (Garden City, NY: Anchor Books, 1955).

124. Gordon, *Assimilation in American Life*.

125. Ibid., 29.

126. Ibid., 26.

127. Ibid., 24.

128. Ibid., 239.

129. Ibid., 37.

130. Ibid., 77.

131. Ibid., 158.

132. Milton Gordon, *The Scope of Sociology* (New York: Oxford University Press, 1988), 11.

133. Gordon, *Assimilation in American Life*, 13.

134. Ibid., 10.

135. Martin Marty, "The Skeleton of Religion in America," *Church History* 41 (1972): 5.

136. African American scholars, such as Alphonso Pinkney and Adolph Reed Jr., quote Gordon's notion of peoplehood in defending their own claims about their "African peoplehood." See Alphonso Pinkney, "The Assimilation of Afro-Americans," *Black Scholar* 1 (1969): 37.

137. "Powell Says He's Trying to Channel Black Power into Constructive Force," *New York Times*, September 8, 1966, 35.

138. Stokely Carmichael, *Stokely Speaks* (Chicago: Chicago Review Press, 2007), 128.

139. Jerry Hochbaum, "The Federation Executive and Our Contemporary Crises," paper presented at the Intermediate Cities Institute of the Council of Jewish Federations and Welfare Funds, August 4, 1968, http://www.bjpa.org/Publications/downloadFile.cfm?FileID=4218.

140. Irving Spiegel, "Drive by Negroes for Identity Studied by Jewish Women," *New York Times*, March 5, 1969, 25.

141. Kaplan, *Judaism*, 230.

142. David Hollinger, *Post-Ethnic America: Beyond Multiculturalism* (New York: Basic Books, 2006).

143. Hochbaum, "The Federation Executive."

144. Mary Waters, *Ethnic Options: Choosing Identities in America* (Berkeley: University of California Press, 1990), 147.

145. See Goldstein, *Price of Whiteness*. Goldstein describes the paradox that while Jews wanted to be considered white, at the same time, affirming Jews as racially white left them without a language for affirming how they were different from other groups.

CHAPTER 2 — STATE OF THE QUESTION: ENDURING ENTITY OR CONSTRUCTED COMMUNITY

1. The museum has updated its Hebrew logo to include both the previous name, Beit Hatfutsot (Museum of the Diaspora), and the new name, Muzayon Am Hayehudi. It appears that the museum has decided to retain both names going forward—a relevant decision discussed below.

2. The reference to Anderson's work was indirect. However, I did find another example by a museum curator that references Anderson directly. See Shelly Keder, "Ready, Steady, Go: Midrashic Applications of Jewish Peoplehood Education," in *The Peoplehood Papers*, vol. 1 (New York: United Jewish Communities, 2007), 3. A very similar reference is made in the very popular recent text by Erica Brown and Misha Galperin, *The Case for Jewish Peoplehood: Can We Be One?* (Woodstock, VT: Jewish Lights, 2009), 90. The overlapping references to Anderson by members of the small cohort of contemporary peoplehood theorists indicate a conscious effort to integrate this theorist of nationalism into the justification and explanation of Jewish peoplehood.

3. Benedict Anderson, *Imagined Communities* (London: Verso, 2006), 168.

4. Shlomo Sand, *The Invention of the Jewish People* (London: Verso, 2009). For responses to Sand's work, see Derek Penslar, "Shlomo Sand's *The Invention of the Jewish People* and the End of the New History," *Israel Studies* 17 (2012): 156–168.

5. Shlomi Ravid and Varda Rafaeli, *Jewish Peoplehood Education: Framing the Field* (Israel: Center for Peoplehood Education, 2011), 13.

6. http://www.bjpa.org/Publications/search.cfm (search term, Jewish Peoplehood; date range, 1980 to 1996), accessed December 2, 2014.

7. http://www.bjpa.org/Publications/search.cfm (search term, Jewish Peoplehood; date range, 1996 to 2014), accessed December 2, 2014.

8. "What Is Jewish Peoplehood?" in *The Peoplehood Papers*, vol. 1, 1.

9. David Hazony, "The Death of Peoplehood," *Jewish Daily Forward*, July 27, 2011; Steven Bayme and David Harman, *On Jewish Peoplehood* (New York: American Jewish Committee, 2008), 3. One of the early articles that sparked anxiety about peoplehood can be found in Irving Greenberg, "Will There Be One Jewish People by the Year 2000? The Demographics of Separation," *Perspectives* (New York: CLAL, The National Jewish Center for Learning and Leadership 1985).

10. The Jewish People Policy Institute developed a series of dashboards that rank the level of bonds between the Jewish people along a scale from "Declining" to "Thriving." See, for example, "Prioritized Strategies for the Jewish People: Challenges and Opportunities: A Conceptual Framework" (Jerusalem: Jewish People Policy Institute, 2012).

11. In 2010, the Israeli Navy boarded a flotilla of ships that had sailed from Turkey to break through a blockade Israel had placed off the coast of Gaza. Turkey condemned Israel's handling of the situation. Ironically, three years; later, the prime minister of Israel, Benjamin Netanyahu, apologized to Turkey for Israel's mishandling of the flotilla incident and the loss of life that resulted from the raid of the Turkish ship.

12. Brown and Galperin, *The Case for Jewish Peoplehood*, 2.

13. Misha Galperin, "Continuing a Peoplehood Debate," *Jewish Daily Forward*, July 11, 2011.

14. "Board of Governors Content Presentation," http://www.bh.org.il/news-item.aspx?99311, accessed January 20, 2014.

15. See note 2 for examples of references to Anderson.

16. An example of the rhetorical link between Jewish peoplehood and support for a Jewish state can be found in Mordecai Nisan, "In Defense of the Idea of a Jewish State," *Israel Affairs* 19 (2013): 259–272. He writes, "The idea of a Jewish state is rooted in ancient Jewish peoplehood based upon essential features of collective identity and ties to the territorial homeland." See also Shmuel Rosner and Inbal Hakman, *The Challenge of Peoplehood: Strengthening the Attachment of Young American Jews to Israel in the Time of the Distancing Discourse* (Jerusalem: Jewish People Policy Institute, 2012).

17. See chapter 1, note 7.

18. Alan Hoffman, "Israel in Jewish Peoplehood Education," in *The Peoplehood Papers*, vol. 1, 24.

19. For an analysis of trends regarding the relationship between American Jews and Israel, see Steven M. Cohen and Ari Y. Kelman, *Beyond Distancing: Young Adult American Jews and Their Alienation from Israel* (New York: Jewish Identity Project of Reboot, 2007).

20. *The Israeli Diaspora as a Catalyst for Jewish Peoplehood* (Tel Aviv: Reut Institute, 2012).

21. Shlomi Ravid, "Jewish Peoplehood: The Israeli Challenge," *Contact* (2012): 12–13.

22. Exceptions include Aryeh Cohen, "Jewish Peoplehood, Why?," in *The Peoplehood Papers*, vol. 8 (Jerusalem: Jewish Agency, 2010), 5–8; and David Myers, *Rethinking Global Jewish Collectivity in a Post-Statist World* (Jerusalem: Jewish Agency, 2010), 8–12.

23. Jack Wertheimer, *Generation of Change: How Leaders in Their Twenties and Thirties Are Reshaping American Jewish Life* (New York: Avi Chai Foundation, 2010).

24. Ibid., 7, 22.

25. The Russian Jewish experience has exerted an impact all the way up to the leadership of the peoplehood movement. Three of the main proponents of peoplehood are Russian émigrés: Jewish Agency chairperson Natan Sharansky; philanthropist Leonid Nevzlin; and Misha Galperin, president and CEO of Jewish Agency International Development, and, until 2010, an executive in the Jewish Federation system in the United States.

26. Steven M. Cohen, Misha Galperin, and Yoav Shoam, *The Power of Peoplehood: How Commitment to the Jewish People Undergirds Tzedakah for Jewish Causes* (Washington, D.C.: Jewish Federation of Greater Washington, 2009), 14.

27. Jay Michaelson, "Peoplehood: There's No There There," in *The Peoplehood Papers*, vol. 1, 10–12.

28. Daniel Septimus, "The Real Peoplehood Problem," *Jewish Daily Forward*, July 14, 2011; Ruth Messinger, "Debating Peoplehood," *Jewish Daily Forward*, July 22, 2011.

29. The lack of interest in peoplehood among "non-establishment" American Jewish leaders is reported by Jack Wertheimer in *Generation of Change*. There has been one grassroots effort to claim the future of the peoplehood conversation. A group called Kol Dor was created in 2004 with the purpose of stimulating connections among young Jews from around the world. Peoplehood, for Kol Dor, meant an implicit critique of current Israel-diaspora relations and encouraged a break away from a perspective of collectivity rooted in one center and the remaining periphery whose job it was to support and protect the center.

30. John Lie, *Modern Peoplehood* (Cambridge, MA: Harvard University Press, 2004), 12.

31. Hans Kohn, *The Idea of Nationalism* (New York: Macmillan, 1944).

32. For an analysis of the turn to history in modern Jewish thought, see Ismar Schorsch, *From Text to Context: The Turn to History in Modern Judaism* (Waltham, MA: Brandeis University Press, 2003).

33. For an overview of modern social thought, see Patrick Baert and Filipe Carreira Da Silva, *Social Theory in the Twentieth Century and Beyond* (Cambridge: Polity Press, 2010).

34. See Ernest Gellner, *Nations and Nationalism* (Ithaca, NY: Cornell University Press, 1983), 1; Eric Hobsbawm, *Nations and Nationalism since 1780* (Cambridge: Cambridge University Press, 1990).

35. Anthony Smith, *Nations and Nationalism in a Global Era* (Cambridge: Polity, 1995), 6. Other perennialists, such as Aviel Roshwald and Jon Hutchinson, join Smith in highlighting continuities between premodern groups and modern nations. Aviel Roshwald, *The Endurance of Nationalism: Ancient Roots and Modern Dilemmas* (Cambridge: Cambridge University Press, 2006).

36. Smith, *Nations and Nationalism*, 55.

37. See Rogers Brubaker, *Ethnicity without Groups* (Cambridge, MA: Harvard University Press, 2008), 17. Scholar of nationalism Elie Kedourie makes a similar claim: "Nationalists make use of the past in order to subvert the present." Elie Kedourie, *Nationalism*, 4th ed. (Oxford: Wiley-Blackwell, 1993), 71.

38. Hobsbawm, *Nations*, 76.

39. Smith, *Nations and Nationalism*, 65.

40. See, for example, ibid., 53.

41. Ibid.

42. Kedourie, *Nationalism*, 71.

43. Gideon Shimoni, *The Zionist Ideology* (Waltham, MA: Brandeis University Press, 1995).

44. See Sand, *Invention*.

45. One recent example of this possibility is Arie Dubnov, *Isaiah Berlin: The Journey of a Jewish Liberal* (New York: Palgrave Macmillan, 2012).

46. Recent works on globalization include Anthony Giddens, *The Consequences of Modernity* (Stanford, CA: Stanford University Press, 1991); Ulrich Beck, *Cosmopolitan Vision* (Cambridge: Polity, 2006); Saskia Sassen, *Territory, Autonomy, Rights: From Medieval to Global Assemblages* (Princeton, NJ: Princeton University Press, 2008).

47. Giddens, *Consequences*, 13.

48. Beck, *Cosmopolitan Vision*, 18, 33, 68, 85, 87.

49. Ibid., 19.

50. Ibid., 2.

51. Ibid., 73.

52. Giddens, *Consequences*.

53. See also Sassen, *Territory, Autonomy, Rights*, 1.

54. Tony Judt, "Israel: The Alternative," *New York Review of Books*, September 25, 2003.

55. The article elicited ire within the Jewish community. See, for example, Leon Wieseltier, "Israel, Palestine, and the Return of the Bi-National Fantasy: What Is Not to Be Done," *New Republic*, October 27, 2003.

56. "Obama Race Speech: Read the Full Text," http://www.huffingtonpost.com/2008/03/18/obama-race-speech-read-th_n_92077.html, accessed April 1, 2013; Barack Obama, *Dreams from My Father: A Story of Race and Inheritance* (New York: Random House, 2004).

57. Susan Saluny, "Black? White? Asian? More Young Americans Choose All of the Above," *New York Times*, January 29, 2011.

58. 1 Judgment "R v Governing Body of JFS and the Admissions Appeal Panel of JFS and others," http://www.supremecourt.uk/decided-cases/docs/UKSC_2009_0136_Judgment.pdf, accessed July 10, 2014.

59. Brown and Galperin, *The Case for Jewish Peoplehood*, 100.

60. Harry Ostrer, *Legacy: A Genetic History of the Jewish People* (Oxford: Oxford University Press, 2012). A critique of Ostrer's argument that genetics can prove the existence of the Jewish people may be found in Nadia Abu El-Haj, *The Genealogical Science: The Search for Jewish Origins and the Politics of Epistemology* (Chicago: University of Chicago Press, 2012). See also Susan Martha Kahn, "Who Are the Jews? New Formulations on an Age-Old Question," *Human Biology* 85 (2013): 919–924.

61. David Hollinger, "The Concept of Post-Racial: How Its Easy Dismissal Obscures Important Questions," *Daedalus* 140 (2011): 174–182.

62. See, for example, Fredrik Barth, *Ethnic Groups and Boundaries* (Long Grove, IL: Waveland Press, 1998), 10.

63. Mary Waters, *Ethnic Options: Choosing Identities in America* (Berkeley: University of California Press, 1990), 17.

64. Nancy Ammerman, "Religious Identities and Religious Institutions," in *Handbook of the Sociology of Religion*, ed. Michele Dillon (Cambridge: Cambridge University Press, 2003), 209.

65. For instance, see Anthony Giddens, *Modernity and Self Identity* (Stanford, CA: Stanford University Press, 1991), 169.

66. David Scott, "Stuart Hall's Ethics," *Small Axe* 17 (2005): 14.

67. Will Kymlicka, *Multicultural Citizenship* (Oxford: Oxford University Press, 1996); Werner Sollors, *Beyond Ethnicity: Consent and Descent in American Culture* (Oxford: Oxford University Press, 1987); David Hollinger, *Post-Ethnic America: Beyond Multiculturalism* (New York: Basic Books, 2006). Sayla Benhabib pushes the critique of inscribed attributes even further, explaining her goal in this language: "To move a democratic society toward a model of public life in which narratives of self-identification would be more determinant of one's status in public life than would designators and indices imposed upon one by others." Seyla Benhabib, *The Claims of Culture* (Princeton, NJ: Princeton University Press, 2002), 80.

68. Rogers Smith, *Stories of Peoplehood* (Cambridge: Cambridge University Press, 2003).

69. Immanuel Wallerstein, "The Construction of Peoplehood: Racism, Nationalism, Ethnicity," *Sociological Forum* 2 (1987): 378–388.

70. Ibid., 85.

71. Ibid., 381.

72. Lie, *Modern Peoplehood*, 42.

73. Ibid., 15.

74. Milton Gordon, *Assimilation in American Life: The Role of Race, Religion, and National Origins* (New York: Oxford University Press, 1964), 28.

75. Smith, *Stories*, 32.

76. Smith, "The Next Chapter of the American Story," *Chronicle of Higher Education* 49 (July 11, 2003): B10–B11.

77. Hayim Ben-Sasson, ed., *A History of the Jewish People* (London: George Weidenfeld and Nicolson, 1976).

78. Jacob Neusner, review of *A History of the Jewish People*, ed. Hayim Ben-Sasson, *American Historical Review* 82 (1977): 1030–1031.

79. Arnold Eisen, "Four Questions Concerning Peoplehood—And Just as Many Answers," in *Jewish Peoplehood: Change and Challenge*, ed. Menachem Revivi and Ezra Kopelowitz (Boston: Academic Studies Press, 2009), 2.

80. Other scholars more directly view their work as affirming Jewish nationhood and peoplehood. Take, for example, scholar David Aberbach's concern that the rise of the secular nation-state triggered the rejection of "the nationalism inherent in Judaism, if not of Judaism itself," or Irving Zeitlin's historical exploration of "The Making of a Diaspora People." David Aberbach, "Zionist Patriotism in Europe, 1897–1942: Ambiguities in Jewish Nationalism," *International History Review* 31 (2009): 268; Irving M. Zeitlin, *Jews: The Making of a Diaspora People* (Cambridge: Polity Press, 2012).

81. Arnold Eisen, *Rebuilding Jewish Peoplehood: Where Do We Go from Here?* (New York: American Jewish Committee, 1996), 23–26.

82. David Myers, *Between Jew and Arab* (Waltham, MA: Brandeis University Press, 2008).

83. Yael Tamir, *Liberal Nationalism* (Princeton, NJ: Princeton University Press, 1993); Chaim Gans, *A Just Zionism: On the Morality of the Jewish State* (New York: Oxford University Press, 2008). For a review of Jewish theorists of liberal nationalism, see Noam Pianko, "'Make Room for Us': Jewish Collective Solidarity in Contemporary Political Thought," *Journal of Modern Jewish Studies* 11 (2013): 191–205.

84. Jonathan and Daniel Boyarin, *Powers of Diaspora* (Minneapolis: University of Minnesota Press, 2002); Judith Butler, *Parting Ways: Jewishness and the Critique of Zionism* (New York: Columbia University Press, 2012). See also Caryn Aviv and David Shneer, *New Jews: The End of the Jewish Diaspora* (New York: New York University Press, 2005).

85. David Biale, ed., *The Cultures of the Jews* (New York: Schocken Books, 2002).

86. See note 81.

87. See, for example, Paula Hyman, *Gender and Assimilation* (Seattle: University of Washington Press, 1995); Marion Kaplan, *The Making of the Jewish Middle Class* (New York: Oxford University Press, 1991); Joyce Antler, *The Journey Home: How Jewish Women Shaped Modern America* (New York: Schocken, 1998); Karla Goldman, *Beyond the Synagogue Gallery: Finding a Place for Women in American Judaism* (Cambridge, MA: Harvard University Press, 2001).

88. Judith Plaskow, *Standing Again at Sinai* (New York: Harper One, 1991).

89. Naomi Seidman, *A Marriage Made in Heaven: The Sexual Politics of Hebrew and Yiddish* (Berkeley: University of California Press, 1997).

90. Hyman, *Gender and Assimilation*; Kaplan, *Making of the Jewish Middle Class*.

91. Ilana Pardes, "Imagining the Birth of Ancient Israel: National Metaphors in the Bible," in Biale, *Cultures of the Jews*, 5.

92. Ibid., 11.

93. Daniel Boyarin, *Carnal Israel: Reading Sex in Talmudic Culture* (Berkeley: University of California Press, 1995).

CHAPTER 3 — IN A NEW KEY: CAN PEOPLEHOOD SPEAK TO A GLOBAL ERA?

1. Ari Kelman, "The Hegemony of Religion," http://www.stanford.edu/group/edjs/cgi-bin/wordpress/2013/10/04/the-hegemony-of-religion/, accessed February 15, 2014.

2. Abraham Joshua Heschel, "The Future of Zionism and Its Role in Judaism," *Proceedings: Biennial Convention of the United Synagogue of America* (Kiamesha Lake, NY: United Synagogue of America, 1959), 76–85.

3. Ibid.

4. Ibid.

5. Robert Wuthnow, *After the Baby Boomers: How Twenty- and Thirty-Somethings Are Shaping the Future of American Religion* (Princeton, NJ: Princeton University Press, 2010).

6. See below for a description of recent literature on changing notions of religion and its practice.

7. "The New Authentics: Artists of the Post-Jewish Generation," http://spertus.edu/exhibits/new-authentics, accessed January 27, 2013.

8. "Faith in Flux: Changes in Religious Affiliation in the US," Pew Forum on Religion and Public Life, April 27, 2009; "Many Americans Mix Multiple Faiths,"

Pew Forum on Religion and Public Life, December 9, 2009; U.S. Religious Landscape Survey, Pew Forum on Religion and Public Life, February 10, 2009.

9. Nancy Ammerman, "Religious Identities and Religious Institutions," in *The Handbook of the Sociology of Religion*, ed. Michele Dillon (Cambridge: Cambridge University Press, 2003), 207.

10. Nancy Ammerman, "Religious Identities in Contemporary American Life: Lessons from the NJPS," *Sociology of Religion* 67 (2006): 359–364.

11. Nancy T. Ammerman, "Studying Everyday Religion: Challenges for the Future," in *Everyday Religion: Observing Modern Religious Lives*, ed. Nancy Ammerman (Oxford: Oxford University Press, 2006), 219.

12. For a different view of Kaplan's theology and religious commitments, see chapter 1, note 100.

13. On the role that religion plays in constructing Kaplan's definition of nationhood, see Noam Pianko, "Reconstructing Judaism, Reconstructing America: The Sources and Functions of Mordecai Kaplan's 'Civilization,'" *Jewish Social Studies* 12 (2006): 39–55, and Noam Pianko, *Zionism and the Roads Not Taken* (Bloomington: Indiana University Press, 2010), especially chapter 3.

14. See discussion of Erica Brown and Misha Galperin, *The Case for Jewish Peoplehood: Can We Be One?* (Woodstock, VT: Jewish Lights, 2009), in chapter 2.

15. Simon Rawidowicz, *The Ever Dying People*, ed. Benjamin Ravid (Cranbury, NJ: Associated University Presses, 1986).

16. Rogers Smith, "The Next Chapter of the American Story," *Chronicle of Higher Education: The Chronicle Review* 49 (July 11, 2003): B10–11.

17. American Jewish Committee website, www.ajc.org, accessed February 2, 2014.

18. See Jonathan Boyarin, *Jewish Families* (New Brunswick, NJ: Rutgers University Press, 2013), for a discussion of changing notions of Jewish families. Rethinking the language of families on a literal level would also contribute to different symbolic ideas of what characteristics would define national families.

19. See Barbara Kirshenblatt-Gimblett, *Destination Culture: Tourism, Museums, and Heritage* (Berkeley: University of California Press, 1998).

20. Natalie Angier, "The Changing American Family," *New York Times*, November 25, 2013.

21. Ludwig Wittgenstein, *Philosophical Investigations*, 4th ed. (Malden, MA: Wiley-Blackwell, 2009).

22. Thomas A. Tweed, *Crossing and Dwelling* (Cambridge, MA: Harvard University Press, 2006), 17.

23. John Heilemann, "The First Jewish President," *New York Magazine*, September 2011.

24. See Paula Hyman's discussion of assimilation as a project in *Gender and Assimilation* (Seattle: University of Washington Press, 1995).

25. The work of Jewish studies scholars, from the earliest progenitors of the German precursor the American Jewish studies, *Wissenschaft des Judentums*, has always been part of the broader context of Jewish identity formation in the post-emancipation landscape. See Michael A. Meyer. "Two Persistent Tensions within *Wissenschaft Des Judentums*," *Modern Judaism* 24 (2004): 105–119.

Index

African Americans, 51, 57, 60–64, 92
Agus, Jacob, 52
Ahad Ha-am (Asher Ginzberg), 31, 36, 40, 109, 127
American Council for Judaism (ACJ), 38, 42–43, 54–56, 59
American-Israeli Public Affairs Committee (AIPAC), 55, 123–124
American Jewish Committee (AJC), 42–43, 59, 105, 123–124, 129
American Jewish Congress, 34–35
American Jewish World Service, 80–81
American Jews: advocacy for European Jews, 29, 34–35; alienation from Israeli nationalism, 76–77; aliyah principle and, 76; American pluralism and, 27; avoidance of *chosenness* term, 47; communal life, 16; decline-of-peoplehood concern and, 15–16, 71–74; dual allegiance issue for, 37–38, 43, 54–56, 58; émigré intellectual foundations, 22; Holocaust intervention and, 14–15; *-hood* suffix as conceptual synthesis, 47; institutional affiliations with Zionism, 35–36, 52–53, 55; *Jewishhood* project and, 138–139; Kaplan's idea of nationalism and, 27–28, 31–34; marginalization in American society, 34; *mifgashim* (American and Israeli Jewish encounters), 77, 124; nativism and, 29; Orthodox Judaism and, 96; Palestinian Arab conflict and, 76; peoplehood claims of, 104–105; Pew Survey of, 1–3, 16, 117; Russian Jews association with, 14, 56; U.S. Jewish organizations, 33, 34–35, 42–43, 54–56, 80, 105, 120; Wise's form of political Zionism and, 35–36, 44; Zionism debates of, 34, 42–44, 47–48. *See also* American Zionism; United States
American peoplehood term, 45–46
American Zionism: as non-nationalist conception, 7; peoplehood concept in, 54–55; pluralist nation-of-nationalities model, 30–34. *See also* American Jews; Zionism
amiyut (Hebrew language *peoplehood* translation), 18, 76, 78
Ammerman, Nancy, 122–123
Anderson, Benedict, 24, 68–70, 75, 82, 131
antisemitism: American Jewish Congress challenge to, 34–35; Black Power movement and, 62; Gordon's idea of pluralism influences, 58–59; Jewish racial categories and, 93–94; *race* term in U.S. and, 30; unifying effect of, 2, 8, 128–129; Wise on external threats, 35–36, 64. *See also* Holocaust; persecution and external threat
Arendt, Hannah, 53–54
assimilation: as diaspora fate, 67; *Jewish project* and, 130; melting pot thesis, 31, 57–60, 62, 93
Auerbach, Jerold S., 141n5

Baron, Salo, 52
Barth, Fredrik, 98
Bauman, Zygmunt, 99
Beck, Ulrich, 89
Ben-Gurion, David, 48–50, 53, 91
Benhabib, Sayla, 157n67
Ben-Sasson, Hayim, 106
Berman Jewish Policy archive, 72
Bernstein, Philip S., 55
Birthright Israel, 77
Black Power movement, 51, 57, 61–63
blood (shared blood concept). *See* genealogy; spirit/soul/essence principle
Boyarin, Jonathan and Daniel, 110
Brown, Erica, 74–75
Brubaker, Rogers, 24, 85–86
Burritt, Elihu, 46

Carlebach, Shlomo, 14
Carmichael, Stokely, 61–62
Center for Peoplehood Education, 73

163

Central Conference of American Rabbis (CCAR), 39
chosenness, 46–47. *See also* spirit/soul/essence principle
chosen people term: adoption of *peoplehood* term and, 45; Christian theology and, 47; divine election implication in, 46–47; as Jewish collectivity term, 10, 30. *See also* spirit/soul/essence principle
class, 60–61, 89–90
Cohen, Eugene, 52
Cohen, Jack, 52
Cohen, Steven M., 15–16
Cold War, 14, 56
collectivity: Anderson's "imagined community" model of, 12, 68–70, 75, 81, 131, 135; contemporary scholarship on, 81–82; decline of post-Holocaust solidarity, 15; early U.S. terms for, 30; *family* as collectivity model, 63, 74, 113–114, 129–133; fragmentation of values and, 75, 92, 97, 99, 111, 125, 128–130, 136–139; gendered representations of, 112–113; genealogical analysis and, 12–13; historical claims for groupness, 20, 26, 102–103; Jewish exceptionalism and, 9, 86–87, 101–102, 104, 109; Lazaron's rejection of universal solidarity, 38–39; membership/inclusion practices, 6, 27, 53, 65–66, 94, 129–130; neighborhood as model, 124–134; open-source models for, 132–133; as people vs. religion, 2; premodern religious community model, 20–25, 72, 82, 85; religious practice and, 119–122; social theory as model for, 83–87; state as representation of, 100–101; sustainable solidarity, 13; *tikkun olam* principle, 74; traits vs. boundaries approach, 98, 110–111; voluntary affiliation, 98–100, 130. *See also* diaspora; *nation/nationality* terms; secular solidarity
colonialism, 69, 100
Commission on the Jewish People, 71–73
communal advocacy: American Jewish communalism, 33, 42, 79–80; black peoplehood and, 62; decline-of-peoplehood concern, 15–16, 71–74; disconnect with critical scholarship, 10–12, 71–72, 79, 108–109; essentialism and, 11, 13; genealogical analysis and, 12–13; interest in Soviet Jews, 56; *Jewishhood* project and, 136–137; peoplehood centrality for, 2–3, 10–11; racial logic in, 65; U.S. Jewish communal organizations, 33; "vital psyche" theme in, 15. *See also* Israel; Zionism
Conservative Judaism, 52
constructivism. *See* genealogy
contemporary Jewish peoplehood: contemporary paradigms for, 70–71; decline-of-peoplehood concern, 15–16, 71–74; descent-based collectivity and, 96, 98–99; as diaspora-friendly Zionism, 76–78; disconnect with critical scholarship, 82, 88, 90–91, 100–101, 104, 107–109; disenchantment with, 80–81, 105–106, 155n29; Hebrew language avoidance of, 78; key events, 2000–2011, 73; multivocal self-understanding approach, 110–111; Palestinian Arab conflict and, 74, 76, 154n11; *peoplehood* as statist code word, 71, 75–76, 78–79; persecution and external threat, 74; postethnic/postracial identity and, 93, 106, 117; postmodern identity models, 70–71; as secular peoplehood, 79; Soviet Jewish immigration and, 16, 76, 79–80; statehood centrality for, 100–101; U.S. Jewish organizations and, 80, 105. *See also* peoplehood
cosmopolitanization, 89
Council of Jewish Federations and Welfare Funds, 62, 64
cultural Zionism: Ahad Ha-am and, 31, 36, 40, 109, 127; American Jewish synthesis of, 30–31, 36–37; influence in diaspora, 36; Israel as font of intellectualism, 26–27; Kaplan's idea of cultural solidarity, 37, 40; Lazaron on multinationality and, 38; peoplehood emergence from, 7; shared culture as collectivity basis, 31; Zionism studies and, 109

decline-of-peoplehood concern, 15–17, 71–74
democracy: ancestral peoplehood in Gordon and, 58–59; contemporary heterogeneous populations and, 89, 91; democratic peoplehood, 16–17, 45–47; influence on American Jews, 29, 40; Kallen's idea of nation-of-nationalities democracy, 31–33; neighborhood solidarity model and, 128; Soviet Jewish advocacy and, 80; voluntary association and, 130, 157n67

diaspora: aliyah (diaspora migration to Israel), 55, 76, 151n119; competing claims for, 11; contemporary Israeli views of, 77–78; as Jewish identity component, 2, 27; as minority religious community, 49–50; multicentered paradigm for, 68–70, 109–110, 155n29; *peoplehood* incorporation of, 9, 49–50, 55–56; *peoplehood* reframing and, 118; pre-statehood *am yisrael* and, 19; Soviet Jewish mass emigration, 16; State of Israel naming and, 19, 49–51, 87; transnational Jewish collective, 50–51; Zionist rejection of, 26, 67–68, 76. *See also* collectivity; homeland
Dinin, Samuel, 44
diversity. *See* pluralism
Drachsler, Julius, 57
Dubnow, Simon, 23, 26, 84

Eisen, Arnold, 109–110
Eisenstein, Ira, 44, 52
essentialism: in communal advocacy discourse, 11; essentialist peoplehood, 100–101; genealogical analysis and, 12–13; moral objections to, 13; racism and, 103
ethnicity: declining significance of, 3; emergence as term for U.S. minorities, 50–51; ethnic pride movement, 63–65; ethnies, 87; *folk/Volk/Stamm/narod* terms, 21–23; Gordon on ancestral and generative peoplehood, 57–61; Herberg's idea of religious peoplehood and, 61; historical embeddedness of, 11–12, 82–84; as inadequate concept for Jewish groupness, 9; as Jewish identity component, 1; postethnic identity, 92–93, 97–98; post-WWI nationalist paradigm and, 21; premodern ethnicity, 85, 109; racial logic in, 63–66; scriptural commentary on, 144n15; traits vs. boundaries approach, 98, 110–111; U.S. minorities' adoption of *peoplehood*, 59–60; voluntary ethnicity, 98–99, 130. *See also* minorities; pluralism; race
European Jews: *folk/Volk/Stamm/narod* terms used by, 21–23; nationalist paradigm development by, 17; political influence in the U.S., 10
exceptionalism, 9, 86–87, 101–102, 104, 109

family (as collectivity), 63, 74, 113–114, 129–133. *See also* genealogy
fascism, 32
Federation of American Zionists (later Zionist Organization of America), 35, 54–55
Feldman, Abraham J., 39
feminism, 112–14
folk/Volk/Stamm/narod terms: European *folk/Volk/Stamm/narod* terms, 21–23; Folkspartei formation in Russia, 23; Herzl "one people (*Volk*)" passage, 35–36, 40, 44–45; Kaplan critique of, 41; peoplehood derivation from, 44–45. *See also* spirit/soul/essence principle

Galperin, Misha, 74–75, 155n25
Gans, Chaim, 110
Geiger, Abraham, 84
gender, 112–114
genealogy (descent and consent): ascriptive color as identity marker, 64; conversion, 95–97; critique of inscribed attributes, 157n67; *family* image in peoplehood conceptualizations, 63, 74, 113–114, 129–133; fractional vs. exclusive descent-based membership, 96–97; Gordon on ancestral and generative peoplehood, 57–61; historical embeddedness of, 12–13; Israeli citizenship as inclusion marker, 53, 55–56; Kallen's grandfather thesis, 31, 96; Kaplan's idea of "spiritual background of a people," 37–38, 61–63; marriage practices and, 11–12, 16, 65, 96; matrilineal descent, 65, 94, 95; national membership and, 21–22; racial (descent-based) discrimination and, 94–95, 131; solidarity with Soviet Jews and, 14
genealogy (descent vs. consent). *See* spirit/soul/essence principle
Giddens, Anthony, 89–90
Ginzberg, Asher. *See* Ahad Ha-am
Glazer, Nathan, 57
globalization, 16, 88–92. *See also* nation/nationality terms; transnationality
Gordon, Milton, 57–61, 102
Graetz, Heinrich, 26, 84

Hadassah, 105
Hall, Stuart, 99
Handlin, Oscar, 57
Hansen, Marcus Lee, 57

Hayes, Christine, 144n15
Hebrew language, 18, 76
Hebrews term, 30, 47
Herberg, Will, 57, 60–61, 122
Hertzberg, Arthur, 52
Herzl, Theodor, 35–36, 40, 44–45
Heschel, Abraham Joshua, 119–120
history: historically situated identity, 11, 26, 99–100; Jewish exceptionalism and, 9, 86–87, 101–102; in key word analysis, 10–11; modernist historical scholarship, 84–92, 99–100; multivocal self-understanding approach, 110–111; nationalist paradigm and, 7; as peoplehood component, 2, 4–6, 8–9, 11–12; perennialism (transhistorical nationalism/peoplehood), 12, 16–17, 24, 83–87, 103, 106–107, 126; primordialism (theory of nationalism), 20–25, 72, 82, 85, 109
Hobsbawm, Eric, 86–88
Hochbaum, Jerry, 62, 64
Hollinger, David, 64, 97
Holocaust: Arendt's *Eichmann in Jerusalem* and, 53–54; Museum of the Jewish People depiction, 67; racial peoplehood and, 63; solidarity as response to, 14–15. *See also* antisemitism; Nazism; persecution and external threat
homeland: competing claims for, 11; in contemporary *peoplehood*, 74–75; cultural Zionism and, 36; diaspora and, 19, 29, 38, 40–42, 49–50; *folk/Volk/Stamm/narod* terms and, 23–24; Jewish collectivity and, 6; multicentered paradigm and, 68–70, 109–110, 155n29; nation-state principle and, 33; *peoplehood* incorporation of, 9, 154n16; *peoplehood* reframing and, 118; Zionism and, 11, 26–27, 48. *See also* diaspora
human rights, 128–129
hybrid identity, 11, 81–82, 96–97, 99–100, 133
Hyman, Paula, 113

identity: aliyah (diaspora migration to Israel) and, 55, 76, 151n119; autobiographical identity, 122–123; as choice vs. collective commitment, 10–11; contemporary Jewish identity patterns, 117; cosmopolitan disembeddedness and, 89, 99; emancipation vs. life politics and, 89–90; fractional vs. exclusive descent ties, 96–97; historically situated identity, 11, 26, 99–100; hybrid identity, 11, 81–82, 96–97, 99–100, 133; identity politics/ethnic pride and, 29, 51, 56–58, 63–65; individualized vs. collective identity, 16; individual religious practice and, 119–122; Israeli citizenship as inclusion marker, 53, 55–56; Kallen's idea of inherited secular group identity, 31; membership/inclusion practices and, 6, 27, 53, 65–66, 94; post-Jewishness, 122; postmodern identity models, 70–71; premodern organic group coherence and, 24, 99; slogans related to, 2, 14, 126, 130, 141n5; Soviet Jewish emigration to Israel and, 79–80
Israel (People of Israel, *am yisrael*), 11, 17–19, 55–56, 113
Israel (State of Israel, *medinat yisrael*): aliyah (diaspora migration to Israel), 55, 76, 151n119; changing attitudes toward, 16; choice of name, 19, 49–51, 87; citizenship as inclusion marker, 53, 55–56; early mainstream Zionist uninterest in, 27; *Jewish project* and, 130; Palestinian Arab conflict, 74, 76, 154n11; *peoplehood* as statist code word, 51–52, 54–55, 71, 75–76, 78–79, 154n16; *peoplehood* term emergence and, 2, 5–6, 11, 48; secular-religious dichotomy in, 124; Soviet Jewish immigration, 16, 76, 79–80. *See also* communal advocacy; political Zionism; state/statehood; Zionism
Israelites term, 30

Jellinek, Adolf, 22
Jewish Agency for Israel (JAFI), 1, 72–73, 76–77, 108
Jewish Emancipation, 20–21
Jewish Federations of North America, 1, 105, 140
Jewish feminism, 112–114
Jewishhood term, 133–140
Jewish Peoplehood HUB, 1
Jewish people/peoplehood. *See* contemporary Jewish peoplehood; peoplehood
Jewish People Planning Institute, 73
Jewish project, 129–130, 133–134

INDEX   167

Jewish psyche. *See* spirit/soul/essence principle
Jewish studies: applied model for, 137–140; disconnect from Jewish community, 139; feminist influences in, 112–114; multivocal self-understanding approach, 110–111; peoplehood study in, 10, 106–109; views of nationalism, 87–88
Joint Distribution Committee, 105
J Street, 123–124
Judt, Tony, 90–91, 92

Kallen, Horace, 30–33, 52, 60, 63
Kaplan, Mordecai: cultural Zionism of, 37, 40; emergence of peoplehood in thought of, 7, 40–42, 62–63, 103–104; on ethical collectivity, 31–34, 52–53, 60, 102, 110; "evolving religious civilization" principle, 79, 121; Heschel's "synagogue" remark and, 119–120; *Jewishhood* project and, 135; Jewish nationalism (pre-1942) writings, 39–40; on nation vs. nationality, 37–39, 41–42; on pluralist nationalism, 31–34; Reconstructionist Summer Conference address, 27–28, 39–42; secular-religious dichotomy in, 124; on the "spiritual background of a people," 37–38, 61–63, 124–125; State of Israel establishment and, 48–51, 75, 78–79; transhistorical presumptions in, 84. WORKS: "Judaism and Nationality" (1909), 32; *Judaism as a Civilization* (1934), 31–32, 63; *The Future of the American Jew* (1948), 34, 42; *New Zionism* (1957), 52–53; *The Religion of Ethical Nationhood* (1970), 32, 50
Kedourie, Elie, 87–88
Kehillah (community center), 33, 124
Kelman, Ari, 117
Kerry, John, 2
key word study: communal advocacy and, 12–13; exceptionalism and, 9; Jewish studies key words, 10; *peoplehood* appearance in dictionaries, 29; *peoplehood* as code word, 51–52, 54–55, 71, 75–76, 78–79; pluralism and, 135; reframing of key words, 116–117; study design for, 5–6
Kohn, Eugene, 44
Kohn, Hans, 83, 88
Kol Dor, 155n29

Land of Israel (*eretz yisrael*), 11
language: *American peoplehood* principle, 45–46; English-language *people* connotations, 36; *folk/Volk/Stamm/narod* terms, 21–23, 35–36; gendered language in collective representation, 112–113; Hebraist-Yiddish debates, 113; Hebrew-language *peoplehood* approximations/antecedents, 14, 18, 76, 78; -*hood* suffix, 8, 18–19, 47, 119, 134; *Jewish people* English-language term, 2, 18; *Jewish-people-hood* reframing elements, 118–119; language families as social metaphor, 131–132; *nation* English-language term, 45–46; *peoplehood* usage frequency analysis, 51–52, 56–57, 72, 152n122; *people/peoplehood* U.S. English-language usage, 4, 6–8, 18, 45; slogans related to peoplehood, 2, 14, 126, 130, 141n5; State of Israel naming and, 19, 49–51, 87
Lazaron, Morris S., 37–39, 41, 42–44
Lie, John, 9, 82, 101–104

Magnes, Judah, 31
Marty, Martin, 59–60
Menorah Journal, 30–31
Messinger, Ruth, 80–81
Michaelson, Jay, 80–81
mifgashim (American and Israeli Jewish encounters), 77, 124
migration: aliyah (diaspora migration to Israel), 55, 76, 151n119; globalization and transnational migration, 88–89; Soviet Jewish mass emigration, 16; U.S. immigration, 33
minorities: diaspora Jews as, 49–50; ethical nationalism and, 110; feminist support for Israeli minorities, 114; human rights of, 128–129; Kaplan's understanding of Jewish minority, 40; Lazaron's "American Jew" defense of Jewish minority, 37; marginalization of American Jews, 34; *nationhood* vs. *ethnicity* as terms for, 50–51; separatism and, 47, 62; in statist nationalism, 32; U.S. minorities' adoption of *peoplehood*, 59–60, 63–65. *See also* pluralism
Moore, Deborah Dash, 110
multiculturalism. *See* ethnicity; minorities; pluralism

168 INDEX

Museum of the Jewish People (formerly Museum of the Jewish Diaspora), 2, 67–70, 73, 75, 78, 104, 106, 130–131
Myers, David, 110

Nadav Foundation, 73–74
National American Jewish Congress, 62
nationalism: overview, 7; American nationalism, 45–46; Arendt critique of secular nationalism, 54; as basis for groupness/peoplehood, 20–21, 28, 44; in contemporary *peoplehood*, 74; contemporary Zionist peoplehood and, 80–81; denationalization, 91–92, 115; European and European Jewish development of, 17; globalization and postnational thought, 88–92; historical embeddedness of, 11–12, 82–84; as inadequate concept for Jewish groupness, 9; Jewish historical narrative and, 26; Jewish scholars on, 88; Kallen's idea of nation-of-nationalities pluralism and, 31–33; liberal nationalism, 110; modernist scholarship and, 84–87; peoplehood as critique and embrace of, 9–10, 66, 118; perennialism (transhistorical nationalism/peoplehood), 12, 16–17, 24, 83–87, 126; postracial identity and, 93; as post-WWI political concept, 21–22, 41; secular peoplehood and, 6–7; traditional societies and, 24–25; transterritorial nationalism and, 23–24; U.S. Jewish organizations and, 33. *See also* nation/nationality terms; transnationality
nationhood: American pluralism conflict with, 6; ethical nationhood, 25, 27–28, 31–34, 75, 110; *ethnicity* term emergence and, 50–51, 63–64; as Jewish identity component, 1; neighborhood solidarity model and, 125–134; peoplehood association with, 9–10, 54–55; peoplehood neologism and, 8; scriptural commentary on, 144n16; State of Israel establishment and, 48–51; transnationality, 50–51; Zionist concept of, 7, 16–17. *See also* globalization; nation/nationality terms; transnationality
nation/nationality terms: Ahad Ha-am usage, 31; avoidance of *chosenness* terminology, 47; English-language usage, 45–46; Kallen usage, 30–33; in *Menorah Journal*, 30–31; nation vs. nationality in Kaplan, 37–39, 41–42, 61. *See also* collectivity; globalization; nationalism; nationhood; state/statehood; transnationality
nation-states. *See* Israel; nationalism; nationhood; state/statehood
nativism, 29, 30
Nazism: American Jewish identity and, 29, 34–35; Arendt's *Eichmann in Jerusalem* and, 53–54; Jewish racial logic parallels with, 95; Kaplan on nationalism and, 32–33. *See also* Holocaust
neighborhood, 125–134
Neusner, Jacob, 107
Nisan, Mordecai, 154n16
Nussbaum, Max, 55

Obama, Barack, 92–93, 133
open-source social models, 132–133
Orthodox Judaism, 65–66, 96, 124

Palestine: bi-national proposal for, 91; Jewish social justice advocacy and, 103; second Intifada, 76; view of Jewish peoplehood, 2
Pardes, Ilana, 113
peoplehood: *am yisrael* as basis for, 17–18; analytical definitions of, 101–102; communalist view of, 3; contemporary paradigms for, 70–71; decline-of-peoplehood concern, 15–16, 71–74; as English-language neologism, 8; historical framing of, 3–5; intellectual sources of, 6–7; key word study of, 5–6; *klal yisrael* principle, 71–72; measurement instruments for, 73–74, 108; modernity of, 72, 115–116; nationalist model for, 20–21, 28, 44; obstacles to study of, 10–11; Pew Survey, 1–3, 16, 117; as sociological process, 9; usage frequency analysis of, 51–52, 56–57, 72, 152n122. *See also* contemporary Jewish peoplehood; peoplehood studies; reframing of *peoplehood*
peoplehood (chronology of usage): *folk/volk/Stamm/narod* terms (1881–1917) (*see folk/volk/Stamm/narod* terms); Herzl's "one people (*Volk*)" passage (1896), 35–36, 40; Russian Folkspartei

(1906), 23; Kallen's "Democracy vs. the Melting Pot" (1915), 31, 38; Lazaron's "American Jew" article (1921), 37–39, 41; Stephen Wise address (1932), 34–36, 54–55; Kaplan's "alternatives to *nationhood*" address (1942), 27–28, 39–42; Steinberg critique of Zionist debate (1942), 43–44; Dinin's nationalist peoplehood article (1944), 44; Kaplan's *Future of the American Jew* (1948), 34, 42; estalishment of State of Israel (1948), 2, 5–6, 11, 14, 48–51; post-statehood usage (1950s), 51, 54–55, 58; Kaplan's *New Zionism* (1957), 52–53; Heschel's "synagogue" remark (1959), 119–120; Gordon's *Assimilation in American Life* (1964), 57–61, 102; civil rights movement and racial peoplehood (mid-1960s), 51, 61–64; crossover into U.S. mainstream (1965), 29, 51, 56–58, 63–66, 102; Ben-Sasson's *History of the Jewish People* (1976), 106–107; modernist historical scholarship (1980s), 84–92; overview of recent events (2000s), 73, 82; Lie and Smith's *peoplehood* publications (2003–2004), 101–104, 106; Obama U.S. presidency (2008), 92; Sand's *Invention of the Jewish People* (2008), 69–70; Brown and Galperin's *Case for Jewish Peoplehood* (2009), 74–75; Israeli proposed designation "nation-state of the Jewish people" (2011), 73; UJA global task force on peoplehood education (2011), 71–72
Peoplehood Index, 73–74
peoplehood studies: overview, 82–83; communal advocacy disconnect with, 10–12, 71–72, 79, 82, 88, 90–91, 100–101, 104; critical inquiry in, 100–102; parallels with older models, 103–104
people of Israel (*am yisrael*), 11, 17–19, 55–56, 113
persecution and external threat: Arendt's *Eichmann in Jerusalem* and, 53–54; black peoplehood and, 64; contemporary concerns with, 74; critiques of legitimacy of Jewish peoplehood/statehood, 12–13, 87, 90–91, 104–105; emancipation vs. life politics and, 89–90; Herzl "distress binds us" passage, 35; Kaplan's idea of cultural solidarity and, 40; nativism in the U.S., 29; as peoplehood marker, 11; post-Holocaust solidarity and, 14–15;

reframing of *peoplehood* and, 126, 133; second Intifada and, 76; Six Day and Yom Kippur Wars and, 15, 66; Soviet Jewry movement and, 14, 56; Wise on external threats, 35–36, 64. *See also* antisemitism; Holocaust
Pew Research Center Survey (2014), 1–3, 16, 117
Plaskow, Judith, 112
pluralism: chauvinistic peoplehood and, 127–128; emergence of American, 6, 27; fragmentation of values, 75, 92, 97, 99, 111, 125, 128–130, 136–139; Gordon's idea of ancestral and generative peoplehood, 57–61; Jewish nationalism conflict with, 6; Jewish people as American pluralism, 64; Kallen's nation-of-nationalities pluralism and, 31–33; key word usage and, 135; multicultural critique of descent, 100. *See also* ethnicity; minorities
political Zionism: American-Jewish synthesis of, 36–37; external threat theme in, 15, 35–36, 64, 66; Lazaron critique of, 37–39, 42–44; *peoplehood* as code word for, 51–52, 54–55, 71, 75–76, 78–79; *peoplehood* term emergence and, 7, 27, 48, 66; rejection of diasporic life, 26; Soviet Jewry movement and, 14, 56; statehood as ambition in, 8, 26; Wise's idea of "peoplehood of Israel" and, 35–36, 44. *See also* Israel; state/statehood; territorial sovereignty
Powell, Adam Clayton, 61

race: declining significance of, 3; *ethnicity* term emergence and, 63–66; *halakhic* descent-based membership and, 93–97; historical embeddedness of, 11–12, 82–84; Kaplan's idea of descent-based nationhood and, 62–63; Obama U.S. presidency and, 92; postracial identity, 92–93; *race* as Jewish collectivity term, 9, 30; racial Jewish peoplehood practices, 94–97; racial peoplehood in Gordon, 59–63; and racism, 62, 65, 94, 103, 131; religious peoplehood and, 61–62. *See also* ethnicity
Rawidowicz, Simon, 50, 110, 127
Reconstructionist Summer Conference (1942), 27–28, 41–44

Reform movement: advocacy for religious Jewishness, 34, 42–43, 59; American Council for Judaism founding, 38; *chosenness* principle and, 47; creedal emphasis in, 39; early peoplehood formulations in, 37, 39; Kaplan's racial critique of, 63

reframing of *peoplehood*: avoidance of essentialism, 118; demystification process, 115–116; *family* as boundary device, 129–133; *Jewishhood* project, 133–140; *Jewish-people-hood* reframing elements, 118–119; *Jewish project* as membership device, 129–130; necessity of, 116–118; neighborhood as model, 125–134; religious Jewish practice and, 119–124; Zionism as component of, 118, 133. *See also* peoplehood

religion: as basis for secular morality, 26, 54; and Gordon's idea of hybrid religious-national peoplehood, 51, 58; Herberg on religious civilizations, 61; individual religious practice and, 119–123; as Jewish identity component, 1–2; post-Jewishness, 122; Reform advocacy for religious Jewishness, 34, 42–43, 59; reframing of *peoplehood* and, 122–124; religious folkways as collectivity basis, 31; secular solidarity and, 87

religious Zionism: chosenness (divine election) and, 46–47; and Lazaron's rejection of universal solidarity, 38–39; messianic return to Palestine in, 26–27, 68, 79, 94–95; religious covenant as basis for, 109–110; religious practice in Kaplan, 40

Renan, Ernest, 21, 25–26
Reut Institute, 77
revisionist Zionism, 26–27

Sand, Shlomo, 12, 69–70
Sandler, Adam, 96–97
Scholem, Gershom, 53–54
secular solidarity: Ahad Ha-am's secular approach, 40; Arendt critique of, 54; contemporary Jewish peoplehood and, 79; Gordon on ancestral and generative peoplehood, 58–61; Kallen on cultural solidarity, 31; peoplehood discourse and, 119–120; political Zionism and, 43, 47–48; Reform movement and, 39; religious Judaism and, 87; role of class in, 60–61; secular expressions of Judaism, 29; secular history as basis for, 22, 25–27; secular peoplehood, 3, 6–7, 20; voluntary affiliation and, 100, 130; Zionist historiography and, 109. *See also* collectivity

Seidman, Naomi, 113
separatism, 47, 62
Sephardic Jews, 30
Septimus, Daniel, 80–81
Sharansky, Natan, 76, 79–80, 155n25
Shimoni, Gideon, 87, 109
Six Day War, 15, 66
Smith, Anthony, 85–88, 109
Smith, Rogers M., 9, 101–104, 127–128
solidarity. *See* collectivity; secular solidarity
Soviet and Russian Jews: American Jews' association with, 14, 56, 66; Folkspartei formation, 23; global Jewish solidarity and, 14–15; mass emigration of, 16, 76, 79–80; *narod* as collectivity term, 22–23; Russian proponents of peoplehood, 155n25
Spertus Museum, 122
spirit/soul/essence principle: absence of women in, 112–113; American Jewish psyche, 5, 15–16; chosenness (divine election) and, 46–47; and ethical basis for collectivity, 25, 27–28, 31–34, 75, 102–103, 110; *Jewish project* and, 129–130; Law of Return and, 26–27, 68, 79, 94–95; modern internalization of peoplehood and, 9, 75; as outdated global-age concept, 13; postethnic/postracial identity and, 106; in Renan's national formulation, 24–25. *See also* chosen people term; *folk/Volk/Stamm/narod* terms; genealogy
state/statehood: absence from early Zionist concerns, 27; contemporary Jewish peoplehood and, 75; European Jewish nationalist paradigm and, 17; globalization and postnational thought, 88–92; Herzl's formulation of, 35; infrastructural implications, 109–110; Jewish security and, 5; Kaplan critique of statist nationhood, 42; minorities in statist nationalism, 32; peoplehood as fundamental principle for, 9; *peoplehood* as statist code word, 51–52, 54–55, 71,

75–76, 78–79, 154n16; scriptural commentary on, 144n16; as site of collective identity, 100–101; solidarity with Soviet Jews and, 14; State of Israel naming and, 19, 49–51, 87; statist Zionism, 33–34, 53. *See also* Israel; *nation/nationality* terms; political Zionism; territorial sovereignty
Steinberg, Milton, 43–44
sustainable solidarity, 13

Tamir, Yuli, 110
territorial sovereignty: effect on nationalism, 128–129; Folkspartei formation in Russia, 23; as fundamental Zionist component, 26–27; Hebrew terms for, 18–19; historical ethnic territorial claims, 85; historical variation as peoplehood component, 20; as Jewish identity component, 27; Kaplan's *peoplehood* formulation and, 41; modernist scholarship and, 89–90; as post-WWI political concept, 21–22, 33, 66; State of Israel establishment and, 48–51. *See also* political Zionism; state/statehood
transnationality: global economic pressures, 91; Obama U.S. presidency and, 92; transnational Jewish collective, 51; transnational migration, 88–89; transnational networks, 89–90, 100–101. *See also* globalization; nationalism; nationhood; *nation/nationality* terms
Troen, Ilan, 110

UJA Federation of New York, 71–73, 108
United Jewish Communities, 73
United States: Black Power movement, 57; civil rights movement racial peoplehood, 51, 61–64; *ethnicity* term emergence, 50–51; government recognition of Jewish peoplehood, 55; immigration and, 33; Jewish dual allegiance issue, 37–38, 43, 54–56, 58; *Jewish people* English-language term, 2, 18; Kallen's pluralist model for, 31–33; *nation* as legal concept, 41; nativist movement, 38; *people/peoplehood* U.S. English-language usage, 4, 6–8, 18, 45; terminology for collective identity, 6, 32;

U.S. 1960s identity politics, 29, 51, 56–58, 63–66. *See also* American Jews
United Synagogue, 52, 55, 119–120

van Rahden, Till, 22
voluntary affiliation/association, 98–100, 130

Wallerstein, Immanuel, 101–102
Waters, Mary, 65, 98
Wertheimer, Jack, 15–16, 155n29
Wilson, Woodrow, 33
Wise, Stephen: emergence of peoplehood in thought of, 7; and ethical collectives principle, 60; peoplehood studies and, 104; Zurich "peoplehood of Israel" address, 34–36, 44, 54
Wittgenstein, Ludwig, 131–132
World Zionist Organization (formerly Zionist Organization), 52, 119–120
Wright, Richard, 144n16
Wuthnow, Robert, 121–122

Yom Kippur War, 15, 66

Zangwell, Israel, 93
Zionism: absence of peoplehood concept in, 6; American Jewish debates about, 34, 42–44, 47–48; American Jewish institutions and, 35–36, 52–53, 55; *American peoplehood* differences with, 46; as condition for peoplehood emergence, 5; Jewish historical narrative and, 26; just Zionism, 110; modernist historical analysis and, 86–92; nationhood concept in, 7, 16–17; political vs. religious vs. revisionist Zionism, 26–27; State of Israel embodiment of peoplehood in, 77, 154n16; statist Zionism, 33–34, 53; U.N. racism resolution on, 94; Zionism studies, 109. *See also* American Zionism; communal advocacy; cultural Zionism; Israel; political Zionism; religious Zionism; revisionist Zionism
Zionist Congress (1897–), 35
Zionist Organization (later World Zionist Organization), 52
Zionist Organization of America (formerly Federation of American Zionists), 35, 54–55

About the Author

Noam Pianko is the Samuel N. Stroum Professor of Jewish Studies and an associate professor in the Jackson School of International Studies at the University of Washington. He also directs the Stroum Center for Jewish Studies and serves as the Lucia S. and Herbert L. Lucy Pruzan Chair of Jewish Studies. Pianko's research interests include modern Jewish history, Zionism, and American Judaism. He has published *Zionism and the Roads Not Taken: Rawidowicz Kaplan, Kohn* (2010), as well as articles in *Jewish Social Studies, American Jewish History, Journal of Modern Jewish Studies, Leo Baeck Institute Yearbook*, and *Ab Imperio*. He received his Ph.D. in Religious Studies/Judaic Studies from Yale University in 2004.

www.ingramcontent.com/pod-product-compliance
Ingram Content Group UK Ltd.
Pitfield, Milton Keynes, MK11 3LW, UK
UKHW041429180426
11947UKWH00007B/356